THE PIGEON WARS OF DAMASCUS

Marius Kociejowski

The Pigeon Wars of Damascus

BIBLIOASIS

BIBLIOASIS

EMERYVILLE · DETROIT · LONDON

FIRST EDITION

Library and Archives Canada Cataloguing in Publication

Kociejowski, Marius
The pigeon wars of Damascus / Marius Kociejowski.

ISBN 978-1-897231-97-5 (bound).—ISBN 978-1-926845-02-9 (pbk.)

1. Kociejowski, Marius—Travel—Syria—Damascus.
2. Damascus (Syria)—Description and travel. 3. Damascus (Syria)—Social life and customs—21st century.
4. Pigeons—Syria—Damascus. I. Title.

DS99.D3K63 2010 956.91′44042 C2010-904593-9

Canada Council for the Arts Conseil des Arts du Canada

Canadian Heritage Patrimoine canadien

ONTARIO ARTS COUNCIL
CONSEIL DES ARTS DE L'ONTARIO

Mixed Sources
Product group from well-managed forests, controlled sources and recycled wood or fiber
FSC www.fsc.org Cert no. SW-COC-001352
© 1996 Forest Stewardship Council

Biblioasis acknowledges the ongoing financial support of the Government of Canada through The Canada Council for the Arts, Canadian Heritage, the Book Publishing Industry Development Program (BPIDP); and the Government of Ontario through the Ontario Arts Council.

PRINTED AND BOUND IN CANADA

to Arcangelo Riffis

The heart which tender thought clothes like a dove

—Percy Bysshe Shelley *From the Arabic: An Imitation*

And many are mad with the love of these birds;
they build towers for them on the tops of their roof,
and will relate the high breeding and ancestry of
each, after the ancient fashion.

—Pliny *Anecdotes of Animals*, Book III. 15

Contents

Prologue

A pigeon fancier said to me, 'If you want to understand the Middle East, just look at my birds.' It was approaching evening and on a rooftop in Damascus, several miles from its ancient centre, amid minarets and satellite dishes, the cooing of Waseem's pigeons, sixty or seventy of them, mingled oddly with the electronically amplified cry of a muezzin in the near distance. Waseem scowled the scowl of one who feigns to despise what he loves.

'They are brutes,' he said, 'just like the Americans are brutes.'

Waseem eyed me sharply, maybe in order to get a measure of my political allegiances. The war in neighbouring Iraq was tearing at everyone's nerves.

'Do you not love your pigeons more?'

'Yes, but they are brutes all the same.'

It didn't seem I'd get terribly far with him, and I felt too that Waseem looked upon me as a guest come from the house of the friend of his foe. Already he had asked me why *ingiltirā*, with all her experience of the Arabic world, was following the lead of a country that had none. Such questions contain their own answers, of course, and so I made no response. I had heard enough, though, of pigeon fanciers and of the crazy disputes between them, some of which ended in murder, to suspect that what he said to me was

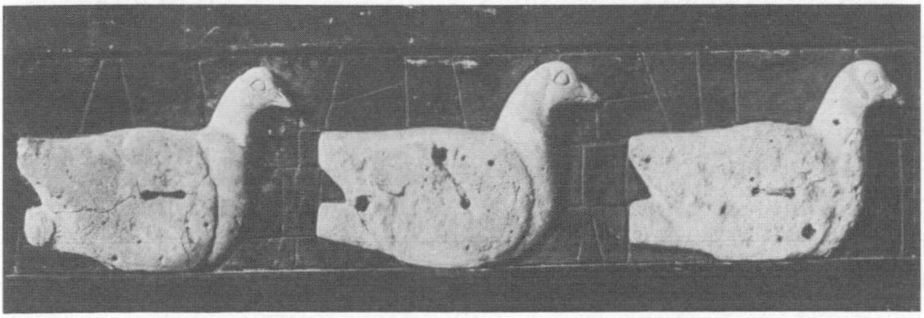

true, and there really was an analogy here for all that was happening in this part of the world. It was one that might reach back through time, to whoever it was, over 5,000 years ago, at al-'Ubaid near Ur, felt it important enough to carve three pigeons in stone.

After all, a dove, a trained one at that, brought news to Noah, which also suggests that its recipient is the earliest *named* example we have of a pigeon fancier. (What is a dove but a pigeon made respectable?) This particular female dove had to have been domesticated because when she returned, Noah 'put forth his hand, and took her, and pulled her in unto him into the ark.' The Muslims, wanting, perhaps, to outpoeticise the Old Testament, say the reason pigeons have red feet is because of the reddish mud Noah found on them, which provided him with proof of the world's drying state. It's just as well his dove didn't alight on Lord Byron's longboat, or, rather, Don Juan's:

> And had it been the dove from Noah's ark,
> Returning there from her successful search,
> Which in their way that moment chanced to fall,
> They would have eat her, olive-branch and all.

Ornithologists will tell you Noah's was probably a rock dove, which is the ancestor of all pigeons, including the ones that were evicted not so long ago from Trafalgar Square.

Noah, then: *pigeon fancier*.

The ancient Syrians considered pigeons and doves sacred to the goddess Ishtar, whose Phoenician counterpart was Astarte, whom the Greeks identified with Aphrodite. Virgins consecrated to Ishtar were called doves (*hu*), a euphemism for prostitutes. The *hu* sound invites one to think of *whore*. One must beware, though, of slinky analogies. Whole belief systems have been founded on a thing misheard or on what one may think is a favourable breeze. Amazingly, though, the notion of a feathered *demi-monde* seems to have survived through onto the streets of nineteenth-century London, where prostitutes were often referred to as 'soiled doves' or 'columbines', a 'carrier pigeon' being one who did her soliciting on the trains. Again, what appears to be cultural transference may be only coincidence. Why *dove*, though, when it is known to be a monogamous creature and has been traditionally looked upon as a symbol of faithfulness? Why *hu* when the very sound came to signify the godhead? When it drifted from ancient belief to become part of the Muslim chant, *Allāh hu?* Whores, doves. Sacred and profane are the two wings of the same bird flying through many cultures. What creature has been made to carry more contrarieties? A brute, then, the highest of all speechless creatures – the Holy Spirit, a dove.

The British Admiralty ought never to have abandoned its pigeon service.

Maybe the thematic weight I'm putting on pigeons is more than they are able to bear. Still, there can be no denying the potency of bird symbolism. The idea of the soul as a winged creature is ancient, and I myself have had sufficient cause to be able to make a connection between the newly dead and a certain bird vying for my attention. Sometimes Ishtar herself took on the form of a dove. She still looks fondly upon Syria, considers it her special province, and wears plenty of kohl about the eyes. The old deities of any place, after being melted down, tend to leave their stain somewhere.

What were these birds to this man? Surely they were more than brutes. Whatever the case, Waseem couldn't tell me, which is not to say he did not have thoughts on the matter but that these might not have been easy, or even desirable, for him to want to articulate. After all, we do not ask of stamp collectors that they be philosophers as well, although one might see, in both philatelist

and fancier, somewhere between the insistence on a stamp's cleanly perforated edge and the high score that comes of a prized pigeon's accumulated points, a shoring up against our own demise. Wherever obsession is, Death watches from some place near.

Waseem had no time for such airy prattle. It was feeding time, and from out of a cupped hand he flung seed in an arc, which no sooner hit the floor than his pigeons swooped and pecked and scrummed for more. So maybe they really were brutes. What were they to *me*? I must confess precious little. A kind of background music that remained inaudible. So many times, without actually pausing to analyse what I saw, although there did seem to be a lovely mathematics in the way they'd move, I would notice flocks of pigeons rise like constellations above the houses, soaring together as if guided by a single thought, their flight accompanied by human whistles, a waving of flags on bamboo poles; and sometimes those floating constellations, one emanating from one house and another from its neighbour, would merge, maybe for just a moment or two, fly as one, and then separate. That was about it for me. I'd be onto something else. It was not until Waseem spoke the words that were either a small nonsense or the proffering of a great theme that I'd either lose, or else come to, my senses.

Such meaning as I would later derive from this nefarious activity came not from the birds themselves but from the relationship between them and men such as Waseem who either squandered their lives on, or else devoted them to, what rises up in the air, goes in circles, and comes home. So why the pigeon wars of Damascus? Why not Karachi, Johannesburg or Tuscaloosa? Pigeons are everywhere, and sometimes they are loved and sometimes they are hated, sometimes they are worth a small fortune and sometimes they are not even fit for one's dinner plate, but it was the fact of them being *here* that would present me, as it were, with a fresh perspective on a city I'd come to love. Damascus was more than just a stomping ground for my enquiries; it was a place that, in dream and reality, both haunted and galvanised me.

Soon I was seeking analogies before I realised I was doing so. Aha, people would say, we know what you're really after. And, scratching my head a little, I'd feign acknowledgement. What did they know that I didn't yet know? This said, it has always been my contention that if one wants to observe what happens at the centre of a society, the best place from which to do so is from its periphery, preferably through the eyes of people who are themselves outsiders. The outcast is, to a degree, made of the very thing that rejects him. As it turned out, I could not have chosen a group of people more deeply reviled by polite society: I would appreciate them for that alone. I would look at them and then I would look at people who were *not* them, all the while seeking parallels that maybe neither side would especially welcome, and it got so I had to resist the temptation to see pigeon wars everywhere. Actually what I was after was something more subtle – echoes rather than analogies, faint shimmers rather than hard edges, sly hints as opposed to verities. Also I needed to keep my eyes not just on the skies but on the streets too. If there were connections to be made, some of them eluded me until my very last hours in Damascus, when a holy fool would pull everything together for me.

Somebody once asked me if I were a journalist and jokingly I told him I was a *metaphysical journalist*. And now, thinking back upon those feathered creatures, on that rooftop in Damascus, swivelling altogether in their separate places, with their colourful beaded anklets that made them look like so many Indian dancers, they seem to me to represent the mysterious, restless powers of the mind, grey matter shot through with occasional flashes of amethystine, and from whose disparate elements – call them random thoughts or memories – one might draw a single, unifying voice.

Chapter One

'Watch Out for your Antennae!'

Since my last visit there, almost five years earlier, I had had several dreams of Damascus. They were none of them auspicious ones. When I dreamed my way back onto the Souq al-Ḥamīdiyya, where I hoped to find Fatina 'Queen of the Souq', the only woman at that time to work in that male preserve, what I found instead was some crazy Arabic equivalent of a western shopping mall, an open hive of small concrete cubicles, one of which was a beauty salon of some kind where a live model dolled up to look like Cleopatra sat motionless in a chair – a plain wooden chair and *not* a burnished throne – and when I asked her *where is Fatina?* she seemed not to hear me, or so she pretended. I repeated my question, but just like a figure in profile on an Egyptian tomb painting, whose eye nobody will ever catch, she continued to gaze straight past me. One dream later, the last in a melancholy series, the Umayyad mosque was nowhere visible, and the area behind it, where the Nofara Café used to be, was now entirely demolished and resembled an industrial landscape, the Barada River cutting through it, black, much wider than it is in reality, and I had to be careful not to slip into it because I was walking along the top edge of a steep incline of loose pebbles. The city I knew was gone. If this were an apocalypse, the dream seemed to be saying to me, it was a self-inflicted one. Worse still, my friends Abed and Sulaymān demonstrated no great desire to see me. When finally I did locate them, on some peculiar housing estate, a group of squat, windowless buildings facing onto a communal square paved with concrete, again nothing such as one would find in Damascus, we sat out in the open air, picking at a meal in bored silence. The loss of any connection to them, this is where those dreams most deeply affected me.

§

When I first met him, Abed spoke of life's vicissis*si*tudes, saying that this was a word he'd picked up from Oscar Wilde. Although he'd never been to university, Abed had an impressive, if slightly eccentric, grasp of the English language. If one wishes to reach into the soul of another people, he told me, one must seek out their language's sharp edge. It was because of him and his ability to translate, such that each phrase came wrapped in the nuance of the original, capturing the humour or sadness of the speaker, that I was able to write my first book on Syria, *The Street Philosopher and the Holy Fool*. What he gave me was actually *more* than language. There came with it the static, the buzz of human existence, without which one has only the surface of another culture and which only with difficulty one brings into one's own prose because the greater part of what one seeks to recreate is lost before it ever reaches the page. Words are mere survivors. Abed was the self-described 'street philosopher' of the book's title. Dostoyevskian in his enquiries into human nature, although Oblomovian in applying such answers as he managed to generate, he soon enlisted me in his quest for a wife. I was to become his counsellor in matters of romance. Now, while I do not wish to claim expertise in this area, I might have been bringing snow to the Sahara, for such was the wonderment with which Abed met my scattered flurries of advice. 'These are things my mother never told me!' While I took notes from him, he took notes from me. What I needed to do, however, and this is where often he failed me, was to disengage him from his pillow, which he clung to until at least midday and to which, as the years went by, he would cling more and more.

When Abed became engaged to a girl of sixteen called Ghufrān he came to me, with panic in his eyes, saying he had never before kissed a girl. 'I understand there is a problem with oxygen intake.' The affair with Ghufrān was to end in failure, as would all his future romances. Abed, who dedicated himself to adventures of the mind, had little to offer in terms of a secure marital, or, indeed, *material*, future. While his greatest fear was of becoming a 'mainstreamer', what he wanted was a girl of traditional values 'pure of mind and body' who had all the mental attributes of a westerner, that is, someone with whom, while she sliced the aubergines, he could discuss Averroes. I was never able to persuade him that truth and happiness, although decent enough objectives, are rarely found on the same plate.

Meanwhile, his bosom friend, Sulaymān, holy fool and alchemist, moved along a path of asceticism strange to even his fellow Muslims. Such was the love between them, Abed told me, that when he dies, amid his putrescence will be found the gold Sulaymān's friendship gave him. (A self-confessed poacher of lines, Abed couldn't recall whether he invented or stole this one, so we decided to call it a proverb just in case.) In this life, on the other hand, Sulaymān was determined to produce *actual* gold, the making of it being for him, as for all true alchemists, as opposed to puffers, a spiritual exercise. *Omnia in Unum.* When I last saw him, it was at one of his alchemical sessions. As we watched the temperature on the digital kiln steadily rise, Sulaymān, pretending to succumb to the effect of poisonous fumes, performed one of his splendid mimes. Over his feigned corpse, Abed explained to me how it had been Sulaymān's ambition to dispense with language altogether and to go through life by means of mime alone. A follower of the great mystic and philosopher, Ibn al-'Arabī, Sulaymān sought to interpret things according to his own lights which at times flickered wildly, as if there were something loose in the connection between medium and source. Whatever the particulars, and he was nothing if not unique, Sulaymān's holy folly had its roots deep in the country's spiritual history. Sometimes the line between it and total madness would dissolve almost entirely, not least the year he spent in a cemetery, communing with the newly dead as they were lowered into their graves. All he ate, during that period of his life, was one date a day, which, as a few desert travellers can verify, is something of which only Bedouins are capable. Sulaymān's father was from of one of the desert tribes. Sulaymān had never been to the desert but always he spoke of it as his spiritual home.

Sulaymān was who Abed most wanted to emulate, while, at the same time, Abed prevented Sulaymān from flying into space. They were, if anything, too close. Such mutual dependency, once fractured, could never be fully repaired. Over the years I knew them they began to drift apart, and it got so they would reunite only for my sake. Oddly enough, the affection they demonstrated for each other at those meetings was real enough although Abed put this down to memories, or, rather, the remembrance of memories. Occasionally, though, Sulaymān would demonstrate his power over Abed and Abed would retreat wounded, asking why such and such a weakness in him had been so cruelly exposed. This would be followed by another period of silence. If, as my dreams portended, I were to lose their friendship, Damascus might just as well be a barren landscape.

There was somebody else equally important to me.

Yasser Saghrjie, although of Turkmen origin, was first and foremost a Damascene. Actually he was *profoundly* Damascene, given his complete absorption with, and love for, the city. Yasser's knowledge of Damascus was encyclopaedic and indeed there is no place he loved more, although Istanbul came close, and because he articulated so well his passion for where he lived it was to him I would go when I wanted something of the city's nature revealed to me. Abed and Sulaymān had taken me into its secret life, showing me things normally invisible even to native Damascenes, whereas Yasser could show me what was there for everyone to see. The latter, as opposed to the multi-faceted gems of bizarre experience, is what one so often disregards or misses.

Another aspect of Yasser's nature was that he attached himself to hopeless causes, which was strange given his absolute scrutiny in the business of daily life. A romantic in the extreme, he was a fool (*majnūn*) when it came to women and wise only when in retreat from them. I noticed later in his copy of Orhan Pamuk's *My Name is Red* that he'd highlighted the sentence: 'Tell me then, does love make one a fool or do only fools fall in love?' A wily businessman, he was also an aesthete. There is little to which he did not give the greatest thought and, like Abed, he was philosophically inclined although he did not tarry too long with anything insupportable. There were no phantom chairs in his thinking nor was there any need in him to flatter or please, which is where so often one becomes unstuck with Arabs who feel it is impolite to offer a negative. Yasser was wholly on the level, there never being any slip or slide. One threw one's junk at him to see what stuck and what didn't. A sturdy presence behind all I wrote, Yasser did not even need to be impolite with me because he had two distinct smiles, only barely distinguishable from each other, one of which indicated assent, and the other, accompanied by a slight furrowing of the brow, nonsense. This he did while appearing to be on his own learning curve.

'A connoisseur of poetry and nomadic textiles' is how he appears all too briefly in *Street Philosopher* and certainly he was most succinct on the subject of his favourite Syrian poet and playwright, Muḥammad al-Māghūṭ. What he told me was beyond the reach of many literary critics, which is to say he had an ability to describe how al-Māghūṭ's work played upon the nerves of ordinary Syrian people. When I last saw him he was reading, in English, Milan Kundera's *The Unbearable Lightness of Being*. As he began to tell me about it he blushed, for the book contains scenes unthinkable in Arabic literature. Worry came to him easily and what troubled him most was his inability to absorb modern English verse. Without any recognisable metre to cling to, he felt left out in the cold, and yet he read poetry deeply and not, as is so often the case with his fellow citizens, by rote. One day I accompanied him on a walk when from out of the blue he recited a line.

'*Stone walls do not a prison make nor iron bars a cage.*'

I asked him from where he got it.

'Richard Lovelace,' he replied. 'It's in my most precious book, *The Penguin Book of English Verse*.'

Would Yasser be there for me as well?

§

A year before, I discovered the 1936 film, *Pépé le Moko*, and, with something approaching nostalgia for a world that never quite was, I watched it several times. *Casablanca* is not a patch on it, nor is *Sinbad the Sailor*. Jean Gabin plays a charming French gangster, confined to the Casbah in Algiers, where he is shielded from the police. The Casbah is a maze. Only if Pépé leaves it and abandons his Arab mistress, Inès, for a floozy Parisian, Gaby, will they be able to catch him. What does he really pine for, though, the dazzling babe or the City of Light, memories of which she reawakens in him? At one point he speaks to her of his longing for the Métro. Other men might have been thinking along rather different lines. As of late, eyebrows have been raised about the director Julien Duvivier's cultural and political attitudes. Soon there may be questions about mine. The film is shamelessly Orientalist in tone. It wouldn't be the great film it is otherwise. What was there about it, though, that made me ache? Could it be that I pined for what Pépé wants to flee? Was I feeling nostalgic for similar dark alleyways, strains of Arabic music and an occasional whiff of spices? Certainly in Pépé's shoes, and I would rather it were *in his time*, I'd have gone for the dusky Inès and the Ali Baba Café. Could it be the film offered the blatant fiction, which, when putting pen to page, I was at such pains to avoid? Was I after a holiday from verisimilitude? I am not given to escapism, however, and prefer the mysteries of the real world to those of celluloid fantasies. Still, one wants for truth of a kind even in movies. One reason the film tickled me so is that the evil it portrays is of a spiritually localised nature, and, no matter how wobbly the premises, the human predicaments as played out in that particular space (which I learned later, to my surprise, was actually a set built in Joinville) felt true. One was dealing with recognisable forms rather than with mere fripperies. The gangster Pépé cares about style; he cares about etiquette; he cares about the French language.

Pépé's world is graspable and somehow delicious, witty and attractive, and it reminded me of Damascus as I first experienced it, when, as in an old movie, I really did enter a play of light and dark. It was not so strange, then, that my planned return to Damascus should be infused with memories, over a decade old, of my first visit there, when I had arrived without so much as a guidebook and also without having secured a room in advance. A petty crook called Eli had said to me, 'Would you like to know the Arabic for *chicken and rice*?' There was a curl at one side of his smile, which he might have gleaned from some other movie. Certainly it had nothing of Pépé's Gallic insouciance. I fell for his line and twenty-four hours later was relieved of my purse. The irony of it all, and I am thinking here of my friends having warned me against going to such a 'dangerous' place, is that, technically speaking, Eli was an American, a New Yorker of Syrian descent. I should have been able to judge him by his doubtful name and his silk flowered shirt, the buttons of which were half undone, but then he looked too much the crook to possibly be one. Eli told me he had been a boxer once. This much was believable. With his shaven head and broken nose, his ballroom dancer's nimbleness, his pointed shoes, and his fingers that he'd open shut, open shut, open shut, Eli seemed a likely enough middleweight, a walking cartoon strip speaking through bubbles. 'Say, you speak good English for an Englishman,' he said in impeccable Brooklynese, and I had no wish to disabuse him of the notion. 'I met this English guy once, didn't know *what* he was trying to say to me.' Yes, Eli had dark cinematic sparkle.

I can say, in all truth, that I had gone with nothing other than a hunger for experience, and that to treat those early sightings as false, which clearly they were not, would be to fall into another kind of trap, that is, of paying homage to what I fear other people may think of me. Should veracity be made to wear a starched shirt? Shouldn't its loose threads be allowed to show at times? It would be another year before I'd find my focus in particulars as opposed to generalities. Still, with that old authorial struggle now firmly behind me, there was something in that film which just wouldn't let go of me. It took me back to a more innocent time, not that such times can be said to exist or, if they do, they are merely silk-wrapped lulls in an endless cycle of violence. I should say rather that in it, in that mythical place, one could entertain certain assumptions about human nature. Whatever could have got into the world's craw that the relentless pursuit of reality, always in the most trashy of modes – 'reality TV', for example – should have rendered the most basic truths false? When's reality not reality but a city made of papier mâché? My alchemist friend told me the new millennium, when it came, might provide a cure. What would Sulaymān say now that the gold he dreamed he could make is nothing more than a hideous alloy of broken glass, steel girders and human blood? What took place one September morning in New York City had changed things forever. Small wonder Pépé's Casbah seems a finer place.

§

Maybe it was because of those dreams of mine that I decided to go first to Aleppo, whereas Damascus I'd approach by slow degrees. Also I would be better acclimatised to any changes I'd have to face. Aleppo is a city whose mysteries I'd never been able to penetrate. My friend Zahed scolds me. By rights, he tells me, Aleppo should provide me with even more material than Damascus. Surely he knows, Zahed with his Phoenician eyes. Aleppo, so he informs me, is even older than Damascus. A new archaeological dig inside the citadel would prove his case. Damascus would be put firmly in its place. The Damascenes, after all, suffer from pride.

Aleppo, Aleppo. ('Her husband's to Aleppo gone, master of the *Tiger*.' Shakespeare's Aleppo is more in evidence than Shakespeare's London. The souq is much as it would have been in his time. There has been a slump, of course, in mercantile activity. Aleppo is no longer in Devonshire Square. Shakespeare, as performed, is barely Shakespeare anymore. There is the running joke that he was in fact an Arabic writer, Shaykh al-Spear, as Zahed is always at pains to remind me.) Aleppo stumps me. All I ever got were surfaces, snippets of information, which I knew not how to make into a tower of prose. The stories I heard were mostly the stories I left behind. They were not to my taste. I can barely articulate what it was I had gone looking for in the first place, but it had to do with making the links between a Christian saint and a Muslim one, with a Jewish prophet in the wings, and that, once made, I would demonstrate how all three had their common roots elsewhere, somewhere deeper than recorded time. Although those origins were pagan, and probably in code, I would be able to decipher them in living faces. I had read F.W. Hasluck's *Christianity and Islam under the Sultans* (1929), which was left unfinished at the time of his early death from consumption. Much ado hides behind the stodgy title. The book is a series of notes really, sketches towards something much grander, which, once amalgamated, would demonstrate a connectedness between things that would light up the whole arena at once. It was one of my secret books, whose identity I now reveal because it no longer has any use for me. Somebody else can take up the cause.

My scheme was quite possibly absurd, a kind of unified field theory regarding matters of religion, which, if made applicable, could be a recipe for world peace. I suffer from impatience. Aleppo, where, at the very least, I would find evidence for an ancient prototype for St. George and his Muslim equivalent, al-Khiḍr, was to prove an endless cable of frustrations. I had been promised a holy fool who would lead me down certain avenues and what I got was an idiot instead. I had to dismiss him. I had planned to go to a religious ceremony so secretive, which I thought was about due, only to discover it had been observed the week before. There wouldn't be another until the following year. I missed appointments or else they missed me. The failures were mine alone, either that or my antennae were not adjusted to the city's hidden frequencies.

Yasser had teased me about my antennae once. I had complained to him about them, saying I hadn't been picking up stories like before. He was greatly amused to inform me that in common Arabic usage such talk of antennae could only mean I'd been cuckolded. It used to be 'horns', he told me, but 'antennae' is more up to date. The sexual connotation remains the same. There is a saying in Arabic, 'Watch out for your antennae!' It means one's wife is on the loose. She may be in Moscow or she may be in Honolulu and she is crazy with desire.

§

One person, sensing my disappointment, fixed up for me to meet a certain shaykh and suggested that if I were to get information out of him I ought first to declare my interest in becoming a Muslim.

'What must I do?'

'You could begin by getting the chop.'

'The chop?'

'Yes, you *know*.' Smilingly he pointed to his nether region.

'And suppose I don't like it?'

'Then we'll give you the chop again!' He winked at me, running a finger across his neck and exploded with laughter.

Shaykh 'Umar was surrounded by various implements, skewers and the like. I had heard of the practice of *shish*, developed by some Sufi orders and frowned upon by others, which involves running steel objects through parts of one's own body. An Anglican priest I spoke to had observed this and was impressed although not sufficiently so to abandon his faith. I asked the shaykh if it were true, that he could run skewers through his body.

'Yes,' he replied, 'through my chest, my arms and legs, my heart even.'

'You will forgive me,' I said, 'if I find this hard to believe.'

'Why so?' he asked.

'I would have to see before I could believe.'

The shaykh, taking a skewer from the wall, said he'd do it right there and then if I promised to become a Muslim immediately.

'What sort of faith is this,' I replied, 'which demands such promises? And surely for me to agree to such a proposal would be to become a Muslim for all the wrong reasons, whereas if I were to *see* such a thing I might be persuaded a little.'

The shaykh, seeing through my verbal transparencies – in truth, while I have little stomach for such activities, my brain dictated otherwise – replaced the skewer on the wall. I still wonder who was more at fault, the shaykh for bartering on matters of faith or me for wishing to witness something on a vaguely false promise.

§

I did have the good fortune to see Nouri 'Ajamī again. I had wondered if he were still alive, the elderly poet who wrote only in English, whose verses were clumsy but true, melancholy Nouri 'Ajamī who had also made it his life's mission to compile a dictionary of Aramaic words that have survived through into common usage, a sheaf of pages that ultimately will go nowhere, yes, Nouri 'Ajamī whose quiet struggles –against poverty, against obscurity, against a history of family misfortune, against the obduracy of a language not his and against which, if need be, he would force his rhymes – speak of what it is to be truly humble. Nouri 'Ajamī has little hope of recognition other than that which I accord him here. I was going to tell him I wrote a few pages on him, that people in England, complete strangers, were reading about him, but when I saw how fragile he was I decided not to. Also I hadn't been too complimentary about his verses. I praised something in him bigger than the actual lines he wrote. He had entered another struggle, which soon he will lose, a serious heart failure, and already he was confined to his home. I did not want to excite or upset him with false hopes.

I was lucky to have found him. The wooden shack, from which he sold socks, and where I first met him, had been demolished and replaced with a metal booth selling parts for sewing machines. The young man working there was able to inform me of Nouri 'Ajamī's whereabouts. The address was in a part of Aleppo that had been home once to Urfalee refugees. They had escaped the Ottoman massacres, and here, amid hunger and disease, Nouri 'Ajamī's parents lived in tents and watched their own and their neighbours' children die.

Afternoon, and Nouri 'Ajamī had only just risen from his bed, and was still in his dressing gown of dark patterned blue. He was like an empty paper bag standing open to receive fresh content, which rustled with each breath from inside, with every breeze from outside. 'Tell me, do you know this word?' Etymology was his favourite subject, as if by getting to the roots of words he could discover the roots of his own existence, the roots that might feed his survival for a while longer, because, after all, there was still work to be done, still words to be found and catalogued, and so it was that for much of the time we were together he threw word after word at me, each more obscure than the last, and incredibly there was not one among them that I had ever heard or seen used. The words, each one of them, seemed endangered species poised on the brink of extinction, whose very survival depended upon an amateur etymologist in Aleppo keeping them alive. The more I shook my head, the more satisfied he was. A daughter appeared, surely much too young to be his, I thought, and then I realised Nouri 'Ajamī was only newly into his decline – he had fathered a child at the age most men retire. Or could it be that he looked older than he was? After all, people in this part of the world age more quickly. What would become of his wife, his daughter, when the breath for which he fought in front of me gave out on him? There was a valedictory note to our goodbyes. I have struggled with, and against, this prose in which I fail, yet again, to capture Aleppo, but now, in speaking of him, I feel a breeze at my side.

§

One evening, at one of Aleppo's finer restaurants, a young man with a falsetto voice sang to me, Niagara Falls about ready to burst from his eyes. 'We should enjoy ourselves,' he said. Ṣāliḥ was to have been my translator if the need arose. It did not arise. Admittedly I was irritable, probably because once again I had failed to find my focus in this most magnificent of places, but this serenade I could have done without in the best of times. And then my guest asked me what the English word was, which best describes the moment the sun or moon first appears on the horizon. The Arabic word, he told me, was *buzūgh*.

'If you cannot tell me the English for this,' Ṣāliḥ told me, 'then you are not a poet man.'

'Sunrise,' I muttered, 'moonrise, *whatever*.'

'No, no, that's nothing!' he protested. 'I mean the *very* instant it appears. I want a *special* word.'

I said I couldn't think of any so precise, and Ṣāliḥ looked at me doubtfully, maybe calling into question whether I was what I claimed to be. I decided right there and then the time had come for me to leave Aleppo. I would put my store in Damascus which had always worked for me.

§

On the way from Aleppo I made a detour and stopped at the coastal town of Tartus where, for the first couple of days, I slogged away at trying to write verses. And when they wouldn't come, I switched to prose. I wrote nothing of significance. The Muse scorns prose. The Muse accepts no substitutes. I did mistake her for a pelican once, which I then noticed was chained to a rock, padlocked too, and not at all well disposed towards the poetic hankerings of human nature. This was near where the boats embarked for the island of Arwad, sadly for the pelican a busy route. I should like to have been able to undo that bird, but I doubt it could have coped with freedom anymore. All day long youths teased her, and young couples, thinking themselves romantic, posed for photographs in front of her, and the usual idiots tried to feed her garbage. Would that she could have shat upon them from above, I'd have supplied her with radar, night goggles too. What I should have thought of then, but failed to, was the pelican of legend, which so loved its offspring it pierced its own breast to feed them with its own blood, an act that later came to symbolise Christ's sacrifice on the Cross: 'I am like a pelican of the wilderness.'

Later, I did what that pelican would most like to have done, at her own table, on her own time, and ate an enormous fish, which I could not identify although it seemed to know me, as it eyed me from the plate. Such are the thoughts one has, when there isn't any sensible conversation to put a brake on them. After reducing that fish to its bones and eyes, I walked along the rather ugly shore, and, not far from where the pelican waited for night to come, just so it could be alone for a while, I watched the sun go down behind a ship in the distance, and, just seconds before it did, the deck of that ship appeared to be ablaze. Greek fire. What was the Arabic word for this, which describes the very instant the sun hovers in air, just *before* it sinks beneath the horizon? Surely there must be one or the Arabs are not a poetic people. Where was my Aleppine with the falsetto voice?

Something happened on my third day in Tartus, which made me feel as though that maybe at last my antennae were in working order. I was sitting amid the Crusader ruins, at an outdoor café, at the inner edge of what would have been the castle keep once. The coffee was superb, easily the best I've had in Syria. The café owner didn't seem to mind my settling there. With my notebook spread on the table before me, I might have cut some kind of figure. The sunlight was coming down at a certain angle, there was a gentle breeze, and, despite recent efforts to make Tartus a major tourist site, there wasn't a foreigner anywhere. Built into the inner castle walls, spread over two or three levels, were fairly new wooden doors, which indicate, each of them, where people today have made their homes. It is a form of appropriation that has always rather appealed to me. Quite frankly, I have never much cared for the antiquities one pays to see, and much prefer those instances, so magical and rare, when ancient stone intrudes upon one's own actual time. This happened to me in Apamea once, when the sun was going down over the Greco-Roman *cardo maximus* or the Great

Colonnade, and I heard the call to prayer, from the minaret in the village nearby, and I found myself at a vortex – pagan, Christian and Muslim – where one world cancels out another and yet remains of it, so as to be, in itself, a species of poetic justice. I felt something like that might happen any moment here, in Tartus.

Straight ahead of me there was a modern wooden pavilion of some kind, around which children ran in circles. There was no traffic, and the children's screams didn't make for a bad silence. I was dwelling on what the mood must have been like, on 3 August 1291, when the besieged Knights Templar put down arms and quit the mainland forever. They would have been grouped right here in front of me. Were there tears in their eyes? Some of them fled to the nearby island fortress of Arwad where they held out for another twelve years. I am glad they had to go, of course, yet I could not help but wonder what it must have been like for them to see their dream of Outremer come to such an anticlimactic end, and also for them to have heard the ticking away of a clock that must have sounded once like permanence. (This is an anachronism, I know. Besides, this isn't exactly how things stood with me that morning. I looked up the aforementioned date only a few minutes ago. Also I discovered there was another group of soldiers, at Athlit, much further south, south of Haifa, who really were the last to leave.) All I knew then, sitting in front of my coffee, was that the Crusades ended here. This was true, of course, if one considers their final stand as being within Syria's present day boundaries. It was enough to provoke if not melancholy exactly, then something approaching mild disturbance. I'm not sure if I really knew what I was thinking or whether I was thinking at all, and also if what one reads into a specific scene bears any relation to what one remembers of it a year hence. A decade from now, who knows, I might have the sun's beams falling at another angle and the café owner will have grown a moustache.

Meanwhile, child's play had turned into child's warfare. One didn't need to speak Arabic in order to understand the cries they made were the perennial cries of some injustice. A few minutes later, all of them had fled save for a boy of maybe six, possibly five, staring at the abandoned shoe of one of his mates. The shoe lay on its side. The boy slipped into another frame, the instantaneous, solitary world that a very young child is able to enter with ease, and which artists spend their adult lives trying to recreate. Certainly he didn't notice me watching him. Gently he turned the shoe upright, positioning it at a slight angle. And then very quietly, very calmly, he pulled down his flies and proceeded to piss into the shoe. I began to rise from my table, the solid citizen in defence of the world's unfortunate, but then I was much too fascinated by the spectacle. It was not one that I had ever seen before. I sat and watched. The stream seemed to run forever. Now, by some happy mathematical chance, added to which the boy's aim was absolutely sure, he filled the shoe exactly and no more. Again I was appalled, but then it struck me – depending on how one looked at it, the boy's revenge was either utterly crude or absolutely exquisite.

I signalled for another coffee. Tomorrow, setting aside my initial failures and surrendering myself to come what may, I would go to Damascus. What I had just witnessed, although I'd be hard put to say what its significance was, somehow inspired me. A small lever in the brain, as fine as any in the workings of a Swiss watch, moved just a fraction of a degree and a brightly wrapped idea, which nobody had ever had before, slid down a spiral chute, and the small thump it made when it hit bottom caused a shutter in the heart to open and then, as if everything inside me had been clotted for ages, my blood began to race.

Chapter Two

The Blue Ball

The street philosopher had acquired a most unphilosophical girth.

Abed who had been so lean, so spry once, waddled towards me. There was a slackening in his face, the atrophy that comes not of age but lassitude. We greeted each other with a clumsy embrace, and then fumbled for words that just wouldn't come. As was usually the case, when meeting him after an interval, I'd have to take a machete to the bramble that had grown over the clear ground that was once our scene of play. And the deeper I hacked for a root cause, the more likely it was a woman's name would leap frog-like to the surface. The last one was a Monique or a Claire, and, after a whirlwind marriage lasting only a month, silly girl, she fled back to France. Apparently she had caught a bad dose of orientalism. She came, albeit just a bit late, to her senses. Abed, silly boy, was going to pursue her, either to woo her back or kill her, he wasn't sure which. I recommended he stay home. So flattened he was, so drained of pride, it required the skills of a forklift operator to get him back onto his feet. I did manage to prop him up for a while, and then, after leaving him leaning heavily against a beam of hope, I heard no more.

The bramble seemed thicker now than ever before. It was almost five years since I'd last seen him, although, given his physical and what seemed to be his mental decline, it could have been a couple of decades. I am reminded here of what a poet in Jerusalem tells me, that this is what happens to young men in the Middle East, especially those with the brightest hopes. Abed did seem to have lost his flare.

We went to our rooftop café, which has nothing to recommend it other than that the clouds of sweet tobacco smoke from the *nargilehs* serve to weigh down the car exhaust fumes. The air quality in Damascus is so bad one *has* to smoke. With every step he took I could hear a wheezing in his lungs, which he explained away with a weak excuse. I said cigarettes – he said no, blocked sinuses. I didn't want to argue. A recent medical report claimed that smokers tend not to get Alzheimer's, which, for Abed ('Allāh be praised!'), was the best news he'd had in ages. Certain things in Damascus will never change, and the café, with its sweet-scented tobacco soaked in apple juice, the click-clack from the backgammon boards, the regulars who shift position only several times in their lives, was precisely as I remembered it. Whether this was cause for celebration or dismay is open to debate. At least it was grimly authentic.

'*Mallam!*' Abed shouted at the waiter.

The word, which translates as 'master', was hurled more like a term of abuse. When I asked Abed what he had been doing the past five years, he told me he had spent most of that time in bed.

'And what did you do there?'

'Well, either I lay flat or else I lay semi-prone.'

Abed has never been anything less than frank with me. When I asked him if he read, he told me he read the Qur'ān for an hour each day, otherwise no, nothing at all, not even the movie magazines which he used to peruse. All this he put down to circumstance, although what this was he was loath to tell me. I assumed unrequited love. When I asked him if he saw Sulaymān he said only rarely, that most of his acquaintances had drifted away from him. Sulaymān's mother, thinking Abed a bad influence on her son, although not so bad an influence as Abed's mother took Sulaymān to be, had been blocking Abed's phone calls to him. The mothers were in an unspoken league. A combination of street philosopher and holy fool was too lethal a cocktail for the conservative Damascene mind, and, as seen from certain angles, doubtless it was true. They had driven each other into inertia. At least Sulaymān was able to give the appearance of being able to move. There was always a project of some kind, although such application as there was did little to advance the fortunes of the human race. The greater the energy he expended, the more likely it was that the things he wanted to make move faster actually moved backwards through time. One had to applaud his industry, though, even if for the want of produce.

'Mallam! Mallam!'

The waiter didn't so much as turn his head. Abed said he had an announcement to make. It was his declared wish that he make my time in Damascus as interesting as possible. The problem seemed to lie in that small word *make*, and that he felt obliged to do what in times past had been so effortlessly *made*.

'Mallam!'

Abed bellowed like a child for its bauble. At last he caught the other's attention. The waiter signalled he'd return in a minute, which, in this part of the world, is one minute short of eternity.

'So who is she?' I refrained from adding the word *now*.

Yes, there had been another young woman in Abed's life, his mother's candidate, Tahani, whom he described as being 'wanton, craven and lascivious', those being the precise words he used, which indicated he had not lost his grip on the English language. Almost always, he spoke in hyperbole. The girl's depravity was probably little more than the cheek that is part and parcel of the marriage game, but which for Abed was akin to higher mathematics. Purity, for him, was the pressing issue. The record sheet had to be whiter than white. Such an approach as his could only mean nobody was sufficiently pure, which, perhaps, spared him having to take a grip on life. As he spoke them, these three words, the way they took shape in his mouth, seemed to prick him alive.

The comedian's gleam was back in his eye.

§

The Queen of the Souq, I am happy to report, is where she always was, with her Marlboros and several packs in reserve, her arthritis, a single braid running down the middle of her back, her owlish glasses and the pigeon's coo that is her tender voice. She, who in our hemisphere would be single, is a spinster in hers. The shop is the closest thing she has to a marriage. She barely strays from the road that takes her there and back home again. When I last saw her a bad storm had rendered one wall of her house unstable. She fixed her house just in time. A bigger storm was yet to come.

This year an increasingly unstable Middle East had been bad for trade, but despite this, despite the big economic squeeze, Fatina remained for me a kind of assurance. Whatever the world's turmoil, and the American shelling of Fallujah was only the latest in a deadly cycle, Fatina's smile temporarily removed all such stains from the mind. The shop was our shelter against dark forces. We stuck mainly to local themes. I'd speak to her of areas of Old Damascus she claimed she had never been to, which are only minutes away, although I wonder if she wasn't teasing me a little.

There is a great sadness in her life. I say this only because she herself was amazed she told me of it. We were sitting in what was the courtyard of a great Ottoman house once, which is now an excellent restaurant, and which would have been mood-perfect were it not for the movie that was suddenly, and at nobody's behest, projected against one of the black-and-white stone walls. When I protested, the waiter laughed. After all, he said, this was freedom. There's no waiter anywhere in the world who is not a master ironist, which may have something to do with food being one of the most temporary of pleasures. The movie, milky with light from other sources, was *The Bodyguard* with Kevin Costner and somehow his squeaky voice grated all the more against stone. And then, just as Fatina got to the crux of her tragedy, there was a car chase with much gunfire and squealing of tyres. Perhaps it was easier for her to unburden herself while my attention was pulled elsewhere. The pity of it was that I had to ask her to repeat what was difficult enough for her to say in the first place. We drank a mint julep, without alcohol, of course, which nevertheless was unsurpassable. The fresh mint was so finely ground one could not see any swimming particles. The lemon and sugar were perfectly in balance. The ice was crushed but not so crushed that it became mush but was more like rock crystals in liquid emerald. 'How's it made?' asked Fatina. The waiter, although he gave us the ingredients, would reveal neither the method nor the measures.

One must listen carefully to Fatina because although she speaks English with perfect confidence, and at great speed, what comes out is a bit of a jumble. She is worth all the power of one's concentration. She has stories to relate, some of them rather fine, such as the one she told me about an Austrian UN soldier, stationed in the Golan Heights, who came to Damascus on weekend leave. 'Can you tell me where the action is?' he asked her. 'What you do mean, *action*?' she replied. 'Well, like, you *know*.' Fatina said, 'Ah yes, of course! What you do is go downstairs, turn right, away from the Souq al-Ḥamīdiyya, and then turn left where, at the end of the street, you'll see a blue door. Go through that blue door and you will find all the action you like.' A few minutes later, the Austrian returned in a crimson rage, saying, 'So what's the big idea, sending me to the public toilets?' Fatina replied, 'Oh, I thought you might find yourself there!'

§

I had chanced upon a copy, in English, of Siham Tergeman's *Daughter of Damascus*, a memoir of growing up in the Saruja area of the old town, which was where my hotel was. I had just read her chapter on pigeon fanciers. And because things for me hardly ever come in one's, I then met Khālid, an Algerian from Paris who was here in order to improve his Arabic, and who had been in Damascus for only a few days. Somehow we got onto the subject of Tergeman's book and pigeons and Khālid told me his landlord, Waseem, was a pigeon fancier. Would I like to meet him? Always a sucker for a story, I said yes, of course. I had spotted a few pigeon terms, in Arabic, in Tergeman's book, and because I had heard that pigeon fanciers are rarely sociable, and by implication, not forthcoming, and also because it is always best to be forearmed with knowledge, I kept a few of those words in mental store.

A couple of hours later, we were sitting in Waseem's living room, which, although I'm sure no pigeon ever took up residence there, smelled like the bottom of a bird's cage. The television was on, and there was the latest report from Baghdad, the deaths of several American soldiers caught in an ambush. There was a triumphant gleam in Waseem's eye.

'So, do you have any good pigeon stories?'

Khālid translated for me, and Waseem whose French was evidently better than Khālid's Arabic scowled at me. Clearly I was there on sufferance. It was interesting to observe how Waseem's sometimes lengthy responses to my questions, when they finally came back to me, in Khālid's uncertain English, were only about a quarter of the original length and sometimes the Algerian, not comprehending the Syrian's French or else unable to translate avian technicalities, simply brushed them aside. I did get this story, however, which involved Khālid too.

'A neighbour stole a pigeon of mine. Young fellow, stupid. I know his mother. She's stupid too. She allowed me to search the roof of her house and, of course, I found nothing there. So I went to the pigeon market and there I was told that a pigeon just like the one I described had been bought and sold that very morning. My suspicions were confirmed. I went back to my neighbour's house, this time found the son there, and beat him. I really beat him. I never did get my pigeon back but, believe me, the idiot never stole another. This was several years ago. A few days ago, I went to the airport to collect our Algerian friend here. I didn't know what he looked like, so I brought a sign with me, with his name on it, written in big letters. I am holding up the sign, you see. Now, would you believe it, our Algerian friend's name is the same as my thieving neighbour's. KHĀLID! And can you believe it, no, it's impossible! My neighbour's mother was at the airport too, waiting for her son to come back from somewhere. She saw me holding up her son's name, and came to me, crying, "Please, please, I beg you, don't beat him again! You made him suffer enough already."'

Waseem then explained to me the business that would give this book its title.

A pigeon war, the Arabic for which is *kashsh al-ḥamām*, although, more strictly, it means 'to call a pigeon in with a pole', involves two or more fanciers keeping their flocks flying in circles while each combatant (*kashshāsh*) seeks to lure his neighbour's pigeon into his own air space. Cowardly is the man who keeps his flock close to home. (Most appropriately, *kashshāsh*, I would learn later, also means 'liar'.) Only with a military precision that comes of much experience, and with the aid of a bamboo pole festooned with ribbons, will he score a victory and lure as many pigeons as possible. When the moment is ripe and he sees his opponent's pigeons caught among his own, he grabs a female bird, a 'hooker', to attract the males and whistles them down. Sexual gratification awaits the first male to arrive home.

There is an old formula that is recognised even today which is, as it were, a kind of ritual lie. If a fancier lives in Bāb Tūmā, say, and he steals a pigeon, he'll put it in a box labelled Bāb Sharqī. When the owner comes demanding the return of his pigeon, he is then able to say to him, with something only faintly approaching truth but which is truth enough for a fabricator of artful dodges: 'The pigeon is not here. It's in Bāb Sharqī where I saw it only an hour ago.' This may be the starting point for negotiation – a bit wobbly perhaps, but such are all peace processes. Should words fail, it may be best then to resort to violence.

Kashsh al-ḥamām, with variations here and there, can be broken down into three basic principles. Firstly there is 'hunting' (*ṣayd*), the rules for which are agreed upon in advance. If one catches a bird it is permissible to sell it without returning it to its owner. Sometimes the birds are killed. The scoring of a 'goal' and any selling operation are conducted with the full notice of the legitimate owner. Secondly there is disengagement or *fikāk*, which means the bird is returned to its original owner upon receipt of a payment. Thirdly there is reconciliation (*ṣulḥ*) whereby a bird is returned to its owner without any money being paid. When the rules are not observed, which is invariably the case, then there is a rise in violence. I had been told of a village outside Damascus where seven people died over a single bird.

A few minutes later, just as the evening call to prayer started, we were on Waseem's rooftop.

'If you want to understand the Middle East,' he said, 'just look at my birds.'

It was at that very moment something crept into my brain that would take another couple of days to re-emerge.

'They are brutes,' he said, 'just like the Americans are brutes.'

Waseem informed me that although a fancier looks constantly to the skies, always with an eye to his birds, he must remember Allāh too. Waseem flung seed on the floor of the roof.

'What can you tell me about *kish*,' I asked him.

Waseem, hearing me use the Arabic word for pigeon training, seemed impressed. With a single whistle, followed by a cry, Waseem got his birds to rise as one into the air and fly in a circle. I asked him about *maṣaḥḥ*, which is the Arabic for when they land altogether. Waseem clapped his hands twice, and the pigeons immediately obeyed, forming a line at the edge of the roof.

There was a fresh urgency in Waseem's voice. The best pigeons are mostly gone, he told me. The air pollution has resulted in all kinds of avian diseases, which can be treated only with the most expensive medicines purchased from abroad. Only the dollared rich can afford them.

'And the Israelis,' he said, 'they are also to blame.'

'Oh,' I answered, 'how so?'

I braced myself for an anti-Semitic rant, not that I had ever heard any here, and in any case for Arabs to speak against Jews as a race would be to speak against themselves, fellow Semites. The argument, always, was against Israel and its policies. This is not, of course, to diminish the anger, which at times borders on the extreme. Actually the majority of people I spoke to wanted to know their neighbours better, and one person asked me whether I could find him an Arabic-Hebrew grammar. 'I want to know the language of these people who I am supposed to hate,' he told me. What Waseem was about to tell me, however, seemed to have more to do with matters of pigeon commerce. A Jordanian had recently bought his top pigeon for five thousand dollars.

'Do you *really* think a Jordanian could afford that price?' he asked me, with a conspiratorial look in his eye. 'No, the Jordanian buys a pigeon in Damascus and then sells it to an Israeli for double the figure. Our best pigeons are now in Jerusalem,' he scowled. 'We have nothing anymore.'

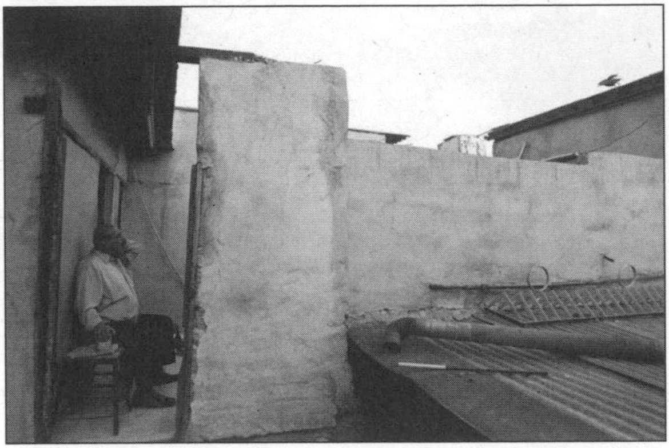

I asked Waseem about *karashtilak*.

'What!' he exclaimed. 'Not even Arabs know this word. Where did you find it?'

I said I'd picked it up somewhere. I already knew that it meant to send one's pigeons among somebody else's, in effect, to *crash* them. There may be an interesting etymological connection here. Waseem looked at me doubtfully and shifted to another sphere. Pigeons, he continued, were being used to send messages back and forth in Fallujah because they alone could escape electronic surveillance. The Palestinians in Gaza had done the same. Then, in what I suspect was a demonstration of tolerance, Waseem pointed out a rusty brown pigeon.

'English,' he told me.

The presence of this drab creature amid others of brighter plumage seemed to me perversely exotic, a kind of Cromwellian stand against beauty for beauty's sake. A few minutes later, my winged puritan flew up above Waseem's head and released the greatest load I have ever seen any bird release. Waseem stood there in a rage, a greenish-white mess slithering down over his bald head, but rather than look at the culprit, he glared at me. Khālid, meanwhile, knew not where to look.

'I wish to apologise,' I said, 'on behalf of the British government for any inconvenience this has caused you. But I will have to inform Mr Blair that I have discovered the weapons of mass destruction.'

It was all Waseem could do not to smile.

A few days later, I bumped into Khālid who had a curious grin on his face.

'Wherever did you pick up that word?' he asked me.

'What, *karashtilak*?'

'Yes, it's not even Arabic. Turkish maybe. After you left Waseem was really angry with me. He was earlier, when you were still there, but because you were a guest he couldn't let on.'

Something in Khālid's face told me there was more.

'What else did he say?'

'Waseem asked me if you were English. I told him I thought so. "The bastards," he said, "they know everything about us!"'

§

Abed, Sulaymān and I were sitting at a small table by the Barada, the river fuller, swifter this year than I'd ever seen it before. We were in a transitional zone, where city gives way to nature. To the right of where we sat there were modern apartment buildings from whose windows one could watch the sheep graze. Across the river from us there was a dollop of the biblical landscape one associates with more remote places, a *tell* of reddish stone. And to the left were small fields and garden allotments and a favourite spot for picnicking, an activity that Syrians pursue with singular grace. A small, wooden hut nearby served coffee. Sulaymān, holy fool turned cabbie, had driven us here. We were speaking of the various changes in our lives. This, incidentally, had been one of the big changes in Sulaymān's life. As things go, this was a bigger surprise than had he actually managed to turn copper into gold. Could one still be a holy fool and drive? The call to prayer, coming from several directions at once, rose above the trees.

Sulaymān's father died the previous year. I remember him well, an elderly Bedouin biding his time, as taciturn as an old grocer sitting in front of his own grocery store. He never had many words for me, but then I don't think he had many words for anyone. An old soldier, already into his eighties, he sat beneath his prize possession, an ornamental sabre that hung on the wall, which was presented to him by the French for his services. Sulaymān's father worked for them as a desert tracker. The Bedouin are famous as trackers though not quite so renowned for their skills as the Druzes. Also they are deemed loyal to whomever they serve, although the object of their obedience is questionable at times.

Sulaymān, his chronology oddly scrambled, spoke of his father's life. Almost always he spoke in collages, which is not to say he was disorganised in his thought but that what he produced was prismatic in effect – one saw all the clearer through the jumble. The man he described was simultaneously dead and alive.

'You would give him a subject and on the following day, after analysing it, he'd come back to you, speak of its defects and shortcomings. When he was young he was a lieutenant in the French army. There was no Syrian government at the time. And he had a motorcycle. After he died, he looked like an Egyptian mummy. A year before his death, I had a strong feeling he would soon die. I informed my family but they said no. I would serve him through the night, move him from room to room, boil water for him, so he'd be comfortable. Three days before he died he said to me, 'You must read the Qur'ān to me.' Sometimes he would joke with me, telling me how right I was, other times how wrong I was. I started reading the Qur'ān and soon he was peaceful, but I knew his days were numbered. He was eighty-six. After he left the army he learned to drive a steam shovel and worked for the government. He trained five people all of whom ended up working in America. My father wanted to travel after the army, but his salary was too small for him to be able to go anywhere. Always he kept in his wallet 18,000 Syrian lira, which was the cost of his funeral. He wanted to be buried in Damascus and there too, in his pocket, he kept an address for his grave. One night I parked my car and entered the house. My father looked at me, and talked to me with his eyes only, saying, 'I'm finished, I'm going', and I answered him with my heart, saying, 'You are a believer. You read the Qur'ān and you have your prayer beads. You are harmless. Go, in the name of Allāh, go then.' I suffered badly because every time he was about to breathe his last he clung to me. I didn't want my father to be ill. If he died naturally, it would be better. The last thing I saw him do was silently point to the Qur'ān and to his beads. When I came in the morning I felt his neck and it was hot. I didn't tell my family. I told my family he was just sleeping, but I felt that he had died just then. I washed his body. He belonged to an older generation, with whom we didn't really communicate. He was from the Bedouin tribes, ours being the al-Bakr tribe, the descendents of 'Alī. We are members of the household of the Prophet. We are the offspring of Imam 'Alī. My father grew up in the desert, travelled to many places – the Syrian Desert, near the borders of Iraq, Medina, Yemen – he was always on the move. We did not belong to any one sect. We are neither Sunni nor Shī'a.'

Sulaymān removed from his wallet a folded piece of paper, which he then carefully unfolded and spread flat against the surface of the table.

'This is our family tree, 133 branches.'

'Was your father nostalgic for the desert?'

'He *was* the desert! The desert was in him. When I looked at him I felt I was looking at the desert, which was cruel and warm at the same time. His physical appearance was of a brutal and hard man, such that one feared him, but when you sat with him he was fine. My father never once hit me.'

As with Abed, I was shocked by the physical change in Sulaymān who seemed to have jumped an age. At least he had done so with grace, whereas Abed seemed to have been wrung through unnatural processes. We soon got talking of other kinds of changes. Sulaymān spoke of them as being scientific and economic in nature, a kind of spiritual stocks and shares, and, although he was at pains to put the years of holy folly behind him forever, I wondered if this were not evidence of a fresh angle to his madness, an extension, rather than a rejection, of his alchemical activities. A young niece of his had pricked him awake, he told me, a chance remark she made to the effect that her favourite uncle had failed to grasp the stubborn facts of everyday existence.

'Where was I for all that time?' Sulaymān exclaimed.

I was not a little saddened to hear him say this, Sulaymān who had been anything but absent from the world although never wholly of it either. Sulaymān told me his dream now was to trade in his yellow cab for a Jaguar. This was the man who had dreamed of bringing a camel to London once. With a Jaguar, he said, he'd be able to take only the most important rides, VIP's, whom he'd take into neighbouring countries.

'So you want to be a mystic driving a sports car,' I told him.

'What I wanted before was to have all one hundred of my prayer beads at once, but now I realise the solution is to go for just one of them. Only then will I gradually acquire the others. The teachings of my Sufi masters were too exclusive.'

Suddenly a blue rubber ball, a couple of feet in diameter, appeared, moving at great, though irregular, speed over the water's surface, throwing odd loops here and there. Surely, though, the ball itself was motionless, and it was the swift current that made it seem otherwise. It seemed to be not a child's lost thing at all, and its appearance, just then, might have been full of adult significance, although not in ways any of us could articulate. We watched it in silence. As I move it now from the water's surface onto the page's, these ever so slightly fake diaries, written months later, could it be that blue sphere summed up all that we had shared before? All this would be a shade fanciful, perhaps, a literary device, were it not that its sudden appearance did reduce us to silence. We were in a state of suspense. It was as if the focus of our lives, which was our small table, had been removed elsewhere. I had just been telling Abed and Sulaymān that one day, perhaps, they would be able to look upon my book as a record of their youth. Moreover, it might have captured the very last of something in Damascene life, caught the bird in flight, as it were. Abed agreed, while Sulaymān, who speaks not a word of English, said he'd have to read it first. The alchemist wanted further proofs, while the other was only too happy to oblige. This was one major difference between them, Sulaymān who for all his folly took care, Abed who for all his love of reason would invariably stumble. And then, as if taking over from our conversation, came that orb as sure, as inexplicable, an image as Wallace Stevens's jar set on a hill in Tennessee.

§

Something nagged at me, and was still nagging at me when I saw Abed the following day. Waseem's words from a few days before had been swivelling about like a pigeon in my brain. The night before, they'd kept me awake. There was something, too, about that pissing boy in Tartus, as if my being able to give voice to his action, which, heartless though it was, had somehow unblocked me; and then, too, the blue ball, which Abed, Sulaymān and I watched in silence, seemed to symbolise a transition in our lives. Yes, I knew which direction I would take.

'Abed, what do you know about pigeons?'

'Pigeons?'

'Actually I mean pigeon fanciers.'

'*Fanciers*?'

'You know, pigeon people.'

'You mean people who keep pigeons? Nobody likes them. They live alone. One hears stories about them.'

'I'm interested in those stories.'

'I don't know anything.'

'Will you help me?'

Abed lit another cigarette. And then, just as the gleam in his eye was about to recede, what I asked may have pulled him towards some promise of fresh adventure.

'Maybe, maybe.

Chapter Three

Allah's Proclaimers

A Short History of Pigeons in the Islamic World (1)

Seven times the Prophet Muḥammad, mounted on his camel, al-Kaswa, circled the shrine of Ka'ba, which was surrounded by 360 idols, chief among them the statue of Hubal, the pagan deity then most closely associated with Mecca. As Muḥammad touched them one by one with his staff, saying each time, 'Truth hath come, and falsehood gone', the idols fell upon their faces. One suspects a poetic embellishment here. Ibn Isḥāq's historical account describing the peaceful conquest of Mecca in 630 is not to be confused with the traditions of which the automatic self-toppling of the idols is one. Afterwards, the chronicler says, the idols were smashed and the pieces dragged away to be burned. We may wince a little to think of the destruction of all this archaeological treasure. What redeems their loss is the epic moment, however, one that has been re-enacted many millions of times since. A pilgrim making the ḥajj to Mecca circumambulates the Ka'ba seven times before entering the place from whose original rooftop the first call to prayer was made. Only then, after the tumbling of the false and the raising of the true, did Muḥammad summon the custodian of the sanctuary, 'Uthmān ibn Talha, to unlock the door for him. In the company of his adopted son Usāma, and Bilāl and 'Uthmān, he entered the Ka'ba, which henceforth would be the destination of every Muslim if not in fact then at least in his prayers and the direction (*qibla*) in which they are made.

Amid the clutter of votive offerings, cult objects, statuettes and painted images (including one of the Virgin and Child, which the Prophet said was not to be harmed) there, hanging from the ceiling, was a wooden figurine of a dove made from a palm tree. The Prophet himself pulled it down and destroyed it with his own hands, with a vehemence that surely points to the object's symbolic importance.

Just what, then, had been destroyed?

The dove, one of the most enduring and potent of all symbols, appears everywhere in the religions of the Middle East, from the earliest times through to Sumerian and Akkadian cultures and beyond, and the names of the goddesses they represent or serve are, at times, close to interchangeable. The dove, or pigeon, was in all likelihood emblematic of the Great Mother Goddess of Neolithic times, and sometimes, in ancient sculptures, the bodies of woman and bird are combined to comical effect. If there is any uncertainty as to the ornithological species, the sculptors themselves are to blame. She would gain sharper outlines in later years. The Sumerians not only sculpted but also named her in their writings as being sacred to various local goddesses, among them Bau, Gula and Ninhursag, Queen of Heaven and Earth. At the temple of the last, at al-'Ubaid, is the row of sitting pigeons of which three have already made their maiden appearance at the beginning of this book.

The Queen of Heaven changes her name from time to time. In southern Sumeria Ninhursag became Inanna, and in northern Sumeria the semitic Akkadians called her Ishtar who is easily identified in her dove form. The Queen of Heaven is also quite mobile. The Sumerian Ishtar became, albeit in a more militant form, the Babylonian Ishtar. She was also the Goddess of Fertility. When she got to western Anatolia, she was known as Cybele, and when the Greeks came she became Artemis or Diana. Ascalon, city of the Philistines, was a centre of a dove-goddess cult and in later years the Greeks said Aphrodite 'My Lady of Trees and Doves' came originally from there. Philo the Jew, writing in the first century A.D., noted that there was an ancient religious commandment that forbade the catching or profane use of pigeons.

Semiramus, sacred to the Assyrians and Babylonians, was the daughter of the Syrian fish-goddess, Derceto or Atargatis, and according to one myth an egg, which fell from heaven into the Euphrates, was rolled ashore by a fish and hatched by doves. She grew up to become Semiramis whose name translates as 'the Dove-goddess loves the child'. When she died she was changed into a dove, which thereafter was held to be sacred. The goddess of legend is backed by a historical figure, Sammuramat, wife of the Assyrian king Shamshi-Adad V, and herself regent 810-805 B.C. Semiramis is also remembered for her sexual excesses.

According to the Book of Leviticus the Jews considered the pigeon clean enough to be used as a sacrifice. Later, certain early Christian heresies allowed the dove goddess to survive as a third member of the Holy Trinity, that is, until the Nicene Council saw fit to remove her. They were probably right to do so, although one might lament her going all the same.

Meanwhile, in Syria, one of her manifestations was to set men's hearts on fire. The Roman poet, Tibullus, wrote:

> The white doves the Syrians of Palestine
> Revere, flutter unharmed through every city.

These doves had a special significance. Lucian of Samosata in his *De dea Syria* (*The Syrian Goddess*) wrote of a deity so libidinous that even in the most recent Loeb Classics edition of his works this chapter alone is thickly veiled in antique prose. For a long time, *De dea Syria* was thought to be a satire or a parody in the manner of Herodotus until scholars realised the sexual heat was for real. Lucian, who was born circa A.D. 120, was a native of northern Syria and would have been acquainted with local religious rites. What is truly remarkable is that the goddess Mylitta, who is akin to Ishtar, was already into her sixth century. She had a while to go. Herodotus identified her with Aphrodite. Of all the female incarnations under discussion she is the most liberated and at the temple of Hierapolis she was venerated amid phallic shapes, eunuch priests and temple whores. She probably gave Babylon its bad name. She was worshipped there, and any woman of that place was obliged to prostitute herself once in her lifetime. She would wait at the temple until a stranger, declaring his faith in the goddess, which seems a fair enough excuse, offered her money for her services. What that amount was, and in all probability it was decided between both parties, it was dedicated to Mylitta. It is not easy to determine which of the prostitutes sold their bodies more than once, but a number of such figures became attached to temples. They were known as doves. The actual dove was sacred to Mylitta, just as it was to nearly all of the goddesses, Aphrodite included, and would be assured of a safe abode. Lucian observes: 'Of birds the dove seems the most holy to them, nor do they think it right to harm these birds, and if anyone have harmed them unknowingly, they are unholy for that day and so when the pigeons dwell with the mean they enter their rooms and commonly feed on the ground.' The Syrian goddess was to survive for a long time, and the sexual musk surrounding her would have been noticeable even from a distance of several centuries when, in 630, amid 360 fakes, the Prophet Muḥammad destroyed her emblem dove or its not so distant relative.

It is ironic that the Prophet Muḥammad, who destroyed the wooden figurine, should himself have become the object of a Christian slander with regard to pigeons. The substance of this falsehood, traces of which yet survive, is most tidily summed up in John Moore's *Columbarium: or, The Pigeonhouse being an Introduction to a Natural History of Tame Pigeons* (1737).

> Mahomet, the Imposter Prophet of the *Turkish* Religion, and Author of the *Alcoran*, is reputed by some Authors, and those of good Note, as *Scaliger*, *Grotius*, and *Sionita*, to have made Use of the following Stratagem, to induce the credulous *Arabians* to believe that he convers'd frequently with the Holy Spirit, and receiv'd from him his mission as a Prophet, and the new Doctrines he was about to broach.
>
> This Imposture he carried on in this Manner: He took a young Pigeon of the kind which we are now describing, and which by the immaculate Whiteness of its Plumage, was not an improper Emblem of Purity and the celestial Dove: The Bird he brought up by Hand, and made it very tame and familiar, till at last he taught it to eat Meat out of his Ear, which he might easily do, especially if he fed it with rape or Hemp-feed there, which all Pigeons are naturally very fond of, till at last the Pigeon wou'd come frequently to search for its Food there. This Bird he impos'd upon the *Arabians* to be the Holy Ghost, whispering the

Dictates of the Almighty, and teaching him the Precepts of his new Law, and from hence, this Bird is call'd after him by the name of *Mahomet*.

Nothing could be more at variance with the Prophet's thinking with regard to the worship of images. Also, the story differs in tone from those related by earlier Christian travellers. When the Italian Ludovicus Vertomannus visited Mecca in 1503 he made reference to 'the doue that spake in the eare of Mahumet, in lykensses of the Holye Ghost' but without any of the snide distortion that appears in later versions. Moreover his informants had to have been Muslims – they could not have been anyone else. When the ornithologist Francis Willughby (1635-1672) visited the Middle East in search of new species he had no axe to grind, religious or otherwise. Willughby's aim, as his most recent editor John Ray noted, was to exclude 'hieroglyphics, emblems, morals, fables, presage or ought else pertaining to divinity, ethics, grammar, or any sort of humane learning, and present him [the reader] with what properly belongs only to natural history.' Surely his informants too were Muslims. There had to be some reason why the Damascene, still considered by fanciers as the finest breed of pigeon, was commonly referred to as 'the Mahomet'. Willughby also speaks sympathetically of this bird's eyes as having the liquid darkness of the natives. Richard Burton, who was as far removed from the Christian faith as can be, he too repeats the story without prejudice. There would seem to have been some tradition regarding the Prophet and a pigeon, whose roots are no longer clearly visible.

It should not be assumed the Prophet was hostile towards pigeons. A most tantalizing glimpse is that provided by the Prophet's own wife, 'Ā'isha, who, according to Aḥmad ibn Ḥanbal (780-855), compiler of the *Musnad*, one of the earliest, and most important, collections of hadiths, remarks: 'We had in our house a kind of pigeon. When God's Messenger, upon him be peace and blessings, was at home, it would stay quiet, but as soon as he left home, it would continually pace to and fro.' 'Ā'isha, incidentally, is one of the most revered women in Islam, and her memories are considered both precious and accurate. Clearly the Prophet kept at least one bird in his home.

With respect to pigeons, the most important tradition relates to the *hijra*, the Prophet's emigration from Mecca to Medina in 621, which on account of its importance stands as year one in the Islamic calendar. The Prophet, seeking shelter from the unbelievers who were pursuing him, together with Abū Bakr, took refuge in the cave of Thawr. There are a number of traditions relating to the cave. Al-Wāqidī says a spider wove a web over the mouth of the cave, and that when the Prophet's pursuers came, which, in some accounts, included Muḥammad's chief bugbear, Umayya bin Khalaf of the Quraysh tribe, they concluded that the web was so thick it must have been there since before the birth of Muḥammad. Another legend builds upon this, with the sudden growth of a tree. A couple of wild pigeons settled at the entrance to the cave, laying their eggs there. When the Quraysh saw this, they remarked, 'Would those pigeons, standing there, still be there if someone were in the cave?' The Prophet, hearing those words, blessed the pigeons, and made them sacred ever after in this most holy of territories, where it is sacrilege to harm them. Islamic scholars still debate over the accuracy of the stories, just as they do with any tradition that stands outside the inviolable Qur'ān. The problem of miracles is for them a vexing one. Whatever the case, the tradition continued to survive. While pigeons in Medina have appeared on the dinner table, those at Mecca are assured of their safety. Ludovicus Vertomannus continues:

> These are seene euery where, as in the villages, houses, tauernes and graniers of corne and ryse, and are so tame that one can scharsely dryue them away. To take them or kyll them is esteemed a thing worthy death, and therefore a certayne pension is geuen to nourysshe them in the temple.

And it was still the case, centuries later, when Sir Richard Burton visited Mecca in 1853. In his *Pilgrimage to Al-Medinah and Meccah* (1855), he observes a young boy going with a pocketful of barley to feed the mosque pigeons and follows this with yet another tradition:

> He went to the place where these birds flock – the line of pavement leading from the isolated arch to the Eastern cloisters. During the day women and children are to be seen sitting here, with small piles of grain upon little plaited trays of basket-work. For each they demand a copper piece; and religious pilgrims consider it their duty to provide the reverend blue-rocks with a plentiful meal . . . At Meccah they are called the doves of the Ka'abah, and they never appear at table. They are remarkable for their propriety when sitting upon the holy building. This may be a minor miracle: I would rather believe that there is some contrivance on the roof. My friend Mr. Bicknell remarks: 'This marvel, however, having of late years been suspended, many discern another omen of the approach of the long-awaited period when unbelievers shall desecrate the sacred soil.'

A dedicated gatherer of information, Burton notes that in many Muslim countries pigeons are referred to as 'Allāh's Proclaimers' because their movement when cooing resembles prostration. Here, again, this religious metaphor is not without historical precedence. Saladin's secretary, Qāḍī Fāḍil, who died in 596/1200, described carrier pigeons as 'prophet birds' or, more literally, 'prophets of the birds' (*anbiyā' al-ṭayr*). This colourful term was derived from the way pigeons perch on their branches in the same way that preachers perch on their minbars.

Two legends survive to this day on the streets of Damascus, one of which concerns the turtledove, which flutters over the grave of the Prophet Muḥammad so that it may be kept cool and shielded from the sun's rays. (The call of the turtledove also marks the end of the midday siesta during which time the bird goes silent.) So esteemed are the members of this breed that it is considered sacrilege to kill one. The other legend speaks of a mythical bird, the *yemāmī*, which was sent to protect the Prophet from the sun's rays. Connected to this is the belief, in certain quarters, that Muḥammad did not have a shadow and that nobody but him could see this bird whose name, in Arabic, is a common generic name for a certain breed of pigeon.

Very close to the Rokaya Mosque in Damascus, on a street that is usually given over to the sale of socks and panties and even bags of cement – not, one hastens to add, the most modish of souqs – some subversive has scrawled a pigeon on the wall, which is visible only on Fridays when the souq is closed and the wagon above is empty of merchandise. An old tussle continues.

Chapter Four

Pigeon Stew

When Yasser Saghrjie first visited London, in 1995, he crept into a relatively secluded area of Hyde Park where he caught, eviscerated, and later, in the room where he was staying, at William Goodenough House, parboiled and then microwaved a pigeon. A man not wholly given over to brute desire, and besides, he regretted having to use a microwave, Yasser added some carrots, tomatoes and red pepper and shared the results with an approving Italian woman who was staying at the same place. One pictures a horribly foreign glee in their faces.

At least he did not employ cheap subterfuge, such as throwing breadcrumbs to bring his quarry closer, but relied wholly on his own physical resources. One might presume the feline elements of speed and silence and, above all, deep concentration. The bird's slaughter was, he insists, *ḥalāl*, which, if we are to reconstruct the scene of the crime, would have comprised a single, clean stroke of the penknife to the neck, this accompanied by a *bismallāh* or prayer of thanks. Any clumsiness, several attempts to kill it, say, would have been *ḥarām* or forbidden. A good Muslim seeks to be *ḥalāl* in all he does. Quite possibly, though, Yasser felt guilt because later he had dreams of irate Englishmen pursuing him with cameras. An act that might seem shocking to Londoners was, in fact, committed with a ritual observance never accorded the common factory hen over which we pour gravy with no memory at all of God or Yahweh or Allāh who first gave it existence.

There's more to Yasser than a corona of plucked feathers with a growling stomach at its centre. It is to be hoped, too, that my reporting this does not deprive him of a visa in future. There were mitigating circumstances, although starvation was not one of them; nor is it useful to point to any marked difference in culture –

a similar act in Damascus would have been equally unthinkable. It might have been even worse had he acted so within the precincts of the Umayyad mosque where the palm dove is a protected species, where there remains, whether consciously or unconsciously, a collective folk memory of pigeons or doves having saved the Prophet Muḥammad's life. So, then, what plea can be made in Yasser's defence? Yearning, I believe. Such yearning, most commonly a precipitate of old age, sometimes, and prematurely, arrives all at once. And so it was that Yasser, on a sunny afternoon in Hyde Park, was hankering after a specific taste, a desire which was bigger than mere want, and which had to do with filling not so much a stomach as a spiritual vacuum. Now, over a decade later, willy-nilly he falls within the scope of my avian theme.

'Why do they keep telling people not to feed the pigeons?' Yasser argued. 'Why did Allāh create them in the first place? They shit on us and we can't even *touch* them! In Damascus, several people get killed over a pigeon but in London a pigeon was killed for the sake of a single man.'

One further justification Yasser provides reflects poorly on the culinary skills of the English native. And if one is what one eats, the judgement is still more severe. When he first visited one of London's supermarkets and set eyes upon the rows upon rows of tinned vegetables, he concluded the English were a 'tinned' people. Only the English would concur with such an unflattering image of themselves. It's one way they have of getting the better of their enemies. Yasser, acting, as he thought, in accordance with the majority of the Anglo-Saxon tribe, ate from tins until overcome by a need for something of greater nutritional value. One might argue that he could have stepped into another aisle and done better for himself, nabbed a chicken, for example, but a pigeon, and a very fresh one at that, was what he then most craved. The flesh of pigeon, I have been informed, has aphrodisiacal properties.

The English as a tinned people.

A not wholly accurate depiction of a people, it is nevertheless an interesting one. A visitor to a foreign place will often construct a major impression on very little. Clearly Yasser had committed an error of Occidentalism, which would have been quite unforgivable had such an observation been made in his country from a western angle, and yet his perception ought not to be scorned. We are equipped only with what we have, the challenge being how to best make use of it, the glass we peer through being either crystal clear or clouded with ignorance. Shapes may be discerned in clouds, however, and although they may be the wrong ones they ought not to be lumped together with the proletarian sin of prejudice. An enquiring mind is always to be preferred over one that does not risk embarrassment. Yasser found a number of things strange in English life, which subsequent visits rendered all but invisible. It is sadly true that familiarity removes the edge from one's early perceptions, which is one reason they remain so valuable. One swallows truths whole along with mistakes. Also, one's receptivity to the new allows for the added virus of adventure. It is in the nature of package holidays that a tourist be innoculated against this. All he is allowed is a camera and the jujubes of experience.

After many visits to Damascus, although the stranger molecules avoid me more and more, I remain at a loss with regard to a thousand daily events of seemingly negligible importance. It is only with much effort that I can analyse them at all and when the day comes that I am no longer inclined to do so, I will have to go elsewhere, or else stay home. While Yasser was telling me of his Hyde Park adventure, a mule went past, pulling a small wagon upon which lay a single quite large tray of almonds still in their green shells, the financial and physical resources expended on their transport remaining for me a thing quite inexplicable.

A bird is not easy to ensnare at the best of times – harder still is trying to capture Yasser in prose. One may just as well use a butterfly net to catch a meteorite. There is something of both aesthete and bruiser filling the same shape. It comes as no surprise to learn that before coming to work he knocks about a punching bag in the gym and when things go badly for him, which is often enough, he punches it all the harder. It comes as even less of a surprise that often, when he speaks of what most deeply moves him, there are tears in his eyes. A man of peace, at times he goes a proverbial purple with rage. I shall never get to the bottom of his many inner contradictions. Whenever they arise in conversation, I remind him of the pigeon or, if that fails, of his ancestral tribe.

Damascenes love to speak of their ancient pedigree, and lament, for example, the recent invasion of people from the provinces who have little respect for, or scant knowledge of, the city's traditions although even here one might pause a little and take the longer view and see in this yet another historical current feeding into the mighty river that is Damascene existence. After all, its history is the history of intrusions from outside, and one wonders, for instance, how differently things might have been had the city fallen to the Crusaders. The Damascenes were spared just in time. A great leader, Saladin, thwarted the enemy advance. A great deal they were not spared, the Mongol invasions, for example, but however violent those collisions the Damascenes would almost always absorb something of their foes. This is what gives them their hybrid nature, which resembles no other in the Arab world, and so deep are the city's memories it is still legitimate to speak of matters centuries old as if they were recent history. There can be no reckoning with the Syrian people unless one pays homage to this fact and there is a solid contempt for the outsider who comes without either yesterdays or tomorrows and demands that they change. This includes regime change. They will, in response, support even what they most dislike. A conservative people, however, are often given to other, subtler kinds of mutation. What they absorb most willingly is often what inflicts the greatest damage, especially when it comes to matters of identity. With Syrians I have argued endlessly, and fruitlessly, for the restoration of the Arabic line, both in its music and architecture, and I have told them how well they'd look in turbans. As the hadith has it, the turban signifies dignity for the believer and strength for the Arab.

All this is pointless talk in a world where now blue jeans rule supreme.

Yasser's uncle worked in the library of the Madrasa az-Zahiriyya whose façade is a classic instance of honeycombed Ayyubid architecture, its nearest rival being the Madrasa al-'Ādiliyya directly opposite, which also contains a magnificent library. When I first visited the latter years ago, there were figures bowed over ancient manuscripts at long wooden tables. A number of fragile documents seemed precariously shelved. Sadly, although happily for their preservation, they have been moved to the bland environs of the modern Asad Library. Yasser's uncle edited one of the most famous histories of Damascus, *Tārīkh Dīmashq*, by Ibn 'Asākir, and while investigating family trees he discovered that in 1610 a man called Yaseen Saghrjie from Saghrj, a village near Bokhara, came to Damascus in order to study the Qur'ān, settled near the Umayyad Mosque and there married a Syrian woman. Although Yasser's family had its Damascene roots here, it soon moved to the area around Bāb al-Salām (Gate of Peace), close to the Barada River, and which has been their neighbourhood ever since. I say this in order to establish a pedigree, because it is still quite something to be a named and documented family within the walls (*sūr*) of old Damascus.

Yasser might have just dismounted the ghost of a Turkmen horse. It is visible in the way he moves, his legs slightly bowed like two parentheses with nothing in between, and he not so much walks as invades the street, making for himself a space which no one dares intrude. After all, he is a Saghrjie and he knows every stone and every stone knows him. A stocky figure, he has scars on the back of his head from when, as a child, he suffered a near-fatal car accident, and he shaves approximately once every three days. An avowed Oriental, with a family rooted deep in Sufi traditions, he wears a Washington University T-shirt, a baseball hat sometimes, and, to confuse matters even more, he drinks his tea white. It is close to unthinkable for an Arab to do so. I should not be deceived by surfaces, he tells me.

A traditionalist among carpet and kilim sellers, exacting in his standards, the one break he has made with tradition is that his prices are fixed. It is not a ploy but certainly it works as one. Yasser's love is not just for the decorative, but for the decorative which has a history, which makes a piece 'honest' in his eyes. I have seen his face change before a textile as another's might before a painting by Fra Angelico. When he came to London once, I showed him a piece of Zoroastrian cloth that reduced him to silence. It was not just its simplicity that so moved him, but also the courage in the way one colour stood beside another, which took him somewhere far beyond what many people are able to see.

Always he has something with which to torment me, and this time it was an extremely fine piece, which he had purchased in

London, in Portobello Road of all places, a nineteenth-century Syrian patchwork, probably Damascene in origin, which was music to the eyes. When he brought the textile home he removed the hideous backing material that was on it and discovered inside a sewn label with the legend, 'The Cloth of Sir Henry Irving'. Yasser, of course, was quick to spot its significance. With such a provenance, although the cloth in itself was more than enough to make me pine, I dithered for several days before being returned to my senses: its price, though fair, was rather beyond my means. I wondered how it came into Irving's possession in the first place, for it was not the standard Victorian fare. It was *raw* rather than refined and it evoked tribal sonorities.

The relationship Yasser has with his best pieces is what marks the attitude of only the very best dealers. The elderly women who come to him, selling their old textiles, are met with the highest respect, which sadly is not the case with many dealers, in particular the younger, brasher ones, who deride their client's wares or else rummage through them as they would at a jumble sale. My fear is that Yasser belongs to a dying species.

'Where would we be,' he asks, 'were it not for these people?'

I have watched him in his transactions, at once firm and gentle.

§

What is it about Damascus that so appeals to people? After all, there are many places more beautiful and where one may actually breathe. Such beauty as one celebrates here is continually undermined by the dismay one feels for its abuse. As to the actual cityscape, travellers' accounts differ wildly over the ages, their impressions being of a place one either loves or hates. So contradictory is the city's nature, maybe all of those descriptions are equally true. The Prophet Muḥammad, seeing Damascus for the first time, at a distance, declined to enter the city, saying it was not for anyone to enter Paradise twice in a lifetime. True to his word, he never did pass through its gates. An irony often lost on Damascenes is that the city he saw would have been Christian in character – a church stood where the Umayyad mosque now is. In later years, for a while, it was both church and mosque, but then Caliph al-Walīd, brushing aside the warning that whosever pulled the church down would go mad, began with his own hands to demolish it, crying, 'Let me be mad; yea, mad in the work of God!'

Al-Muqaddasī, describing Damascus in 985, writes: 'The City is in itself a very pleasant place, but of its disadvantages are, that the climate is scorching and the inhabitants are turbulent. Fruit here is insipid, and meat hard; also the houses are small, and the streets sombre. Finally, the bread there is bad, and a livelihood is difficult to make.' The geographer Idrisi, who never actually set foot in the place but drew heavily upon the experiences of others, paints a contrasting picture; in 1154 he writes of 'the most beautiful city of Syria, the finest in situation, the most temperate in climate, the most humid in soil, having the greatest variety of fruits, and the utmost abundance of vegetables.' Bad fruit, good fruit? The Spanish Arab Ibn Jubayr visited Damascus in 1184 and provides a detailed description of the Umayyad Mosque, also known as the Jāmī', and, drawing on the city's traditions, collected by the Sufi, Sufyān al-Thawrī, notes that 'one prayer said in this Mosque is equivalent to thirty thousand prayers said elsewhere.'

Abū al-Ṭālib, 'the prince of fools', would agree. Abū al-Ṭālib, whose shop is directly opposite the visitor's entrance to the mosque, claims that the air in the square mile containing the mosque is the cleanest in the world. Would that he knew – best, though, he doesn't. Another of the mosque's wonders, which Ibn Jubayr relates, is that no spider ever spins its web there.

One of the earliest European accounts, arguably the first 'modern' one, was that of the Bolognese Ludovico di Varthema who visited the city in 1502. His *Itinerario* was first published in Italian in Rome in 1510 and an English translation, deliciously rendered by Richard Eden, appeared in 1576: 'It is in maner incredible, and passeth all beleefe to thinke how fayre the citie of Damasco is, and how fertile is the soyle. And therefore allured by the marueilous beautie of the citie, I remained there many dayes, that learning theyr language, I might knowe the maners of the people.' This remarkable figure, also known as Vertomannus, appeared to seek adventure for adventure's sake. After adopting Islam, or else pretending to, he enlisted, under the name of Yūnus, in the Mamlūk garrison in Damascus and from there he made his way to Mecca, the first Christian to have made that dangerous pilgrimage. Later, when he was arrested as a Christian spy, one of the sultanas of Yemen secured his release, which suggests he may have been in possession of certain winning qualities. As inconstant as he may have been in matters of faith, he wrote with a steady eye, and, according to Richard Burton, 'for correctness of observation and readiness of wit [he] stands in the foremost rank of Oriental travellers.'

There are many other travel narratives down through the ages, for example, those of Alphonse Lamartine and Isabel Burton, Richard Burton's wife, and Mark Twain too, if only he weren't so facetious. He rode a bit too easily, one suspects, the wave of his newfound celebrity, either that or the Mississippi really does flow through Damascus. Why make *everything* a running joke? Although Isabel Burton speaks of her relationship to her husband as 'the mere bellows player to the organist', she writes about Damascus with many a splendid insight and her prose compares favourably to his. Clearly she loved the place, describing it as 'my beautiful white City with her swelling domes and tapering minarets, her glittering old crescents set in the green of every shade, sparkling with her fountains and streams.' She kept there a menagerie, so varied its species, a hyena and a panther among their number, it was all she could do to keep them from devouring each other.

The city as it is today swings between the dour and the sublime – cement vies with stone. One sends out one's phantom wrecking crews and one's phantom conservationists and all to no avail because the obdurate would seem to have been raised to the status of a principle. Who could have been so foolish as to place against the wall of the Umayyad mosque a buttress made of cement rather than of stone, with crudely inscribed lines to indicate where the separations between the stones are? True enough, there has been a fresh awareness in recent years, a recognition of things already sacrificed to the wrecking ball, a call for things to be preserved, and the very houses which people abandoned for new, are now being restored and sold at prices that rival those of many of the world's richest cities. What happens, though, when the rich move into the houses of the poor, which were the same houses that in the 1960s the rich abandoned for modern apartment blocks? What happens when many of the finest old houses are turned into restaurants and cafés or, as most recently has been the case, into a fashion boutique?

§

Clearly any answer to these questions lies in things invisible or in what one may term the soul of a city. Why is it that very little of significance happens to me until I pass through the walls of old Damascus? Why would the conversations which one has here, within the *sūr*, the walls, only rarely occur on the outside? There are many fine descriptions of the city over the ages, but very few of them touch upon its magnetism, and it is in this respect that Yasser, without ever having to leave his seat, was to prove my best guide. It was he who came most closely to describing the city's soul while locating it in what is materially there.

'This may sound strange, but I'm one of those people who believe that good things and good people and *dhikr* (prayer) release some kind of physical energy, which becomes invested in a place. When I go to London I visit old churches and graveyards, always finding in them areas of peace. Some people say it's to do with the architecture or with the spots chosen for them, but if this were true why is it that when one comes to old Damascus, with all its crowds and pollution, one feels good here? Actually, when you look at it closely, the old city is a mess. Go and look at the wires outside, go and look at the water system, which, when they dig up parts of the city, I've seen with my own eyes. Go and look at the traffic system, the pollution it causes. If you saw the laws governing this city, you'd be amazed it still survives. And yet we survive because we have this something, which is stored within the city, which we are losing, by the way. All these good things will come to an end if you don't keep feeding them. There is a hadith which says that at the end of time, whenever that will be, Damascenes should have at least a place where they can tie a horse. We have many such hadiths here. They are the traditions relating to the Prophet, things said by him, which stand outside the Qur'ān. They are categorised according to their reliability. Some of them, particularly those relating to Damascus, are weak (*ḍa'īf*) hadiths; others that are a step away from being false or which have been forged to fit a purpose are (*mawḍū*) hadiths, which many people cling to nevertheless; there are hadiths which are simply rejected as being unreliable (*munkar*); those that are completely false (*bāṭil*) of which there are probably many thousands, some of them purposely inserted by unbelievers; and then, finally there are the strong (*ṣaḥīḥ*) hadiths that are absolutely authentic, supported with a reliable evidence. One strong hadith has it that the Prophet prayed to Allāh to bless Shams and Yemen. Another says Damascus has always forty saints (*awliyā'*) and that when one of them dies another will replace him. The historians of Damascus will tell you of the many companions of the Prophet who settled here. They came from the desert and found the Barada River and trees. They were good people who did good things and this released a lot of good things, which, for me, are actually the physical things within which we still live. You do not have to go far to find proof of this.

'When Ibn Baṭṭūṭa came to Damascus, he described it as heaven. I don't think Damascus was for him the nicest city he'd ever seen. There were many nicer, but there is something about this city, you know, there's something so exciting about it, something that lives. There is another hadith: Allāh is generous not only to the good person but also to his neighbours and to the street as a whole. The hadith says when you want to buy a house, choose carefully where you buy it, choose your neighbours before you choose your house. The walls mean nothing on their own, but the whole, the walls *and* what they contain, does. There are treasures within the walls of this city. And not only physical ones. I know of people who always dream of finding treasure, and who dig for jars of old coins, but there are far more obvious treasures one finds here. There are people within these city walls whom you'd never meet on the outside. When you were here last time, and you described how it was you used to be able to stand in one place and things would just come to you, it was because of these reservoirs of energy, this holy ozone. Go to some of the mosques here, and in the middle of this mess and pollution, which is some of the worst in the Arab world, and you feel your soul is swimming.'

'And which is your favourite mosque?'

'It is just down the street from here, on the right side of al-Qaimariye, the Fathī Madrasa, which I think has the nicest mosque in Damascus. Who was this Fathī who built the mosque? This man whom nobody remembers was one of the most evil characters in Damascene history.'

§

Fathī Efendi al-Falāqinsī was perhaps the single greatest threat to Ottoman rule in eighteenth-century Damascus, not because he failed entirely to represent the interests of his fellow Damascenes but because he so outrageously pursued his own. A grandson of a weaver from Homs, in 1735 he was appointed *daftardār* or minister of finances, hence the name by which he is more commonly known, Fathī al-Daftarī. It has to be said on his behalf that, materially speaking, he brought some good to Damascus – the reconstruction, which the chronicler Budayrī describes as the most important of his achievements, of the two minarets of the beautiful Sulaymaniyya Mosque, and then, in 1742-3, Fathī built the road that connected Damascus to Salihiyya, described by one English traveller as being better than those of Europe. This was a shrewd move because Ṣāliḥiyya had always been considered the breeding ground of holy figures, in particular the various Sufi orders whose support Fathī was keen to have. As a *sharīf* or descendant of the Prophet he was by default *in* with the religious community. Certainly it was unusual for a *daftardār* to busy himself with public works and in this respect he probably won for himself the admiration of most Damascenes. Also, given his humble origins, he could appeal to the sentiments of the *Yerliyya*, the local janissaries who doubled as merchants and members of the Sufi orders and he enjoyed, too, the company of musicians and comedians. In 1744, he built the *madrasa* which houses Yasser's favourite mosque. There he installed as *imām* and *khatīb* (orator) the poet Sa'īd al-Sammān who just happened to have written a poem in praise of the *daftardār* and who then produced a dictionary of literary biography which included only those who were astute enough to single out Fathī for praise. Fathī, who by this stage was acting more like a *wālī* or governor, might have remained a local hero were it not that his outward expressions of faith were rarely manifested in private. Not only did he drink prodigiously and in public, but also he was given to lavish public spectacle. On the occasion of the wedding of his daughter, to his nephew, he invited the whole of Damascus to several days of festivities, and did so in order of social standing, on the first day inviting the *wālī* Sulaymān Pasha and his retinue, on the second the emirs, on the third the *'ulamā*, on the fourth the merchants and tradesmen, on the fifth the Christians and Jews, on the sixth the *fellahin* or peasants, and on the seventh – and here Fathī seems to have given full rein to his own true nature – the city's many dancing girls and prostitutes. A man who took the law into his own hands, he often went into prisons and set free whoever he liked, which did not necessarily bespeak a magnanimous nature, and once he even went so far as to send his thugs into the Umayyad Mosque where they set upon two people, one of them 'Alī al-Murādī, the *'alīm* of a prominent Damascene family, who was revered by the common people as championing their cause. This ill-judged action would prove to be a test case in the struggle for power in Damascus.

What was more troubling was his relationship with the ruling *wālī*, who, by this stage, in 1743, was Aṣad Pasha al-Azem whose uncle Sulaymān had just died. Fathī, in what must be considered an act of utmost nerve, put under seal the late governor's possessions and arrested members of his household and family. Such was the disrespect in which Fathī held Aṣad Pasha al-Azem that he did not so much as stand up in his presence. Also Fathī owed much of his boldness to the fact he had powerful allies in Istanbul. Aṣad, for his part, knew he was in a vulnerable position and acted with a circumspection that at the time shocked observers. The populace openly ridiculed him, saying 'The lady is sleeping.' Meanwhile, al-Azem was biding his time. In 1746, he struck, first summoning his private troops, which provoked the *Yerliyya* into attacking not them but the townspeople. Al-Azem was now able to act decisively, and with the execution of many of the *Yerliyya*, he at last secured the prestige which he been hitherto denied. He sent, together with a petition from the Damascene notables complaining of Fathī's activities, a letter to the Sultan Maḥmūd in Istanbul, promising him 500,000 piastres from the confiscation of Fathī's fortune. Sultans have always loved the smell of coinage. The sultan, clearly touched by al-Azem's thoughtfulness, sent back an imperial *firman* ordering Fathī's execution. On July 5th, 1746, Fathī visited the governor's residence, was presented with the *firman* and beheaded on the spot. The 500,000 piastres were sent to the sultan together with Fathī's head while the rest of the corpse was stripped naked, mutilated and dragged by horse through the streets of Damascus for three days. The body was then dumped just outside the Souq al-Ḥamadīyya and left there for the dogs to consume.

§

'"If anyone takes this body and buries it, I will bury him next to it."'

Yasser, for whom all of Damascene history occupies a living moment, cited As'ad Pasha al-Azem's edict as if it had only just been declared.

I visited the madrassa, which still bears Fathī's name, and it was, as Yasser said, a place of great peace. And then, just minutes away, in the spice souq one may pay the entrance fee to the Azem

Palace, of which al-Budayrī wrote: 'It is said by those who had travelled and seen things that there was nothing like it in the Ottoman Empire, not even the palace of the Sultan.' Certainly it is the most beautiful palace in Damascus, the woodwork and mosaic the finest of a period that had already begun to go into decline. As for As'ad Pasha al-Azem himself, he was a paradoxical figure, just to the poor and not so just to those who *have*. 'I have fleeced the rams,' he is supposed to have said, 'and not skinned the lambs and the kids.' A man of just rule, he had scant regard for human life. People were executed for the most trivial offences, while murderers were often set free; a good Muslim, he was tolerant towards Christians and Jews, although this, of course, was, and has always been, the hallmark of a good Muslim; and as for the prostitutes, whom Fathī allowed to charm his hours, As'ad, in the face of the *'ulamā*, refused to expel them from Damascus, choosing instead to tax them on their income. All in all, he was a competent *wālī*, and the period following his suppression of Fathī and the *Yerliyya* was one of peace. Later, though, he was to fall victim to the intrigue of the sultan's court, and, in 1758, after being transferred to Aleppo, was put to death. As one contemporary put it, 'He passed away as dust and as though he had never existed and his palace was left sealed and forsaken.' As the madrassa remains the outward sign of Fathī's misrule, so the Azem Palace remains a sign of its builder's firmer rule. Both are beautiful.

'I was talking to one of the shaykhs in the Umayyad Mosque,' Yasser continued. 'I asked him, "How can someone with such a nasty history build such a magnificent mosque?" He replied, "I will tell you one thing. It was not *him*. When Allāh wants a mosque to be built, He brings things to it." You can read the history of Fathī al-Daftardār, although nobody in Damascus remembers him, but then you read about how they built the mosque. Every single worker before placing a single stone had to do ablutions (*wuḍū'*) and pray to Allāh. If, for some reason, he lost his *wuḍū'* he would have to do it again. They had to be in this state of ritual purity all the way through the construction of the mosque and they would use only the best people with good personal histories. A mosque is built with honour, which is why it survives. This is why you can go to a certain mosque in the new city, which may be fabulous to look at, and you think so much money has been spent in its construction, but you know it has no soul whatsoever.'

And then, drawing from his massive reservoir of hadiths, legends and anecdotes, Yasser illustrated the above with a story.

'There was this caliph who wanted to build a mosque entirely at his own cost. Nobody else was allowed to put a stone there. We have this saying here that if one can afford to put ten million lira into the building of a mosque and another person can afford only one lira, and both pay, then the second person's one lira is equal to the ten million. This caliph decided everything must issue from him. An old woman who was passing by during the construction of the mosque said, "Take this little stone." She was stumbling, carrying it on her back. And the workmen said to her, "No, no, the caliph said everything must come from him." She answered, "For God's sake, what is this one stone going to do to a huge mosque like this? Please don't let me die without doing this for me." A builder took the stone and placed it in the body of the mosque. After the mosque was completed the caliph saw himself in a dream in front of Allāh who then congratulated him for the mosque which he built together with the old lady, saying they both did well. The caliph, thinking the mosque was entirely his, went crazy. He called together all the people who worked there, and demanded who put the old woman's stone there. But it was too late. The building of a mosque cannot be undone. One can drag this analogy further. To put one thing in the right place, to put one good word to make people come together, this is a great thing.'

§

Another mosque where, despite the presence of green fluorescent tubes, one might feel one's soul swimming is the Madares Assad al-Dīn in Ṣāliḥiyya, which houses the tomb of the great Sufi mystic, Ibn al-'Arabī. Step out of the mosque and one finds oneself in the pedestrian thoroughfare, Souq al-Jumaa, at the far end of which used to stand Richard Burton's house and a stone's throw from there is Abū Zayd's place. Ṣāliḥiyya has a rich spiritual tradition, as is evidenced by the extraordinary number of mosques and madrassas and the souq is a string upon which hang many places of worship. It is in Ṣāliḥiyya, too, where one finds the greatest number of pigeon fanciers in Damascus.

Abū Zayd, himself the possessor of some of the finest birds in Damascus, is the son of the son of a famous pigeon fancier who in the 1930s was dubbed 'the shaykh of pigeons'. Abū Zayd proceeded to tell me stories from this earlier period when pigeon fancying was largely the province of the elite, when it was still possible to say with pride, 'In my house I have a well and ten pairs of birds.'

'My grandfather "the shaykh of pigeons" was a modest man. He lived about 500 metres away from here. Now there was another pigeon fancier, an imam at a nearby mosque.'

'An imam who was a pigeon fancier?'

'Yes. The pigeon is strong in Islamic tradition. It drinks water and looks up to God, thanking Him. We love this bird because of its reverence to God. Anyway this imam went to Aleppo and reportedly purchased some fine birds and my grandfather, because he had a good eye, wanted to inspect them. He went to visit him, wearing his traditional work clothes, and the imam, seeing him so casually dressed, wouldn't let him in. "Who are you?" he cried. "Get out of here." So my grandfather left the mosque and went up the mountain a little and from there he studied the imam's movements, figuring out at what hour he flew his birds and so forth. My grandfather trained his birds to fly from this new place, took a female over there, and flew the males in the direction of the mosque. A man greatly skilled in *kashsh al-ḥamām*, he brought back fourteen of the imam's birds. The imam discovered who the culprit was and came to my grandfather's house to demand their return. "Yes," my grandfather replied, "you can have them back but only on condition that you go back to the mosque, shave your beard and remove your headdress and then speak to me. Religion and pigeon fancying do not mix. Choose one! All the big shots in the city come to my home, and they welcome me in theirs, but because you did not welcome me the door of my house is closed to you."'

I was still trying to get to grips with this when Abū Zayd told me another, more recent story.

'There were these two friends, one of them an imam, who always hung about together. They shared everything, their food, why, even their wives were close. One day the imam, doing *kashsh*, caught one of his friend's birds, a rare and beautiful creature, and took it back to the mosque. Later, the friend came to visit him, asked after his whereabouts and was told by the imam's wife that he was at prayer. "In that case," he told her, "I will go up onto the roof and look at his birds." And there he saw his prized bird. He hit it so it wouldn't land in that place again and, released it, sending it back home. And then he went to the mosque to see the imam who at that moment was leading the prayer. When cross-examined, the imam swore on the holy Qur'ān, placing his hand on it, saying he'd never seen any such bird. "What do you mean?" the friend cried. "I was on your roof just a few minutes ago and freed it!" The imam insisted. "No, if I am lying I will divorce my wife and forfeit my children." This is a true story. This imam died a month ago.'

'Where is he now?'

'In hell!'

If the clergy were occasionally corrupt, so, too, were the police.

'The head of the police precinct came once to visit my grandfather. He saw a beautiful red bird and, exploiting his position, tried to bully my grandfather into giving it to him. My grandfather wouldn't let it go. The police chief left and sent his men to remove all the birds, saying to them that the red one was to be put in a separate bag, and that all the birds were to be brought to the station. My father who was never really into birds started gathering them, and then my grandfather said to him, "Gather them up, but make sure you leave the red bird for me." "No, no," said one of the policemen, overhearing him. "We must have that bird." My grandfather threatened to throw him from the roof. "You can bring the whole city up here, but you are not getting that bird." My grandfather then went to the Minister of the Interior and because he too was a fancier took him a gift of several birds. My grandfather explained the situation and the minister picked up the phone. The head of the precinct was demoted and sent to a remote county in the north-east of Syria. My father said to my grandfather, "What's going to happen if they send the police again?" "Well, I will take the red bird and I will go up to the cave. They can come to my house and live here if they like, but I'll leave my wife and children and take my bird with me and live up there."'

Abū Zayd pointed to a cave in the distance, which he said was one of the many hiding places used by Sa'īd 'Akāsh who, depending on how one wishes to interpret his career, was a bandit or revolutionary and perhaps even both.

'When you transport your precious children you evoke God to protect them. When my grandfather transported his birds he always said "Allāh!"'

'My grandfather was so experienced he could tell from the eggshell whether it contained a male or a female. My grandfather had a friend who bred a different kind of bird. "Why don't we trade some eggs," he said. They both had newly-laid eggs. My grandfather said, "I give you four of mine and I'll take just those two." He picked the ones that would later produce the males, which requires some considerable talent because not many people can tell the sex from the eggs alone, whereas the four his friend chose all hatched females. Usually when a female lays two eggs the first is male and the second is female, but it turned out that with those two batches all four of them were female. When the males grew a little he went to visit his friend to see what he had to say about the eggs he chose. "So, how do you get on with my four?" he asked. "They were all females." "What can I do? What I gave you were two batches of newly laid eggs. This is up to God." "No," his friend replied, "God knows and *you* know."When you have two fanciers one might ask for 100,000 lira from the other and he will give it to him. But ask him for a bird? Never! Some of the pigeon wars get serious and people are killed. If I lose a bird they'll bring it back to me because I give them money. I won't lower my standards to their level. A lot of them are poor people, so I won't fight with them over birds. Anyone who needs help comes to me. My father was one of the people who established the Baath party and they have a reputation of helping people.'

'What about the violence?'

'Wherever there is ignorance and poverty there is crime. This can happen anywhere.'

'Do you feel that the traditional code is breaking down between fanciers?'

'Yes, of course! It used to be for the sophisticated, the elite, and people with a sense of aesthetic. It takes someone whose eye can appreciate the beauty of a bird and so that person must be of a high calibre. Even the top brass in the military appreciate birds and they are bird fanciers, but nowadays the ignorant, the unemployed and the punks, they buy only the cheapest birds. They start fighting and that's how problems arise. If I were to do *kashsh* it would be my loss because I have the best birds. All this is being ruined by the newcomers. The true fanciers will get to know each other and will sometimes exchange birds, but not the punks. Society should help these other people.'

'Am I right in understanding that pigeon fanciers often have their own judges?'

'In any community people will know who the right person for the job will be, someone with a good reputation and who is wise and honest.'

'I have heard that with the breaking of the code many people choose judges who are themselves criminals.'

'If the dispute is between two sophisticated fanciers they will find a judge who is equally sophisticated and able to adjudicate. People come to me, from time to time, to adjudicate in disputes. A neighbour can complain and the authorities will remove the birds. If it's punks in dispute they will fight and the fight gets so out of hand sometimes that the authorities have to become involved.'

'What happens to the birds the police confiscate?'

'They take them to a secret place and bury them alive.'

'If your birds were confiscated, what would this do to you?'

'I would be very upset, of course, because these are pure creatures that don't harm anyone. This whole business with bird flu is a conspiracy set up by a rich man who owns a drug company in America. An American ghoul has exported this.'

'Are the police here using this as an excuse to remove people's birds?'

'We are genuinely concerned about bird flu.'

'Can you summarise what your birds mean to you?'

'It's part of my private, my inner being.' Abū Zayd struggled a little. 'How would you describe a red rose? How describe such beauty?'

CHAPTER FIVE

A Cure for Djinns

With Abed I always had to find some combination of words that would goad him into action, maybe a hint of some temptress at the end of whatever path we were about to take, although trussed up she would be nothing more than the chicken he always plumped for at our little restaurant off Shuhadā Square, *The Rose of Damascus* – the rose not quite a rose, a flowering weed more like. Abed, Sulaymān and I would convene there in order to take stock of the day's adventures, or, in this instance, the day's failures. We had spoken earlier to a pigeon fancier so witless no story he began ever got anywhere. And if a plot was not something he could finagle, then he'd resort to lies.

The *Rose* had not changed in twelve years, same menu, same faces, except maybe for an old tourist poster of a pretty Syrian girl that had faded to pale greens and blues. She was in all likelihood a grandmother by now and probably her daughters covered their faces not because they were forced to but because that was how their world had changed, by going into reverse. Abed always made the same choice, chicken and rice, prefaced with a double order of pickles, the pale pink turnips in particular, vinegar solidified, which he drove, wedge after wedge, into his mouth at such speed he could barely manage them and his cigarette at the same time. I called for another plate of pickles. Sulaymān, always unpredictable, ordered liver and chips, which he slowly ate. Whereas Abed gorged, Sulaymān savoured, and mentally too they were opposites – Sulaymān soared, Abed was slow to move.

Sulaymān would have been rich if so inclined. I have never observed madness so perfectly contained in a human frame. Always quick to grasp a situation, he had an ability to move into even the most dubious zones and yet lose nothing of that inner equilibrium of his, which may be compared to those weights the sellers of gold use, every milligram accounted for, all absolutely true. Although mentally he moved at a great speed never once, in all the years I've known him, did he sound a wobbly note. I sat with my back to the window where, on the ledge outside, a stray cat waited for me to smuggle him the occasional bit of lamb through a hole in the mosquito netting. *Allāh provides.* Our conversation was punctuated with regularly spaced meows. We made no mention of our earlier failure. The cat was closer to catching a pigeon than we were. The girl in the wall poster was badly in need of blusher.

I ordered more olives.

'Mallam, zaytun.'

Such Arabic as I know is confined to absolute necessities.

Sulaymān was back on the subject of his father and his Bedouin origins.

'The Ottoman government of the time employed our tribe to protect pilgrims travelling to Mecca. There was always, with sometimes six months of travelling by camel, considerable risk involved. I'll tell you how my father came to be in Damascus. You know we have this thing about revenge between tribes, a vendetta that can be inherited from generation to generation. Sometimes, in later years, when tribes fought each other, the French would interfere. Once they used planes to settle a dispute. Tribe would fight tribe over water, over green pastures, over a woman sometimes, and in such conflicts upwards of a thousand people could be killed. The leader of our tribe got my father into the French army. This man had been in Turkey where he studied the art of warfare and he was referred to as "the inspired one". Nawaf al-Ṣāliḥ he was called, Nawaf being a very Bedouin name and *al-ṣāliḥ* meaning "righteous", and it was he who reunited all the tribes. My father said to him, "I want a job," and so when the Syrian government came into being in the 1940s Nawaf got him one. What really surprised me was that one of my ancestors was first assistant to the famous Ottoman sultan, Mehmed, who reached Vienna over 300 years ago.'

At this point Sulaymān, a man not always aware of the treasures he had in his own store, took me by surprise.

'My grandfather knew T.E. Lawrence, smuggled arms for him. A Bedouin should never be without a gun. He should always be ready in the night. There are photos of Lawrence with some of my ancestors.'

'What did they think of him?'

'They neither liked nor disliked him. The tribesmen knew he was an informer for the British but because of their rules of hospitality they couldn't kick him out. So they ate and drank with him. Their nickname for him was "Abū Barīs". *Barīs* is a white gecko. *Abū* in this instance means not so much "father" as having the qualities of that creature. The gecko lives with us, in our homes. The Arabs used to believe that if you touched one you would become an albino. They'd cut off the tail if it were still alive. A blond man, Lawrence could not see after sunset nor was he eligible to marry our girls. This gecko, they said, sowed dissension between the tribes.'

'Surely, though, he brought them together.'

'Maybe, but all this is gossip. When he returned to England and spoke favourably of the Arabs they sacked him.'

I began to wonder how, in the light of this fresh amphibian angle, I might rewrite Lawrence's biography but Sulaymān had already moved on a generation.

'It was because of such historical connections that my father worked for the Syrian government first as a soldier and then in civil defence where he was involved in the restoration of buildings and so forth. Anyway, to get back to the tribal disputes, ours had killed the leaders of another tribe. This was a serious business because you couldn't offer to pay compensation to their families because these were tribal leaders and you couldn't pay gold for them. They were "expensive" people and the price was that instead of paying compensation we would have to emigrate. Money wasn't of any use – the only thing we could do was to leave forever. Any crime involves the whole family. You have to know the meaning of the tribe, and that in such cases everything, even the sheep, join in the battle. There is a Bedouin saying, "If your tribe goes crazy, your mind will become useless." The only solution when your tribe is in trouble is to defend yourself as best you can. Bedouins are very aggressive people.'

'Was your father involved in the actual fighting?'

'I don't know. We never spoke about this. My father, when he was young, used to be able to carry 250 pounds weight on his back. I think he had a warm heart though. I don't think he would ever kill an innocent person. Only if the other were a criminal would he do so.'

'I remember him as a proud and strong man.'

'He was an honest man, would never take anything from anyone. He would ask me to bring him things but only out of love. Many tribesmen, some of whom now live in Damascus, visited us when he died. He never had an enemy.'

'I thought he worked as a tracker for the French.'

'He was a lieutenant.'

'How did he feel about the French?'

'There were no such prejudices at that time. There weren't the pressures we have now.'

'Traditionally, though, aren't the Bedouins faithful to whomever they serve?'

'A Bedouin, if he is honest, will not continue to follow you if he doesn't wish to, not even if you offer him money. He is either with you or against you. There is no grey area such as you get with Damascenes. This is our Bedouin nature. A Turk told me he wanted to go to Homs, so I agreed to take him there. While on the way there, this man made some problems for me. Here I was, taking him to this group of people, Bedouins, and all he did was backbite them. They were going to offer him everything. "Why do you backbite them?" I asked him. "These people you are going to see, you are going to be their guest, so you shouldn't be speaking about them like this. This is a matter for deep shame." Also I could have got myself into bad trouble. Those Bedouins notice things. Anything can stir them, a single hiccup or a wrong move. You are entering their lands, their habits, their codes. So I told him I didn't want to be with him anymore and returned immediately to Damascus.'

Sulaymān had never been to the desert. The Bedouin seemed never to have quit him, though, and maybe this more than anything explained his hawk's eye, his being able to steer by the Pleiades even when one couldn't see them through the blanket of pollution covering Damascus. I was about to ask him the question to which I already knew the answer, if only for the pleasure of hearing it again from a slightly different angle. I remember once he took me to see a friend of his and we walked for an hour, winding through narrow streets, turning this way and that, and when finally we reached our destination I was surprised to discover that not only did I know it but we could have taken a direct route and arrived there in fifteen minutes. Later, when I asked Sulaymān why he had taken such a complicated route, he said it was because he thought it would give me pleasure. I had been given, at that instant, one of the keys to his character. I was happy to let him take me the long way anywhere and this time our conversation would take me to where he now lived, in the village of Dera, which is on the edge of Damascus, a fairly new development that is also at the edge of arable land. A good many farmers of Bedouin origin live there.

'Do you still feel the Bedouin blood in you?'

'Yes, although I don't know why. In the area where I live they think I'm Damascene, but I'm not. When I first went to Dera, they immediately began their offensive against me. It was psychological warfare. They wanted to know who I was, whether I was harmful, why I was there. They could not believe a Damascene would want to go and live in such a place. I told them I was sick and needed fresh air. You can see the mountains from there. I invited them to tea sometimes. After two months, I was beloved of them. When I told them I wanted to move, they refused to let me. They gave me water, electricity, shared their food with me, and even now, while I am sitting here with you, they are watching after my wife and child. Every day I visit maybe two or three neighbours. If I had reciprocated their hard feelings towards me, things would only have got worse. One should understand the mentality of other people. Villagers are different from Damascenes. Here, in the city, you find a business-like atmosphere. Where I live, there is more mental space. A Damascene is hard to please, but a villager you can satisfy with an apple.'

'Are you hard to please?'

'Human warmth is enough for me. So many different civilisations came here and we ended up with this Damascene type. A Damascene will ask, "What do you want of me?" Peasants are more merciful.'

'Are they really though?'

'They know how to feed the cows and to be with nature. They are instinctive. This is my experience. All other Damascenes who tried to settle in Dera failed. Why? Because the Damascene thinks he is best, and knowing this the peasant will be automatically prejudiced against him. But if you go and live there and say to him, "You and I are the same, and agriculture is the best thing of all because you are feeding the people" then he won't think you are aloof. But if you pretend you are better than he is! A peasant told me, "Look, I feed those city people and they scorn me." On the contrary, I see the peasant as a great thing. I'm not a farmer, but I consider the land as holy because it gives and so one must encourage farmers. One must never despise them.'

I would accept what Sulaymān told me, although from my own experience only rarely are farmers such paragons of good nature. Brutishness and narrow-mindedness are frequently companions to the virtues he described. I wondered if his quest for the 'simple' was not merely a mask for even deeper complexities. The man most solicitous of simplicity in his life will often be the one who jumps through the greatest number of hoops to get there.

'Are you still treating people?'

Oftentimes, in the past, Sulaymān had treated people with mental problems or else possessed by djinns, those invisible beings which, once they enter a human being, can take control of his mind. Djinns predate Islam, and are said to predate humanity itself. Islam recognises them; the Prophet himself exorcised several tribes. Whereas men are made of earth, djinns are composed of smokeless fire (*sūra* 55.15). They take on innumerable shapes and sometimes have no shape at all. Although separate from men they share with them the qualities of intellect, moral discrimination and freedom of choice. Some say they are visible only to those who are possessed of them. They tend to come out after late afternoon prayer and hang about until sunrise and are particularly fond of lavatories. They seem to be especially prevalent in Morocco, and so various are the ways by which a human being may be possessed of one, anything from jumping out of bed naked to pissing in the shade of a fig tree, it's a wonder one gets through the night unscathed. The word has its root in the Arabic *jinna* ('angry' or 'possessed') and it is not wholly surprising, when one thinks of Shakespeare's 'fine frenzy', that *djinn* and *genius* share a common root. Disruptive, although not always so, they seek compensation from people, which can take the form of an offering or sacrifice. There are as many djinns as there are people. Djinns can be male or female and can reproduce through sexual activity, although exactly how they do this is a bit of a mystery given that they are invisible. A female djinn or *jinnīya* can enter a male body and cause havoc there. A bitch, it can turn him against his wife. Djinns are not always insensitive to the power of prayer and in fact the greater part of any treatment for a person possessed by them comes from the recitation of Qur'ānic verses. Some djinns are wholly pagan in spirit and do not respond to Islamic encouragement and for this reason they are the most dangerous of all, often posing a threat to their victim's life. Although at odds with modern psychiatry, there is a booming trade in the exorcism of djinns. Sometimes this involves traditional practice. Other treatments are of a more suspect nature. The removal of djinns can be costly business and many thousands of families have been financially ruined. A *majnūn* ('fool') is said to have been invaded by a djinn. Where black magic is practiced, and its effects are sufficiently well-known to dispel any doubts as to its efficacy when used against people who believe in it, it is impossible to put a spell on anyone without the help of a djinn; conversely the removal of that spell involves communicating with the same djinn, although frequently a second djinn will be employed to drive out the first one. The burning question is whether or not they exist, yet if to know one's demons is to master madness, we may as well become friendly with them. Some say that what is really meant by them are the evil inclinations and tendencies of a corrupted soul and that likewise angels may be said to represent the good in ourselves. Such an approach makes them that much more explicable. One can be a *majnūn* for love, for example, and, in this respect, where's the mad lover who does not feel himself possessed? What is poetically is not always demonstrably true.

I asked Sulaymān how *he* would describe a djinn.

'It is a mass created from fire. If it is an atheist djinn that possesses someone, then this is a serious case. A person I know thinks he can stop the sun. This is atheism, delusion. If you want to save someone like this you need to be strong because you will be attacked for sure. Sometimes the djinn will resort to threats, saying, "If you do this, I will do that to you." Basically a djinn destroys whomever it possesses. Once I healed a girl and was sick for two days afterwards. Such treatment requires someone who is strong. I get affected by patients sometimes and suffer and afterwards stay unemployed for a while. Actually this business is getting to me. I don't want to do it anymore. It pursues me. Now I treat only essential cases, whereas I won't touch anyone who has multiple problems. It is easier to deal with a spinster or a child because they are relatively quick to treat, there is less pressure, but those with chronic psychological problems can go to the shrink. They misunderstand themselves when they say they are spiritually ill because really they are psychologically ill. Sometimes, of course, you find someone who is both psychologically ill *and* possessed by djinns. You learn from experience. I have had to endure many spiritual and psychological shocks. Sometimes you get a patient who is completely ill, who has no internal hardware or software.'

'We are bringing this up to date!'

'You have to give such a patient the spirit of hope. First, psychologically speaking, you have to say to him, "You exist." The Bedouin do this when they poke a patient in the waist, so that he feels he exists. I poke either with my spirit or my hand. It is like an electric shock. I say, "Look at me. You exist!" So the patient will be encouraged because he knows he exists. The patient feels himself pulverised. I was on a minibus once when I heard this man talking to himself, saying, "God, I am in prison, between my house and my profession. When will it end?" It turns out he was a craftsman who had been doing his job for fifty years. I asked him whether what he said was really true. "You are serving people," I told him. "You are important." If he feels he is helping people and making tools for them, he will not feel so greatly this pain of imprisonment. This man was psychologically ill. He was not hit by djinns.'

Sulaymān and Abed looked at each other briefly, and I thought I caught some flicker of discomfort in that exchange. I didn't realise then how close I'd come to discovering the reason for this. Although estranged, they kept up appearances for my sake. I suspect, though, the love between them had not been wholly extinguished.

'No so long ago, I treated a girl possessed by djinns.'

'So what does one do with her?'

'If she is beautiful, what we call "a green girl", I will be assisted by Khiḍr and the prophets. I read the Qur'ān to her. I am afraid to be with her on my own, so when I start with my treatment I bring other people. What is her target? It is to attract me to her beauty, so I bring four important people in our society, maybe a tribal leader or a mayor, strong men, usually in their sixties, who have had such experiences. They come and I say to them, "Stay with me spiritually." So then I put her in a room and I cover her with a blanket. There is no other solution.'

Abed and I burst into laughter.

The beauty in the poster was a 'green girl'.

'Well, look, if I were alone with her, I might be aroused. I do my best not to be alone with her, because when you add benzene to fire you get nuclear sex.'

Sulaymān started on another topic.

'No, wait a minute! You've put a blanket over her head. Is that the end of the treatment?'

'You set a dry branch from an almond tree on her head as well, on top of the blanket, and then start reciting verses from the Qur'ān. The almond branch is inherited from pre-Islamic times. You can use a sword instead of a branch. The sword is symbolic. If she is possessed, the djinns will start speaking through her. They might be foreigners; they might be ancient Assyrians – they will begin to talk to me. "What do you want?" they ask. We start to converse and the invisible war begins. If she is very beautiful, they won't leave her immediately. A beautiful girl needs about three months' treatment, which involves expense. There is a famous hadith: "Beware of a beauty brought up in a nasty environment." What do we mean by a nasty environment? It can be an alcoholic one, with prostitution or belly dancing, maybe even sex orgies.'

'It happens here?'

'Yes, but it is well hidden.'

'Let's go, then!'

Abed slapped the palm of my hand with his.

'It is a dangerous environment,' he continued. 'Such things exist everywhere. This UAE girl, one of my previous girlfriends, I married her. When I entered her room, I saw the photograph of an old friend of mine. This is treason. I was about to hit myself.'

Sulaymān had just performed another of his famous swerves.

'I don't understand!'

'No,' said Abed, 'neither do I! He can be so ambiguous at times.'

'I married her.'

'Who?' we both cried.

'The girl from the United Arab Emirates.'

'Mentally?'

'No, for real! This was about four years ago.'

Abed was at a loss for words.

Sulaymān continued, unruffled.

'I thought she was divorced with two children. She had a house. She didn't tell me she was married and that her husband was my old friend.'

Abed roared, 'Shame on you, you married a married woman!'

'I didn't know! She was a Palestinian living in the UAE.'

'There's something I still haven't got clear here. What happened to the woman under the blanket?'

Sulaymān seemed to have completely forgotten about her. His mind was full of these abrupt turnings without so much as a GO SLOW sign. What he was doing now was settling an old score. Meanwhile, Abed, still thunderstruck by the news of a hitherto unheard-of wife, shook his head in disbelief.

'I was surprised to see the photograph of my old friend at her house. I felt I was in the movies. "Who is this?" I asked her. She answered, "This man is part of my history. He's gone." It turned out she was still married to him, so I made my escape. She pleaded, "Stay with me, I will give you my house." "Impossible," I replied. "You didn't tell me you were married. You stabbed me in the heart. This man was a staunch friend of mine." I left.'

'What about the woman with the blanket on her head?'

Sulaymān finally got back on track.

'So while reciting the Qur'ānic verses I begin to wonder whether she is psychologically or spiritually ill. What type of illness she has – mental, devilish, djinn, what type? There are big differences. Maybe, with this woman, she has sexual hunger or she just wants to get married. You never know what you'll find. It's like when you open a box; you never know what's inside. There is no other solution.'

'So what happened to her?'

'This is the programme one follows for the treatment of a girl with djinns, but if during the recital of the Qur'ānic verses you get an erection then you must stop immediately and leave because this means that her instinct and her appeal are more powerful than you are. If you become sexually aroused this means that all you have done thus far amounts to zero. If you want to start this business, you need special tools, but if you are sexually aroused your spirit will not benefit her. You should go and have a shower. From her waist up is one thing and from her waist down is something else. If you want to mix the two then the girl should be immaculate. This can mean marriage, and you may even reach perfection, but this is true for only one out of a million girls. It is rare to be able to join the two halves. Also, you need this barrier between her and yourself. She is not your wife. You have no legitimate right over her. It is like driving a stolen car. She is not yours. If she attracts you, this will be your ruin. You might leave your wife and then you will find the world an ugly place. She will cause problems for you. There is another Arabic saying, "Before starting a real dance, you should shake a little."'

'Surely this treatment is very rare!'

'All Sufis use this, well, at least the strong ones do. I am still doing this. If I have an ugly old woman, I don't use this treatment with her.'

'That is both sexist *and* ageist!' I joked.

Abed roared with laughter at this intrusion of western liberal values. People started looking at us from the neighbouring tables, wondering what all the hilarity was about. The cat took the final mouthful of lamb that I had intended for myself. Abed was onto his third cigarette.

'I will talk logically to you. If you have ten kilos of gold, will you carry them in the street? You might get killed. A beautiful woman in a nasty environment is dangerous. I am not trying to scare you, but watch out for beautiful women because they are pursued by a thousand males, all of them staring at her, some of them from our world and some, the djinns, from the other. People do not realise the poison is in good meat. Sugar will attract bees. Beware! Don't go into the dangerous zones. What happens when you try to get away is that she will provide you with facilities. Don't accept those facilities. This is dangerous. The more beautiful she is, the more dangerous. A money changer I know was in love with a beautiful girl. Shiny like gold she was, and very dangerous, and he would pursue her, asking for her hand in marriage. "Tread on my grave," he cried, "but accept me." Once he was in an alley. There somebody hit him with a stone, saying to him, "Stay away from this girl." So he changed his mind. He no longer wanted to marry her. He was about to be killed. When I see a beautiful girl, I see her surrounded by a spider's web. I see her being chased by ten people. It depends on your luck, either you will be killed by *them* or you will be killed by her. If she is very dangerous, you are approaching hellfire. She will embrace those ten in your presence, although not necessarily with her hands. She will give you the impression she is in love with them, and then she'll rule you. Who is assisting her? Satan. And you will burn like a candle. She will give the impression there are a thousand alternatives. I answer her, "Many girls are looking for me too." Allāh has mentioned their wickedness. Allāh says that such girls have great wickedness, particularly in Western countries, open societies, where the law is on their side. The government and business are with them. So where are you? Everything is on her side. The judge will say to her, "Take half of his fortune and tell him to get out. We will feed your babies. He can go, sleep in the streets." This is a dangerous topic. If I wanted to marry a Western girl, I would have done so twenty years ago, but make the slightest mistake and it's goodbye. This man I know married a German girl and had four children by her. Now she eats a lot of chocolate, and teases him, and he is about to have a heart attack. He came crying to me, told me his children will be taken, his house too. "Go, find a rubbish bin and sleep in it," I tell him. "The law is on her side, the whole European community. What do you have? Go find yourself a job. The tyranny of Syria is better than the tyranny of western countries. You should have married a Syrian girl. She wanted you to get life insurance so she could inherit from you. Once a battery loses its charge, it will be thrown into the garbage."'

'You ought to have an office and five telephones!'

'My ambition is greater, to deal with nature, to build a human being with nature. It's what I'm looking for and I will find it.'

'How can you tell when a woman is possessed by djinns?'

'It is very clear. She will have a heavy tongue. She will not speak fluently but heavily as if anaesthetised. Also you'll see a change in her eyes. There are many symptoms. If she has had a psychological shock she may vomit.'

'What you seem to be saying is that ultimately there is no cure.'

'There is a cure, but it depends on the problem. Some are easily cured. The easiest to cure are children because they are innocent. The older she is, the more difficult. Usually you find an electrical charge in her. A djinn-possessed girl likes to wear nylon. You will feel she possesses great energy. She will start hunting with her eyes and will make certain movements. And, depending on your luck, she might hit you slightly or you might take a long time to heal. Such a girl knows when to strike. Once she possesses your heart, she will have a free hand to do as she likes. She will hypnotise you. This process we call *salb*, which means "stealing" or "occupying". She will steal everything from you. There is the story of a famous Sufi master and a girl called Fatima Barī. This story is part of our heritage, especially in Sufi circles. She used to take and steal other people's hearts, even those of great men, ascetics too. She had a miraculous energy. She could steal even the hearts of saints. Once a man saw her, he became a servant to her. She would steal everything from him. She did that with one thousand people. Aḥmad Bedawi was a Sufi master. The girls couldn't defeat him. He was celibate. He spent forty years on a rooftop, worshipping God. He was near Ka'ba once when he saw another master called Aḥmad Rifā'ī. "Salaam aleikum," he said. "My cousin, how are you?" They were spiritual cousins. Then Rifā'ī told Bedawi, "There is a girl who has destroyed one thousand men, and the only person who can deal with her is you. I will send you to her. You must rescue those people whose hearts are being stolen by her." So Bedawi went to her, but because there were so many djinns and devils serving her Fatima knew he was coming. She called to one of her servants, saying to him, "Bedawi is coming to kill me." The servant said this was unbelievable. "I saw him in my dreams," she answered. Bedawi, when he came, pretended to be dumb, not only dumb but an idiot too. Fatima said, "This is the man." The servant said, "Impossible, he is an idiot. We will make him take care of the camels." So Bedawi took care of the camels. Many of them died. He screamed he was losing his power. Fatima called her devils and then a war started between them, an invisible war. Then he was rescued by saints. Fatima made her repentance and they married.'

'And you're saying *he* won?'

I would discover later that one of Sulaymān's closest friends, another Barī, was the descendant of this fabled one. Damascus, historically as well as socially, is a village.

Abed was becoming increasingly agitated.

'This very story,' Abed told me, 'when I first heard it some years ago it made me go crazy inside. This is part of our culture. I had a readiness for paranoia, and such a story appeals both to it and to one's manhood.'

'I feel we are back in crazy times!'

'Sulaymān doesn't change,' said Abed angrily. 'Such people are immunised by God, but to enter their world can drive one insane.'

'I am still worried by the woman under the blanket.'

Suddenly our laughter was as empty as the plates in front of us. There were only olive stones and chicken bones. The cat outside knew enough to go elsewhere.

Abed pounced.

'These backwards methods will drive her even crazier, they could even kill her. I'm not betraying Sulaymān, but I have to say this. This is all fakery. We are supposed to be enlightened. Freud showed us the way out of this. These things, I am sorry to say, are what make this a Third World country.'

I had triggered a disturbance, and the proof of it was in Abed's face. Maybe he too had been possessed of a djinn or *jinnīya*, a female creature that interrupts all commerce, all the channels between oneself and the world. This much I could recognise from before, only this time the parameters were not quite the same. I couldn't smell the perfume.

'I've seen djinns,' he said, 'so I know they exist, but I prefer science. A good psychologist will look at your face and know what you have been through. There are creative people like my shrink. Jung and Freud, this is tangible knowledge. This is civilisation. Maybe you disagree with me, but I've been through this.'

'It is easier for me to believe in djinns than in Freud.'

'We are not talking about Freud in particular. We are talking about psychiatry. Those impostors I mentioned have become a big problem in the Arabic world. They are using it to collect money. They are causing divorces. A wife will pay a fortune to regain her husband's love and she will go to a magician who tells her when her period comes to put her bloodied tissues in her husband's tea so he will love her more. This is driving us back to the dark ages. This craft is the result of ignorance and backwardness. It is breaking up households. The Arabs are suffering. Millions of dollars are taken from ignorant people by those who claim to be assisted by djinns.'

'And yet you believe in them?'

'Yes.'

Djinns are said to be fearful of many things, the Qur'ān, water, etcetera. It is to be wondered, though, whether what djinns fear more than anything is modernity. The French ethnopsychiatrist Tobie Nathan who has been known to use amulets and talismans with his immigrant patients writes on the subject with great clarity:

> The world of djinns is a world of thoughts, not a world of belief. It is both supported by and different from philosophy and religion. It resembles philosophy in its search for the characteristics of these beings, in the same way philosophers seek to identify new concepts. But it also resembles religion, because the beings in question are alive and have intentions. Interacting with such beings has consequences. Where religion builds groups, contributing to the creation of social spaces and to the intelligence of the weak and the deprived, the world of djinns leads those who venture in it to explore the margins, the other side, the escape hatches.

> Religion sets up order; the world of djinns gathers those who are excluded from this order, treats them, and facilitates their reintegration in specific niches. If religion builds walls, the world of djinns creates openings. The philosophical world resembles the world of the djinns by its obligation to create, but it is less accountable to life's demands. Identifying the right djinn leads to the healing of the patient or the worsening of the patient's illness. The construction of a 'good' concept has much less obvious results in life. But philosophy is able to disintegrate worlds by emptying them of meaning, by deconstructing them. In the end, a healer, an ally of the djinns, is a religious person without a religion, a philosopher lacking that hatred for the world as it is.

If Abed spoke out against djinns it was not because he disbelieved in them, but that talk of them had taken him back to a point in his life which now set his teeth on edge. So desperately he wanted to become modern, to push away the antique world where once he felt so comfortable, where he and Sulaymān would join forces unto the grave. That old Damascus of which he so badly wanted to be an emblem was rapidly on the slide. Would Freud be his escape? The irony was that Abed could never keep apace with Sulaymān who, while dipping into the past, was always looking for fresh modes. Then again, there had been a five year break in our communication, which contained a story that was as yet untold. Whatever it was, Abed wasn't telling me.

As to the matter of djinns, Nathan concludes:

> And finally, what do djinns want? They want to stop the movement of the world, to freeze life; they dream of being like their human brothers: settled down, territorialized. But they want to stop the world to their benefit, to become the only organizing principles of the universe, from which all the others would be derived. Here is the secret: The djinns want to become God. Sometimes, they succeed.

What had crept into Abed's life to make it freeze?

Chapter Six

A Demon Chasing a Demoness

A Short History of Pigeons in the Islamic World (2)

It may be argued that the Prophet Muḥammad's hostility was not so much towards what men made of pigeons as towards what pigeons made of men. It was the licence they gave to man's moral frailties that he sought to revoke. Abū Bakr, who was Muḥammad's companion, when he was made caliph, the first of that line, was unsurprisingly apprehensive of the great burden thrust upon him. One day he entered a garden and saw there a ringdove in the shade of a tree, and he heaved a deep sigh and said, 'Happy art thou, O bird, that eatest of the trees and seekest shelter beneath them, and art not called to account – would that Abū Bakr were like unto thee.' What was objectionable were not the pigeons themselves, but those human sluggards wasting their livelihoods and energies on them.

Muḥammad, it is said, once called a man running behind a dove 'a demon chasing a demoness' (*shayṭān yatba'u shayṭānah*). There is no certainty as to whether the hadith is an authentic one, and, if it were, whether the words fell harshly or gently from his lips. As repeated by believers, however, those words are early evidence of the hostility pigeon fanciers inspired in them. What is not immediately clear is the degree to which those critical of pigeon fanciers believed their activities were unIslamic or whether religion was used as an excuse to come down hard on a seemingly harmless foible. The idea that pigeon fancying is just one more thing to distract people from their contemplation of God finds its expression in the writings of the great Persian mystic al-Ghazālī: 'Similarly with the man whose hobby is pigeons, who may stand all day in the hot sun without feeling any pain due to the pleasure he takes in his birds, and movements, flight and soaring about in the sky.' – *On Disciplining the Soul* (*Kitāb Riyāḍat al-nafs*).

The pigeon fanciers became a despised people, all of them considered liars by nature, many of them little better than alcoholics, drug addicts, pimps, ragmen, garbage collectors, singers and dancers. Among them were said to be thieves. What they would do was to release birds inside other people's houses in order to create a diversion so that they could sneak in and burgle the place. If caught where they ought not to be, they could justify their presence by saying they were only trying to retrieve their birds. One wonders how often they were able to employ such a ruse. And for every bird that accidentally flew into another person's house, how many fanciers had to answer to false charges? The list of accusations continues. They were accused of tormenting children who'd been attracted by the young pigeons. With crossbows especially designed for the purpose they'd shoot hardened mud balls at innocents in the streets below, often breaking their noses or teeth, even blinding them sometimes. And then there was the damage caused to the environment, falling tiles, for example, which had been brushed against and loosened by the pigeons. If stronger language were required, then one could add to the list all manner of sexual vices, especially pederasty, which would serve to explain why most fanciers did not have wives, or, if they were not guilty of sexual deviance, then they were mocked for their impotence. And in those rare instances where fanciers were married, quite often their devotion to pigeons, which by far exceeded the devotion they showed to their wives, resulted in divorce. Women tried to ban their husbands from keeping company with pigeons, which, with a pinch of sin added to pleasure, would almost guarantee that husbands would redouble their passions in the opposite direction. A perennial complaint, which one *still* hears, is that from the rooftops they were able to peer into the courtyards of neighbouring houses and observe the unveiled women there. And because of all the above, whether real or imagined, the testimony of a pigeon fancier had no validity in court. And if they were dishonourable in the eyes of their neighbours, they were equally so in eyes of God because with so much of their time focussed on the skies they were distracted from saying their prayers.

Islam forbids games of chance. Human destiny is too serious a matter to be brought down by such trifles. According to *Reliance of the Traveller*, a classic manual of Islamic sacred law dating from 769/1368, compiled by Ibn al-Naqīb, 'It is not permissible to conduct contests for prize money that involve birds, foot-racing, or wrestling.' This applied to even seemingly harmless games, the silliest of all, perhaps, being one in which men tried to outrun pigeons. The most popular pigeon games were those involving speed (*musābaqa, sabq*) and it is one of the peculiarities of human nature that wherever there is speed there are usually prizes to be won. This is a perplexing issue, not least because the Prophet himself said that the only thing one may win from races is a dromedary's foot (*huff*), a horse's hoof (*hāfir*) or arrows (*nasl*). These would seem to have been trophies rather than items of monetary value. And what sort of races were these for which one could win prizes? The Hanafites, whose religious school was founded by Abū Hanīfa (d.767), maintained that the only competitions allowed by the Prophet were races with donkeys, mules, elephants and cows. Some people argued that as long as there was no prize for the winner, races involving pigeons might be allowed given their practical use in wartime. After all, the rapid transmission of news might ensure the triumph of Muslims over their infidel enemies.

The problem with any school of thought is that sooner or later it meets an opposing one. Sāfi'i and his disciples sought a wider interpretation of the terms *hāfir* and *huff* and so approved elephant races. It would be something to have been able to sit in on those debates. It is not hard to imagine the raised voices of those on either side of the issue. And even at this remove, they bespeak the complexities that marked the development and codification of Muslim law. One had first to look to the Qur'ān for guidance, and if the answer was not there, then to decisions the Prophet had made with respect to certain cases, and if these failed there was the law of Medina and, finally, the wisdom of the judge. All would have to be seen to be in accordance to what would have been the Prophet's wishes. The constant danger here is the admittance of forgeries. Finally, the Hanbalites (not to be confused with the Hanafites) distinguished between two different kinds of competition: the first allowed a prize for the winner but only in competitions involving horses, dromedaries and archery, all three of which could be called into the service of *jihad*, whereas the second group, which did not directly benefit religion, and which involved runners, elephants, mules, donkeys, javelin-throwing, boats and pigeons, were not allowed prizes. And even the definition of a prize could be a perplexing one because, after all, whatever form it took it had to be acknowledged, it had to be seen, and it had to have a value. It could be something concrete like money or some kind of golden effigy or else it could be payment in kind, a quantity of wheat, for example, or even a combination of the two; it could be immediately winnable or it could be deferred to a future point in time; it could even be some pious undertaking such as the winner promising to give a slave his freedom.

Ibn Taymiyya (1263-1328), the famous Hanbali scholar in Qur'ānic exegesis and jurisprudence, sought to take Islam back to its grassroots and in later years his example was to inspire the Wahhābīs in their denunciation of all frivolities. The Savonarola of his time, he allowed nothing to escape his puritanical eye. This man whose every decision was based on the most literal reading possible of the Qur'ān, such that he even condemned as idolatry the visiting of sacred shrines, set an equally grave face towards the antics of pigeon fanciers. All forms of competitions other than those with dromedaries, horse and arrows, which might be seen as contributing to jihad, were condemned as having no benefit to religion.

While conservative Muslims put pigeon races in the same category as games of chance, in more liberal quarters attempts were being made to bend the rules. There were even occasional efforts made to give some form of sanction to the games. A stranger to the competition, for example, a sovereign or governor or someone paid by the public treasury, could offer a prize, or else it could be provided by one of the competitors or by the owner of the pigeons or whichever animal was involved in the race. If the prize was provided by both the participants in the race, the race would be allowed only if there were a third person involved who did not stand to win anything. The mere presence of this 'legaliser' (*muḥallil*) was enough to ensure the competitors were not playing a game of chance. And then, of course, there were those who did not play by the rules at all, who cheated, and it was here that passions would rise.

Attempts were made from time to time to excise pigeon fancying altogether, one of the earliest being that by the third caliph 'Uthmān, normally a man of peace, who ordered that the wings of pigeons be broken. Attempts were made to surprise the suspects by arriving unannounced at their houses, but such vigilance required more than any caliph was capable of. After his death, the games resumed or else people simply turned a blind eye to them. In later years, further attempts at suppression were made. In Kufa and Damascus the craze inspired by pigeons became fatal to the pigeons themselves. The Umayyad caliph 'Umar II ibn 'Abd al-'Azīz during his short reign of only two years 99/717-101/720, had all the flying pigeons killed and spared only those who had already had one wing removed.

In 467/1075 the caliph Muqtadī's vizier Faḥr al-Dawla b. Gahīr ordered the inspector of the markets to get rid of all the pigeon coups and pigeons. Muqtadī used the old excuse that pigeon fanciers had been peering at women in neighbouring courtyards. Again, this attempt to ban pigeons failed. All the dovecotes, which had been destroyed, were rebuilt and repopulated and the games started up again and the fanciers quickly took up their positions again on the rooftops.

The fifth Abbasid caliph, Hārūn ar-Rashīd (c.766-809) loved pigeon games. The hero of the *Arabian Nights*, he was the most brilliant figure in the annals of the caliphate, a scholar and poet, and yet his failings were equal to his successes. A deeply religious man, who prostrated himself a hundred times daily and made the Hajj to Mecca nine or ten times, he was also given to pleasure. Arabic culture benefited hugely from his exquisite taste. The *qāḍī* Abū l-Baḥtarī Wahb, in order to curry favour with him, added the term 'wing' to the tradition which until then had allowed only competitions involving the aforementioned feet, hooves and arrows and at a single stroke legalised pigeon games. At first he was richly rewarded, but then Hārūn ar-Rashīd repented and had all the pigeons in Baghdad killed. A term had been fraudulently attributed to the Prophet and for this, rather unfairly, the pigeons themselves were held to blame.

Amid all the ravages we get a curious glimpse of a pigeon fancier, not of an actual one but of someone who pretended to be one. A Khārijite from Kufa, called Abū Bayhas, fled from the terrible Oriental master, Ḥajjāj, who had a practice of cutting heads off members of his sect, mostly, it appears, for pleasure. When Abū Bayhas arrived at Medina he disguised himself as a pigeon fancier, grew his hair and beard long and covered his hands with henna. One day, while standing in a crowd, he heard the governor read out a proclamation, which had been sent from Kufa to Medina, calling for Abū Bayhas's arrest. The man standing next to Abū Bayhas identified him, grabbed him and handed him over to the authorities. After a short-lived period during which he seems to have been held in favour he was deemed a heretic and had his hands and feet amputated. Finally, in 713, he was killed on the orders of the caliph.

The most brutal treatment of pigeon fanciers was in 301/913-914, in Baqra, when a number of them were accused of being spies and of corresponding with the enemy by means of pigeon post. After being forced to eat their own limbs roasted, they were then burned alive. Mostly, however, one hears of pigeon games only when they have been proscribed. We hear, for example, that in Seville, the sale of pigeons was prohibited in the 6th /12th century in order to prevent people looking into neighbouring courtyards. In the province of Ardabil, some official of the Savafid shah, Ṭahmāsp I (930/1524-984/1576) banned pigeons two years after coming to power. And so we get reports through the ages. In 1969, in Teheran, the police enforced a ban so as to prevent collisions between birds and planes and then when the ayatollahs came into power they tried to purge the country of pigeons altogether, thereby surpassing the rigors of earlier times. Since a seemingly infinite number of birds rendered the mission impossible, the massacre was suspended and today pigeon fanciers are back to doing what they have always done.

In Syria, in 1966, the authorities, fearful of Israeli spies operating in the country, banned the use of carrier pigeons and private owners who continued to keep them risked three years in prison and a heavy fine. However, this prohibition was useless. First of all, the existence of clandestine dovecotes in the pay of foreigners was highly improbable. Also, if a solitary pigeon were spotted flying that would enable anyone to locate from where it came and to where it was going. Most recently, for religious reasons, the Taliban in Afghanistan banned pigeon games along with such frivolities as music.

A man born to a love of pigeons inherits a whole history of blame. And such is human nature that when man is labelled a beast he frequently acts as one. The pigeon fanciers, pushed as they have been to the outskirts of society, do indeed include among their number murderers, gunrunners, thieves, drug addicts and dealers, and pimps. The situation has, if anything, worsened. The first to admit this are the old style pigeon fanciers themselves, who want for nothing more than to be allowed to fly their birds in peace.

Chapter Seven

The Daybook of Yasser Sagherie

It is used to be said of the Souq al-Arawam that business there was so tough whenever Satan walked through it he'd roll up his trouser legs so as not to get them soiled. If you met a girl and fancied her, it was best to tell a white lie and say your shop was just around the corner, in the Souq al-Ḥamīdiyya, because to be from the Souq al-Arawam was akin to having a mark on your forehead. It was also where one found only the very best carpets and antiques. The villagers would gravitate there, trading in their old hand-woven carpets for machine-made. Competition was fierce. And even today, at the annual market, there are fisticuffs when pilgrims from afar bring goods with them to cover their fare to Mecca. Damascus is a difficult place in which to survive at the best of times, but to have survived the Souq al-Arawam in its heyday was to have survived the world. The area has become relatively tame, which no doubt had to do with the spread of similar businesses throughout Damascus in order to meet a growing tourist trade.

The souq, even at its most savage, or maybe *especially* at its most savage, is conducive to a certain poetic. One imagines the markets of Shakespeare's London were alive with a rich demotic, just as, not so long ago, Spitalfields Market was. The disappearance of such places amounts to the death of human drama. What replaces them is the shopping centre, and it was fear of the emergence of such sterile palaces that crept into the nightmare that I relate at the beginning of this book. Things have not sunk that far. The souq is still a place where one fights to survive, and it is also where one does so with the munitions of language. The souq is full of stories. I asked Yasser to tell me his.

'I don't sell carpets. I sell kilims. Did I ever tell you why? When we worked for our uncle there were just us three kids and a foreman in charge. Only the boss and this foreman were allowed to handle the carpets, which were expensive. We were allowed only to fold them and place them neatly in piles. Kilims, on the other hand, were okay. The boss would turn a blind eye if I showed a kilim to a customer without consulting him first. This was what took me in the direction of kilims. They were *close* to me. I could handle them. I come from a family, which had a rich and a poor branch. Mine was the poor, well, to be honest, from somewhere in the middle. There were poorer people than us and, in the other direction, there were wealthy aristocrats. I always hated the attitude of the rich towards us and this, in my thinking, was also the carpet's attitude towards me. The kilim, on the other hand, was somehow friendly. We would spend whole days in the shop, with our boss, and he would never speak to us. This was the tradition in Damascus, and he was the last of a conservative school in which a boss maintained his pride by never addressing his inferiors. If I were sitting there, and the foreman was there, he'd ask the foreman to tell me to do this or that, but he would never talk directly to me. And he was my uncle, from my mother's side! We lived fairly close to his house and in the mornings when we went to work with him by car we had to sit in the back seat and *never* look into the mirror which was for his eyes alone. These were serious rules. We weren't even allowed to tell customers our names. If a customer asked mine, I'd have to say, "I work for Mr So-and-so". At the beginning it wasn't such a big deal but it got to the point that I was a university graduate who could not speak his own name. It's like when you read Dickens' *A Tale of Two Cities*, where the man in it has a number, and it's as if you do not own your own being. There was some logic behind this. Our boss would think, "What if he leaves and goes and works in another shop, then people might follow his name."

'When it came time for me to have a shop, I said to myself, "No carpets". My neighbour warned me, saying I could never survive on kilims alone. Adham, my assistant, always says we should try carpets. It was tempting at first to buy the workshop products because they looked so perfect but now that I have sufficient clientele, I'm going more in the direction of things that were made for authentic purposes. I have very little that would satisfy, say,

Americans. I know what they want, but it's not a direction I wish to take. You need to be all the more knowledgeable. You must have an *eye*. You require not only the enthusiasm but the passion to go and look for these things because they are not readily available. This is their poetic for me. The other rule, which is a strict one, and this is my weakest point, which I'd never admit to another dealer, is I decide whether or not I'll buy a piece even *before* hearing the price. There have been many times I bought a kilim at ten times what anyone else in the market would pay for it, but because I loved it I always managed to sell it.'

'And when it comes to selling what you like to someone you don't like?'

§

A couple of days before, I had been sitting in Yasser's shop when a group of eight Americans came in, four couples, and although all of them were in their twenties, they seemed to occupy positions of responsibility quite beyond their years and experience. There was a married couple, one of whom, the female of the species, was attached to the State Department in Washington; another was an NGO who struck me as pretty vacant, and his wife who seemed to harbour a ghost of intelligence, who had eyes one might look into for maybe more than a minute; a third couple I took to be a soldier on account of his shaved head and his GI muscles and his wife or girlfriend who had a face that never left the floor upon which it first gazed, which no spark of curiosity ever threatened to ignite; and the remaining couple were so impenetrable I could glean nothing about them whatsoever except that one of them was called Charlie. They were all en route to Iraq. They positioned themselves in a semicircle at one end of the room and Yasser stood at the other where he displayed his wares and I sat cross-legged at the middle of one side of the room, which was close to where the door was, quite prepared to make my escape, except that I got hooked, observing the curious manners of the eight people. One of them grabbed a woven camel halter which he tied about his waist, and then did an obscene wiggle, thrusting his hips back and forth, making the coloured tassels dance, saying he'd wear it naked to the disco. The others, except for the woman with the intelligent eyes, squealed with delight. Yasser smiled the arrested smile of one watching the end of the world come. He then displayed a deep red and blue Turkmen oven cover and when he explained its purpose, which was to preserve the heat of the food underneath, two of the women replied, 'Cool, cool' and again Yasser smiled, this time a different kind of smile. And then he held up a small prayer rug and explained the significance in its design of the *mihrab*, saying it should be pointed always in the direction of Mecca when one of them, the NGO, shouted, pointing to that sacred spot, 'Say, Charlie, you can stick your photo in there!' Yasser froze. Any smile he had pretended to was in an instant gone.

The couple from the State Department were about to make the purchase of a small kilim from Afghanistan, a handsome piece, which is not to say it was rare or expensive, but, to cite Yasser, it was 'honest' and from where I was it scooped up light from distant places. I greatly liked it and I wondered what it was about this particular rug that so appealed to the couple. Or did they even *know* they liked it? And if they did like it, did they like it because of what it was or because it fitted their domestic scheme? And what of whoever made this, could he or she have pictured such a fate, the journey it would soon make? I couldn't bear it anymore. Without saying a word I got up, crossed the room, folded the kilim twice, tucked it under my arm and walked out, saying not a word to anyone, not even to Yasser who produced yet another kind of smile, this one visible only to me. Apparently, immediately after I left, one of the Americans asked, 'Who in the hell's that, Jack the Ripper?'

The above passage was almost too easy to write, and the reasonable side of me questions whether these people ought to be allowed to represent anything other than themselves, and yet, considering the deadly game of consequences, which is what the politics of whom they serve has become, one need look no further than their faces for what a poet friend of mine calls 'the small fascisms of the spirit'. What also troubled me is that they seemed to exude confidence of a kind I had not witnessed before. The victory they smelled, however, was already the stench of failure. The Afghan kilim is close to the desk where I write, and, looking at it, at this object which I might not have bought otherwise, may Allāh forgive me, but I feel not a little proud to have wrested beauty away from ignorance.

§

'What of those people who buy beauty and cannot see it?' I asked Yasser. 'You must develop a relationship with these objects.'

'Yes, on the other hand if you have such a relationship with the things you love, you'll never become rich. Did I ever tell you about the man who runs a brothel in Trebizond? Trebizond for a long time was the capital of prostitution in Turkey. All the wealthy businessmen from Istanbul, Bursa and Ankara would go there. As you know, in our Islamic culture this is shameful. We daren't speak to each other of such things. This is Turkey's so-called "Russian" city, and, especially after the opening up of the border, Russian prostitutes go there to work full- or part-time. Many girls work in the shops by day and then go to their hotel where they can stay in return for having sex with one customer a night. The people who run these places, cheap hotels designed for this purpose, and the more obvious brothels too, are mafia-rich. They all have miserable lives, but also they drive the biggest cars, wear the most expensive suits. There was one brothel-keeper, however, who was dirt poor. This brothel had fantastic girls. Everyone said this about him, that he had the best prostitutes. One day we were sitting in a café, smoking a *nargileh*, and the others there were making fun of him, saying, "You're no good at this business." I asked him, "How did you end up like this?" The man replied, "What do you do?" I told him I dealt with kilims. "Are you rich?" I said no. "Do you love your business?" I said yes. "Well, then," he said, "there's your mistake. You'll end up like me. Every time I bring a prostitute to my brothel I fall in love with her. And it is painful for me to see her making love with someone else. And it is painful to take money for it and sometimes the meaner the guy who makes love to her the more difficult it is for me to take money from him. I'll never make it. If you love your business, you'll never make it." This has always rung true with me. If I buy something I love, I never make good money from it.'

I wondered how Yasser's parallel between kilims and whores would go down with a western audience. I wondered whether I really cared. What I appreciated most in my many conversations with him was his ability to illustrate his arguments with analogies. And these he could pluck from his beloved Qur'ān and its many surrounding hadiths and also from the mundane. There had always to be a story and the souq remains a live culture for stories. There were some things modernity had not yet squeezed lifeless.

'When you speak in terms of a poetic, there must be something else. Surely you are not driven by bitterness from your youth. Those may be the circumstances that pushed you in the direction of kilims, but I have a sense you are involved in the language of what you deal with.'

'I must admit that I'm driven by both. First of all, I have a vivid memory of going to Mecca. My father taught first in a village called Baḥra, which means "The Pond", and then we moved from there to Mecca where we stayed for three years. This is how we started, and I remember the first time when I went to Ka'ba I prayed to Allāh that we should never be poor. I never really saw hope, though. I worked out mathematically what I'd need in order to start a shop and when I might achieve this goal and it all seemed impossible. But I believe that if you have a passion for something, you are going to do something about it. Somebody somewhere will find out about you. I am a Believer. This is something else. I believe in Allāh. If I believe in Him, He has to be fair. If He is not fair, I'm not going to worship Him. This I believe, and as long as I have this passion and I am not cheating people, my boss included, then surely He'll take me there. If He is sometimes unfair to me, His wrongdoing does not justify my bad response. If you keep on like this, you have to get there. Now there are better believers than me, who'll think that if He is not going to give it to you in this life, He'll give it in the next. I am not that good a believer, but He has ordered me to treat people according to their minds. When you talk to a child, it's not like when you speak to a professor. So I believe at this level and that He should give me what I want and He did. I am now one hundred times better, financially speaking, than I used to be. I came from nothing, from scraps, and now I have two shops, a piece of land, a house, two children, everything I could possibly want. Thus far He has been up to my standards. It is dangerous to believe like this. The other believers think that if you go wrong, He is going to punish you here, but at my level if I go wrong now He might take everything away from me, which means I have to stick to the right road. This was one drive. The other drive, when I started this business, was that I hated it. I worked in a restaurant, which I liked more. You are dealing with people whereas in this business sometimes you sit for days without meeting anyone. It is like fishing. You have to be patient. A whole week goes by like this. I hated this as a kid. I wanted to meet people. So I tried working as a carpenter for a whole year and it didn't work. I was half-hearted. I was stuck with this man, the most successful in our family, and because I was given the opportunity to work for him my mother would have killed me if I wanted to do something else. I did. I tried carpentry, tailoring, painting houses, I even worked as a rubbish collector during the night. I sold used clothes! I preferred anything to what I was doing at the time, but then it got to the point I was the best English-speaker in the shop, probably in the whole street. My boss's brother is the most successful orthodontist in the Middle East. When he studied in Boston he'd send me books on carpets. My boss couldn't read English although he could speak it to a certain level. So my job was to sit and read what is written about this or that tribe. *That's* when I started to love it. I started being able to get the right things in the right places. I would know things my boss didn't know. Although he appreciated me more, he became afraid of me in the same way I was afraid of him because suddenly I had the wider knowledge, even in an academic sense, which speaks to the Western mind more, and as I became more powerful the customers would begin to ask for me. He was afraid that I might leave one day. So now I became passionate about it. I wanted to see more, learn more, even if it meant making mistakes. At a certain point, I must confess, I got bigger than myself, but I wanted to be at least as big as I saw myself and it was then this business became a passion for me. I have always loved languages, poetry too, and this was when I found a connection between what I was doing and the things I love. The gates had opened for me. This is when I had the two dreams that brought me my shop. My boss, incidentally, was one of the three best dream interpreters in Damascus. Many people would go to him to have their dreams interpreted.'

'A dream interpreter! Is this still a stock figure in Arabic life?'

'It depends. We cannot talk of Arabic or even Muslim life as a single entity anymore. You have all different kinds of people. You have people who think of themselves as modern, who do not believe in these things or else are too embarrassed to be thought of as believing in them. There are those people who still believe strongly in dream interpretation, but Islam has an attitude towards this although even here, depending upon where you come from, there are different schools of thought on the matter. There are schools that try to interpret miracles scientifically, for example. Where I come from, which is a rather conservative family, we believe that when you have a dream you are really looking for something or someone. Still my neighbour will ask me to go to my uncle about a dream he has had. My mother is a big dream interpreter also. So you go to these people. I think it is very human. You want to know what is going to happen. When there is something to support this human side of you, you cling to it. In Islam, dream interpretation is just one of forty parts of prophecy, which is to say forty such parts would make a prophet. That is actually part of being a prophet, being able to interpret dreams, and in the Qur'ān there is strong emphasis on dream interpretation. There is an entire *sūra* called *Yūsuf,* which is about a dream that comes true. At the beginning Yūsuf has a dream in which he sees the ten planets kneeling to him, the moon and the sun too, and throughout this *sūra* he interprets dreams for the Egyptian pharaoh and when he is in prison he interprets dreams for people there, and in the end his dream comes true – all ten brothers and his father and mother kneel to him when he becomes responsible for Egypt. A dream interpreter must have a good reputation, and should be seen to attend to his prayers, and to have been on a Hajj to Mecca and actually to have successfully interpreted dreams. Islamic dream interpretation is completely different from Freudian. We have dreams, for example, which require no interpretation. If you go to sleep thirsty and you dream of water, all it means is that you're thirsty. There are certain times, if you pray at dawn, for example, when a dream might be sent from God. Such dreams weigh on you, ask that they be interpreted, and that's when one might seriously consider going to a dream interpreter. When it is a bad dream, one shouldn't ask for an interpretation. There is a hadith about how a dream rests on the wing of a bird. The minute one talks about it, it falls, and so if someone interprets a dream in a bad way it will fall on you. So it's important to know your interpreter, to be sure he is not evil, because, whether right or wrong, the interpretation of that dream will fall on you. That's why people go to my uncle, also because with him there is no money involved. It's a dodgy area. You can have fake interpreters. Also, from where does it come, from inside or outside oneself? What is the machinery? You can be the best literary critic but not a writer or vice versa. You can be a deeply religious person who hasn't got the ability to interpret dreams.'

'Is there a forest of images to which people refer?'

'I am not of this school, but 95% of people will go to the big book by Muḥammad ibn Sīrīn, *Muntakhab al-kalām fī tafsīr al-aḥlām* (*The Interpretation of Dreams*.) He is the biggest dream interpreter in Islamic history. He'll tell you a fish means this, a horse means that, or that finding a jewel means something else. If, in your dream, you see rain in a rainy season then prosperity will come to you, but if you see rain in summer then it means it's probably going to rain trouble on you. This book has almost everything in it – animals, stones, men and women – and, as I said, 95% of people will go to this book, but the contradictory thing is that these same people will still go to someone for interpretation. It is not just a matter of language. Only the whole dream, the whole story, makes sense.'

'You were about to tell me of your dreams.'

'In my first dream I saw my boss wearing a very tight suit with short pants, looking very uncomfortable. I went to him, saying I had this bad dream, and he said, "Don't tell me!", because, in Islam, when you have a bad dream you shouldn't tell anyone what it is. You should look to your left side and say, '*A'ūdhu bi-llāhi min ash-shayṭāni ar-rajīm*' ['I take refuge with God from Satan the accursed' although, really, it is 'Satan the stoned', but then we don't want to add drug-abuse to his many other sins.] But it nagged at me. I said, "Look, I really want to tell you this dream." When I told him he went bright red and said, "This means one of us will feel some pain on account of the other." That was the first dream. After some time, I had another dream. My boss had five shops at that time. In this second dream he took from the top of his safe five jars of honey. He offered me a spoon of honey from one of the jars. *Wallāh,* the dream is so vivid in my mind! I was always a proud kid. Even when I wanted something I would never ask for it, especially from a rich man. I would sooner ask a poor man. So he offered me a mouthful of honey from one of the jars. At that time we had a big argument. I wanted to do things in a different way. The conservative way of selling a rug was that when someone comes into the shop you begin by showing him the rubbish and then work your way up. And in order to show a fine piece, you must first show a crude one. I agreed with this. We had thousands of pieces in the shop, which meant it could be an endless process, although once the customer likes something you should never go further. The point now is to make him feel this is the best. You then go backwards showing him the worse ones so he'll feel he has already seen the best. These are strict rules. When my boss started like this, he was one of four main dealers dealing with foreigners but now it was the beginning of the 1990s and there were maybe twenty such shops, all of them dealing with foreigners. This system was not working anymore. If a customer sees you are wasting his time with rubbish and if he knows a little, he'll walk away. I would see my customers walking away and buying from someone else. So I started this argument with him, saying, "Let's do this with tourists. They are time wasters anyway, but when you get a real collector let's hit the target. Maybe show him just two things.' He wouldn't let me do this. Then I said, "Allow me a free hand in just one shop and in the other shops you continue as before. If it works, it proves I'm right. If it doesn't, then you're right. We'll go back to the old way." He wouldn't let me. This is when I had this dream. I wanted honey from one shop only. In the dream, he said. "Do you want this?" and I said, "No, I have two jars already." I don't know why I said I had two honey jars when I didn't have anything at the time. Shortly after, an American company offered me a job as their buyer in the Middle East. They'd buy things from Iran but at that time there was an embargo and so they'd ship them to Istanbul, put labels on them saying MADE IN ISTANBUL. All the American dealers did this. I kept saying to myself, "Should I tell him about my dream?" When I told him, he said I'd have more than one shop. A couple of years later, I had my first shop. And always, in my mind, I was asking. "Where is the other jar?" Well here, where we are now sitting, is my second shop.'

Yasser then told me when he opened his shop he had only two carpets, the sale of which was absolutely essential to his being able to continue. It was all he could do to pay for the space, which is the one he still occupies, which one must step down into, as if into a cave. On that first day, over a decade ago, a woman from Argentina, attached, so she said, to her country's embassy in Amman, said she would purchase both carpets but only if she could have them at a discount. Desperate though he was for a sale, Yasser had already decided he'd fix his prices, a policy from which still he refuses to deviate. She said she'd return with the money half an hour later. Two hours passed and she returned, paid the asking figure for the carpets, and then handed him an envelope, saying it contained a message for him but that under no circumstances was he to open it until the following day after she had gone. Yasser, a man of honour, kept his promise. When he opened the envelope he discovered a thousand American dollars, the receipt of which would put him on a steady course. Yasser immediately phoned the Argentine Embassy in Amman only to be informed that no such woman worked there. What this says about her is anyone's guess, but what it says about Yasser is that he draws women who are quite inscrutable.

§

We continued our conversation later.

'A friend of mine gave me a book that was written in the mid-1700s by a barber in Damascus. The barber was the place where people talked. He was a dentist too. If you wanted to buy a house, you went to him. The stereotype of the barber is that of a talkative person, the Reuters of the place. Aḥmad Budayri al-Hallaq or, more simply, Ibn Budayr, wrote this *yawmīya*, which means "the daybook of a worker". The history of this book is almost more interesting than its contents. It was sold as a manuscript at the Umayyad mosque and was not taken seriously until the beginning of the twentieth century. Only its future editor saw its value, thinking, "Who else but a barber would give me the average man's history of Damascus?" Arabic histories concentrate only on great people. Barbers, normally, never wrote, but this one did, day by day, and he wrote about so many things, especially the prices of meat, bread and coal and how they'd change according to the situation in the country. If, for example, a new governor arrived the prices might change. He documented everything.

'This inspired me to write one. I am writing this for myself and, if he ever takes over the shop, for my son. I love the history of this city. Always I want to know who was here before. It is like fixing one's frame. I decided I'd write about this street from its beginning to its end. People here are willing to talk to me. Although I am an outsider, I'm originally from this neighbourhood, my grandfather was a highly respected man, and also I mind my own business. I am here when my neighbours need something translated into English. I wanted originally to document the Souq Arawam where, remember, the devil walks with rolled-up trousers, but it has completely changed after twenty years, so I'm writing about here instead, my street, starting from the Umayyad Mosque and going towards Bāb Tūmā. If you are a Muslim you always start from the right-hand side, so I begin with the first shop on that side. Yesterday, however, I realised I missed the most important thing, which is the Nofara Café. Whereas in Ibn Budayr's book he tried to write in general, what I need to do is make a microcosm. This souq is a mirror to Damascus. You have almost everything here – we have all the different sects – Shī'a, Sunni, Christians. The Jews have mostly gone. In old times this souq was mostly Damascene but now it has people from all over. It also has all kinds of people, educated, many of them with university degrees, and then the completely illiterate who can't even write their own names. Also we have the most religiously conservative people and then we have those, mostly young, people, who ask foreigners, "Do I look Italian?" The shops here cover everything from luxuries to basics such as bread and sugar. What this book will capture is a moment of time in the city's history. The traditional mercantile life of this part of the city is vanishing and being replaced by tourist shops.

'So I start with the young people at the beginning of the street, who are illiterate in English but they can speak it because they grew up in the market. In my youth, even if you worked for ten years in the same shop, you were still a boy. You could not start a shop and be a boss until you had maybe fifteen or twenty years of experience. Your boss would then vouch for your character. Now these guys come and work in a shop for one year, they see what the boss sells, they speak a bit of English, they know about selling to foreigners, and the next day they rent a shop at a huge price they can't really afford even if they are doing well, and then get themselves into debt. It used to be that getting into debt was considered a deep shame. If you did not have the money, you waited until you had it. Say these newcomers have 100,000 lira to spend, they'll buy a million lira's worth. They pay it back week by week. They spend money on expensive clothes with brand names, Diesel, Armani. They start a shop, which goes in a very new rhythm. On Saturdays the prices are high whereas on Thursday the prices may be lower than cost because of their *jam'īya* or money that is due. If they can't pay they'll sell off their goods cheaply to another dealer and they go bankrupt and disappear. People ask after them. They might start up somewhere else in Damascus or even in another city. I am talking about a society that is still trying to hold onto whatever is left of its social values. We say here that one's reputation is half of what one has. People must trust you.'

'So what you describe is a tearing away at the very fabric of society?'

'Yes. This one guy disappeared with a debt of two million lira, which would take me six years to make. This he lost in a single year. People say, "Oh, he's just a boy working for someone else" but he told me many times, "I gave a hundred dollars to sleep with a Japanese girl." He is seventeen years old. A bit of what he says may be true, but probably most of it is bullshit. He spends money on restaurants, girls and clothes, yet the shop costs him 2000 lira a day, which is more than my average daily takings. He pays this to the owner and then he closes the shop to be with a girl! Once someone came by and sold me an ordinary kilim, which cost me 1000 lira, which I then sold for 1700 lira. So one of the boys says to the customer who bought it from me, "What did you buy? What did you pay for it?" Such behaviour in our business is really shameful. This is like going uninvited into someone's house. This boy then sells him the same kilim for 1000 lira, which I know for a fact cost him 1500 lira. So the customer returns the piece to me. I may sound like an angry businessman and although at this level I am, I am much angrier at the violation of the rules of the game – the social game, the business game. After all, the greater part of our life is a game. I am angrier about this than about losing a customer, especially when the profit we are talking about doesn't even cover the price of a meal.

'Another man here sells shawarma and he represents a particular mentality in Damascus. For the longest time, he was the only one here to sell falafels. All the tourist guides mentioned him as being the only falafel shop in the area. He was really successful, as was his father and grandfather before him. This guy across the street opens a shawarma shop and this, too, was successful. The owner of the falafel shop then decides he will sell shawarma as well. The shawarma he sells is seriously disgusting. Meanwhile, he has lost his reputation as a falafel shop, which was named everywhere. And now, most of the time, he smokes and kills himself with envy at seeing his neighbour's success. You'll now see three falafel shops which are doing quite well. *Isn't it sad?* The next shop sells sugar and tea and all the things we need. He is too busy to get dressed properly, and although he looks poor he is hugely successful – he changes money, rents houses, and is one of the people who control the shares market in Damascus. If the dollar is about to go up, he buys all the dollars available. You see again the mentality; he is rich in the true sense of the word. And then there is another man who sells batteries, etc, but where he makes his money is selling tea to Iranians, which is a big smuggling business. Syrian candies have a good reputation too, so his shop is always crowded with Iranians.

'I even documented the street vendor who used to sell orange juice. This man would press fresh orange juice. People, especially foreigners, would pass by and say, "Poor man, let's help him." So this man came with his orange squeezing machine, and out of curiosity I began to watch him. Soon he had five people working for him, busy from morning to night, selling fresh juice. He did not pay taxes, and the biggest tax in this country is for cleaning, which is why the streets are always dirty, and every day he would leave piles of orange peelings that stank, which sometimes stayed there till the worms came out of them. The street is called Nofara which means "water fountain" and there is a little reservoir there. The space this orange juice vendor occupied was, in the end, actually five times the size of my shop. This, again, is the mentality in Damascus. We have this proverb: "A beggar (*shaḥḥādh*) gets two thirds of the world." Say we are both eating falafels and a beggar comes, I would give him half of mine and you would give him half of yours. He gets a complete sandwich and we are each left with half. Anyway this man came and by the end everyone was annoyed with him. He was always shouting and stealing customers from the Nofara Café. All these connected people came to him for fresh juice. You couldn't talk to him anymore. If you challenged him, he would talk to one of his customers who would then make trouble. This really happened. Once the café owner's son came and said he would have to move his wagon otherwise he'd go to the city council to complain. So the juice vendor sent two men around and they broke all the nargilehs at the Nofara Café. Later, because he annoyed someone big enough to be able to take revenge, he disappeared. He was a phenomenon in this street but you can see his like everywhere.

'Did you ever notice the tiny mosque? I am really interested in the history of these mosques. Next door is the huge Umayyad Mosque and at that time, when Damascus was small, it could hold all the city's inhabitants inside. So why are there all these tiny mosques surrounding the big mosque? They may have been Sufi tekkes where they would sit and recite, or rooms given to people who worked at the big mosque or to students of *sharī'a*. Now, if you go to Umayyad Mosque at the busiest time, like when the muftī of Syria died, even with people coming to pray from other places, still there aren't enough people to fill the mosque. So what is the point of these little mosques? If we are really Muslims we should believe in the unity of Muslims and so we should aim at people praying in the same mosque and not taking away from it. I counted them. There are probably sixteen tiny mosques around the Umayyad, some of which will have only six or seven people praying in them.

And they have running hot water twenty-four hours a day, and I know one of them has a constantly leaking faucet. A famous hadith says, "Save water even when on the bank of a flowing river." And according to the Qu'rān, spenders are the brothers of Satan. Why do we need these mosques? What's the point? A mosque cannot be de-sanctified, it is always a mosque, but this tiny one nearby serves as a storage for the surrounding shops; it is their source of water, a place to take a nap and everyone thinks he owns the mosque to the point that some of them who have the key to it, if they don't like you they'll kick you out. If the shawarma seller has a customer who wants to wash his hands he is sent to this little mosque where there is hot water. What do you call this? If this mosque were a shop the money from the rent alone would bring in a minimum of 28,000 dollars a year. One thing that would benefit the mosque would be to bring back the big toilet behind it, which was closed for no reason. You close a toilet that people need. So you close a toilet and open a mosque? What is it about us Muslims? If I say any of this to a fellow believer he'll say, "Shut up! Are you saying a toilet is better than a mosque?" I am not saying a toilet is more important than a mosque, but I'm talking of relative matters. In this case, it is ten times more important than a mosque. All these things I write about, sometimes they are painful, other times funny.

'The most educated house in this street is also the poorest. The people in it are all educated, all the men and women have university degrees, they are always clean but dress poorly, and yet none of them can afford to make it through to the end of the month. They are the poorest people here and in this respect they reflect the value of education in this country. One of these kids I spoke about earlier makes ten times what these people make. One of them works for the foreign ministry, another for the city council. Any one of them, if he were to use his position to manipulate others, could make money. Even the father has a key position where by altering just one line of what he writes he could have made big money at a time when corruption was rife here. They live miserably in two rooms, half the house theirs and the other half rented to a bastard. This reflects the situation of many people in this country who refuse corruption. They can't survive. For how long do you think they could survive? One of them is my age, 36 years old. When he comes from work he stops to say hello. I say to him jokingly, "When will you be happy in your wedding?" He answers, "Well, if I calculate my salary now until I reach zero when I have paid all my debts, I will need another four years salary but ten years after, with maybe a salary increase, then I might be able to ask the hand of a girl but by then I will be fifty and no woman will be interested in me." This is so painful, even though he said it in a comical way. You can't afford to marry here. The minimal rent for a house where there is room for a wife is 8,000 lira, which is the average salary. I would say fifty percent of women are not working and even if they were, they are not supposed to pay whereas men have to. 8,000 lira! Tell me, how can one be expected to pay the rent? They are not pushing you, but they are actually putting you on top of a mountain and telling you to go and steal and be corrupt. This is what they expect you to do.'

§

After what Yasser told me about his street and the breakdown of a business code, all I could hear was a flapping of wings, and although the analogy is something I would rather suggest than force, I began to see pigeons everywhere. The danger here was that I would make my argument fit, even if it meant making adjustments to the world as it actually is, and indeed there's nothing so full of holes as a literary scheme. One falls deepest into those which one takes to be projections of one's own intelligence.

Always to be avoided are those forced unions, the idea or image pushed into the service of a bigger scheme, which result in ungainly convolutions, although here, too, one might find pigeon analogies. The experienced pigeon fancier knew, well before genetics was ever on the syllabus, that putting just any male and female in the same cage was less productive than allowing pigeons to have mates of their own choosing. So there we have it: the songwriter ambles back to his score. The best pigeons come only of true love.

There is even more to startle a permissive age. Breeders have also noted that forced unions can also alter a pigeon's sexual preferences, so you get males that want to be only with other males.

And you get females that bed down with females. And then further confusion enters the picture: sometimes females mount males but refuse to be mounted themselves, and others are so docile they'll allow themselves to be mounted by anyone. Would that it stopped there, but in such artificial relationships pigeons will often lay 'clear' eggs, eggs that are not fertilised, and which, in Arabic, are referred to as 'eggs of the wind' (*bayḍ al-rīḥ*). One might think this a neat Arabic turn of phrase, but despite the pleasant noise it makes the wording was invented not by pigeon fanciers, nor was it ever in the Arab demotic, but in all likelihood goes back to antiquity in ancient Greece. Aristotle's *Generatione animalium* was translated into Arabic under the title *Fī kawn al-ḥayawān* and there one finds the word *hypenemien* meaning 'windy' which, when capitalised, appears also in Rabelais in a context too obvious to repeat here. The ancient breeders wouldn't allow nature to take its course, but forced only the best pigeons to mate so as to preserve the pedigree. The Arabs took the opposite stance and would never allow inter-breeding between close relatives for fear of poor results. The Mogul emperor, Akbar, also a fancier, was the first to cross different pedigrees. Ordinary pigeons mate for life, but when pent up together they look towards their neighbours' wives.

§

Some while later, I visited the Māristān Nur ad-Dīn, the old lunatic asylum, which is now home to a fine medical museum, and there I saw a wooden barber's chair dating from the eighteenth-century, which, in my heart of hearts – a most trustworthy and unreliable place – I knew had to be Ibn Budayr's.

Was the barber's ghostly chit-chat true? Was I pushing too hard at my chosen theme?

§

I will never know why, after such a shaky start, when I rattled his cage with a word so obscure I could only be working for another planet's intelligence, Waseem suddenly offered me his assistance. I ran into him again and he seemed to have got over his earlier soreness with me. Actually he seemed pleased to see me. The incident with the English pigeon seemed to have been forgotten as well. If I were seeking analogies, he no longer seemed to care what they were. Our relationship would be nothing as strong as friendship, but although he was always busy he made time for me. It could be, of course, he believed I might do well for his side. Already I had moved among some of the most despised people in Damascus and got on with them and didn't laugh at their foibles. Maybe I'd write about the injustices visited upon them.

'Will you be free tomorrow? There's somebody important I want to introduce you to, a friend of mine who is a judge.'

'A judge?'

'You'll see!'

Chapter Eight

Meeting the Judge

One day, while walking through the Christian Quarter, I turned a corner only to discover the way ahead blocked with preparations for a funeral parade. There was nothing for me to do but step aside and wait for death's traffic to be done. Should I have turned back, sought another route? There was no suppressing this inner voice, which tells me always to observe. Almost a hundred women flowed out of the church opposite, virtually all of them weeping with the same intensity, such that it was impossible to distinguish family member from acquaintance. A priest stood alone. Some musicians, slightly bored looks on their faces, brandished drums, trumpets and trombones. Suddenly, and at no given signal I could see, several men hoisted the open coffin as high as their arms could reach, and with only their flattened palms to maintain its balance, span it in a dizzying circle. The coffin rocked to and fro, from side to side – and now a cliché forces itself on me – like a small boat on choppy waves. I backed away from what seemed to me sure catastrophe. A young man, presumably the deceased's son, his face bright red and stretched with sorrow, put his fingers to the bottom centre of the coffin and tapped upon the wood as if looking for signals from the other world. The coffin was then tipped forward to allow bystanders a final glimpse, a chance to say goodbye, and its occupant appeared, a man in his late sixties, dressed in his Sunday best, a piece of cloth wrapped longitudinally about his face, presumably to keep his jaw in place, and another band of cloth tying his wrists together. The way the coffin was made to dance, one could feel gratitude for at least this small precaution. A bass drum sounded, and the procession began to move. The band played what sounded like an Arabic version of a New Orleans funeral march, with almost the same jazzy tonalities, with the same flatness – which is not quite the same as being out of tune – except that here, at the end of each bar, the trumpets rose on a suspended high note. It was a most haunting sound, simultaneously ancient and avant-garde, utterly simple, and yet not at all easy to reproduce. An entire symphony could be constructed upon the upward curve of that final melancholy note. Assyrian blues. At the head of the procession walked a young man, another son perhaps, carrying the coffin lid in front of him like a shield. The priest followed, and behind the coffin the band and then the mourners, the men chanting, the women ululating from time to time. The procession would halt at certain places associated with the dead man's life. One of them was a café where presumably he spent much of the time. Maybe his ghost sits there still, calling for another coffee. The parade threaded its way through all the streets of the neighbourhood. I made my escape only to meet it again as it came down another extremely narrow street. It seemed to appear all of a sudden out of nowhere. The position of the band was hard to place by sound alone, so convoluted were the streets and so fine their acoustic. What was I to do? Rather than turn and find myself leading the parade I climbed some steps to let it pass, and when it did the dead man's face was almost level with mine.

§

The Judge, when I first saw him, was extended like a gargoyle from the window of the third or fourth floor of a modern apartment block, his hands gripping the embrasure. All tense with expectation, the upper half of his body formed a perfectly straight line. When he saw us below he signalled once and then withdrew like a cannon into a ship's hold, an absurd image, granted, but it did strike me so at the time. The movement was made in one, without any sacrifice of bodily composure. We waited for the sound of the buzzer and then filed in, Waseem, Abed and I.

There are certain events in our lives that acquire a magnitude quite out of keeping with the world as it actually is, when outsized we move as if through a miniature village. We were about to enter a mini-kingdom that was all but invisible to a casual observer, which had its own hierarchy, with Waseem somewhere in the middle, and the man we'd come to see at its very pinnacle. A rather dapper figure, the Judge had the gypsy features of a gigolo in a 1930s movie, whose slapstick entreaties would have been taken seriously once but were now laughable. I'm pretty sure, although I have a poor eye for such fripperies, he dyed his hair and thin moustache. Black, black. Clearly the Judge was as far from bachelorhood as Waseem was from matrimony, the place where he lived being immaculate, without so much as a whiff of pigeon, and, if one is sufficiently generous in according a man his place, he was, with his exquisite manners, his gold-filled teeth, and his panache, what we might call a kingpin. A kingpin is so only in the smallest of worlds. The Judge brought a tray of coffee from the invisible source that was his wife. When I asked him if he really were a judge, he replied 'more or less' but that, *more to the point*, he was a man of deep experience.

Some fanciers I have spoken to deny the existence of pigeon judges, while others tell me they are merely temporary adjudicators in the disputes between fanciers and that there is no such given title, while still others explain that in times past judges were selected from the most honest fanciers but that nowadays they are recruited from the criminal elements, especially those who have served time. After all, who but a criminal is fit to judge? Waseem told me of one who adjudicated with a grenade in each pocket, which seemed an effective enough way of settling a dispute. Our judge, whose existence is indisputable, was a gentleman of the old school who took every care to see that his guests were made to feel as comfortable as possible.

'This hobby,' he began, 'used to be the preserve of upper class people.'

The word hobby, at least in translation, was suggestive of gentility.

'It was employed as a means of social introduction. If I caught another man's pigeon, I would take it to him just in order to meet him. Money was never mentioned. Pigeons would be exchanged as gifts, and their owners would have meetings and talk shop all the time. They would fly their birds for hours on end. Each fancier would be reputed for a single breed and he would adorn his birds with fine ornamentation, anklets and breastplates. There were no mulattoes, only the purest breeds. There weren't really any problems at that time.'

A man who speaks of a Golden Age usually thinks of himself as having to endure a badly tarnished one. Also he will have a poor memory for any flaws in the picture he presents. I asked him if it were true, that once upon a time disputes were rare. The Judge, being an astute man, must have registered the doubt in my voice.

'Okay, so it was inevitable that maybe ten per cent of the people were bad but any trouble they made did little more than ruffle the mood of the other ninety per cent. The rubbish would keep low-quality birds and try to steal from the wealthy but, by and large, there was trust between people, whereas nowadays money always intrudes. Make a pigeon fancier a high enough offer and he will sell you his rarities, which is why there are no longer any pure birds here. We imported German and French pigeons and married them with ours and now we have even Indian and Chinese. There was no way of transporting them before. We have a hundred times more varieties, but then we also have many more diseases. There were no vaccines at that time. We grew our own food once, which was the best, but now we import American which contains all kinds of impurities.'

Was this wholly true?

'As the breeds began to disintegrate, so, too, did the fanciers themselves?'

'Yes, the percentage is now reversed, with ninety per cent making trouble. To employ another example, in the past singing was like poetry in that when you heard a song it contained a meaningful story beautifully sung whereas now the songs are noisy and sexual in content. The same thing has happened with the pigeon people – ninety per cent of them are rubbish and ten per cent serious. I am from the ten per cent who are poets, as opposed to pimps, and who look upon this as a hobby, but now I am going to have to sell my pigeons just because my neighbours are making problems for me. A youngster will follow me just in order to steal from me. He wants to make easy money. This is where our government has made a big mistake. We have no animal rights in Syria. The mayor should print licences for pigeons and impose a tax, which the rubbishy people with their cheap birds would never be able to afford, and there ought to be special committees to check on pigeon fanciers and to inspect the health of their birds and to determine whether their owners should be granted licences. One should be able to make complaints to the proper authorities so that the wrongdoers will be punished. This will prevent the scum with their cheap birds from following masters like me. I have been in this for forty years and now a youngster who has been doing this for only two has managed, because of his stealing, to make this profession hateful to me. All his pigeons put together are worth 5000 lira while I have a couple of pigeons that are worth that alone. I even had thoughts of killing him, but, look, I have children. I am a grandfather. I am a sane person, but you have others who can't stand it anymore and who are impatient and who will settle their disputes with knives. I realise that if I sell my pigeons life will be more comfortable for me. So I will eliminate my hobby. This will be the price I have to pay. Also, because of the theft there has been deterioration on my side. I have cheaper birds than ever before. The problem lies not just here, however. The punk who steals my birds will boast and make fun of me.'

'What is your response when he steals one?'

'I have severed most of my relationships with pigeon people. It has got so I am rude to another fancier simply because I do not want to have any problems with him. So my response to the thief is, okay, let him keep the bird, sell it if he likes, and spend the money on whatever. This way I develop immunity to him.'

If this were really the case, what was jangling his nerves? The Judge, clearly, was close to breaking point. Was he still fit to judge?

'Can you tell me specific stories about these wars?'

'Last year, in Babira, which is a suburb of Damascus, there were three brothers from Aleppo, all living in the same house. They started to make *al-tomas* with another person. This other man made problems for them. He stole one of the brothers' birds. One of the brothers went to talk to this man. They quarrelled, the other swearing he never stole his bird. "Get out of here!" he screamed. The man from Aleppo said to him, "Whether you like it or not, I will take back my pigeon by force." So the thief attacked him with a knife and wounded him. The wounded man crawled back to his brothers. Meanwhile, the neighbourhood sided with the thief. So began a war by the end of which two of the brothers died. All this happened in the space of twenty-four hours. The surviving brother set fire to the killer's house.'

'Do you have any more stories?'

'Yes, many. There was another war between two pigeon-keeping families whose members used to make constant fun of each other. One of them, an automobile mechanic, stirred things up between the families. Seizing a wrench, the mechanic hit one of the pigeon fanciers who used to work for him. Somebody in the garage went to the brother of the wounded person. This man was a baker who, although he had nothing to do with pigeons, sided with his brother, grabbed a gun and killed the mechanic. This developed into a major feud between the two families. There are now widows, orphans. A lot of mediators or judges get wounded in the process of effecting reconciliation. Once I was trying to bring together two people, one of whom stole a pigeon from the other. I said to them, "Look, rather than give it back to me, from hand to hand, let the pigeon go, release him back into the sky, and I will recapture him." The thief released the pigeon only for it to be stolen by yet another fancier. A third party! The original owner accused me of cheating both of them, saying he would force me to bring the bird from the third party, which, of course, made for further difficulties. Sometimes it happens that a fancier knows you are a judge and that you have a good reputation, so he asks you to go and buy back a stolen pigeon. "I will give you 1000 lira," he says. "It is worth 5000." So what happens then is the judge goes and pays the 1000 lira, brings back the bird to its original owner who then doesn't pay up. The judge loses, pays the costs, and no one shows him any gratitude.'

'Are there bad judges?'

'Yes, in the bad neighbourhoods, but not in our immediate circle. The quality of the judge depends on the area where he lives.'

'Are there judges who are themselves criminals, who are chosen for this very reason?'

'Yes, they are chosen mainly because they alone can intimidate the warring parties. They will be afraid of him and return the pigeons to their rightful owners. Previously the judge was a wise, respectable figure and birds were returned not because of any fear he inspired but because he could make a thief feel ashamed. A bird would be returned out of deference to him. There is something important you must learn here. There was a code once, which was observed by every fancier. For example, if you found a pigeon on your roof and you didn't know where it came from, you kept it for three days until you had a chance to discover the owner and return it to him. An anklet would identify the pigeon's owner. After three days, if nobody came, then the responsibility would be no longer his. He was free to sell or keep the bird. Any reconciliation by a judge had to be effected within those three days. We are living in dirty times. It is no longer a hobby. I'll show you. I will fly my pigeons and you'll see how the others try to steal them.'

'Do you see a parallel between the pigeon world and what has happened in society as a whole?'

'Yes, there has been a change in the construction of the universe. You go to court and the criminal will be innocent and the innocent guilty. Right is wrong, wrong is right. America says the resister is a terrorist and the occupier is a liberator. That's why nobody argues with an educated pigeon fancier because he understands the game. This addiction is all the more despised because it is done in the public eye. A pimp will come home in the morning and people will say oh, he's been working all night and no accusation is ever made against him, but when I fly my birds, in full view of my neighbours, I am condemned.'

'We are looking at something thousands of years old. For the government to ban this would be to remove something culturally rich from Damascene life.'

'Actually the government is the cause of the troubles. If a government-sponsored pigeon syndicate were formed and taxes imposed, medical help and food supplied for the pigeons' upkeep, it would become a source of revenue. This would put an end to all the thievery. What is happening instead is that you have informers making their reports to government people who then come to investigate, not knowing whether one is a good pigeon man or not. I was one such victim. My neighbour, an army lieutenant, a widower, spent his whole time harassing me. "Even if it costs me 10,000 *lira*," he said to me, "I will have your birds removed." This enmity towards me arose out of nothing other than the bad reputation of pigeon fanciers. All kinds of stories, most of them lies, influenced this man. So I visited him, expecting him to have all these prejudices dating from his childhood. "What's bothering you?" I asked him. The lieutenant replied, "You are a good person and everyone here respects you, but I don't like you being in this profession." I explained to him that I took this from my ancestors and I was not a novice. The lieutenant replied, with the usual nonsense, "A fancier is a drug addict, a homosexual and a shark who looks at other men's wives." So I answered him, "Look, I have a friend who is an army colonel. I know four lawyers, three doctors, all of them pigeon fanciers. There are many merchants, engineers, even members of the Chamber of Commerce who are pigeon fanciers. So you see, there are good, highly respected people in the pigeon world." The lieutenant's son arrived and mediated and we separated on what I thought were good terms. What happened next is that this same man went to the mayor and informed on me. I had to pay a bribe of 2000 *lira* to the mayor just so I could be left in peace. Later, there was a change of mayor and the lieutenant went to him, same thing, and I had to bribe him as well. A third time, now this was getting serious, he went to the chief prosecutor to inform on me. So I went to the police department. They know I am a respectable person. The police came here, while the lieutenant watched from his building to see if they'd remove my birds. I am wise to such situations. The constable came to my house, asked for my ID, said my neighbour had informed on me. "We are going onto the roof to have a look." I took him up there. I had about 140 pigeons at the time. The constable, after I bribed him, said he'd make a report saying there were only thirty. The lieutenant who now was waiting downstairs said to the constable, "What, you haven't seized his birds!" The constable told him, "You have done what you had to do, and now it is my turn to do what I have to do. It's *my* job." So he produced his report and took me to the police. There weren't any handcuffs put on me. The police accepted the report in which it was written that there were only thirty pigeons and they belonged to my daughter who originally had only two birds, one male and the other female, and that those two gradually became thirty. The report was presented to the judge in court after which I had to sign a pledge saying that I'd have the birds removed within a week. After two days only, the lieutenant informed the prosecutor again, saying I had bribed the police. This is the problem we have here. Anyone can inform and be seriously listened to. Meanwhile, I sold all my pigeons. I went to the court. There was a female judge who told me I could be imprisoned for either three or fifteen days or else for three months, which are the three levels of punishment we have here for pigeon fanciers. I told her, "Look, I'm raising pigeons and I'm to be imprisoned while there are drug dealers, addicts and thieves walking free on the streets. *They* are not in prison. All I do is raise pigeons and you want to imprison me! If you put me in prison for even just one day, it will convert me into a criminal because as soon as I'm released I will go and shoot this man. *Why?* Because in my whole life I have never been in prison, but for the sake of my hobby you'd put me in one. I'll shoot him!" The lieutenant then said he would collect signatures from the neighbours, saying that I was bothering them. I said to the judge, "If just one of those neighbours claims I'm bothering him, then you can sentence me. I'm harmless and am loved by my neighbours." She asked if I'd sold the pigeons and I said yes and she said she would send someone over to check. So I took back my identity card and went home. A month later, I received a government fine, 240 *lira*, for arguing with administrative procedure. I pray five times a day. I am a committed Muslim. After every prayer, I made a supplication against this man. "May Allāh kill him," I prayed. "May Allāh remove him." I was so tired and he'd been so unjust to me. If he accused me of keeping pigeons that would have been fine, but he also accused me of being an alcoholic, a drug-dealer, everything under the sun. I was even accused of being involved in anti-government activities. He was not a good person. He is well known for being filthy. So after every prayer I made this supplication against him. "May Allāh make him die." After nine months, quite suddenly, he died. *He died!* So now if anyone has problems similar to mine they come, asking me to make prayers on their behalf.'

There was a burst of laughter in the room.

'After the court business, this hobby was forever blackened in my own eyes. Now I have returned to it, but sooner or later I will decide to stop. It has become an embarrassment. I am not a bad person just because I keep pigeons.'

'Do you really think it's possible to stop?'

'The Prophet Suleiman, peace be upon him, was the only prophet to speak to birds and in the Qur'ān you will find he spoke to ants too. A pigeon came to him, bringing him news of the Flood. It is common scientific knowledge animals can predict floods and earthquakes. Suleiman was happy with this pigeon and wanted to reward her. "May I make a supplication to God, asking that every feather of yours be turned into gold?" She replied, "No, I'll become extinct because then I and my children will be hunted for our gold feathers." So then the Prophet Suleiman said, "Okay, I am satisfied with this response, but I will make a different, more powerful, supplication for you. *Those who love you shall not forget you. Your love will not be erased from our minds.*" You may quit this hobby for forty years, but then will return to it out of love. It's not like these people who are after money only.'

(What was interesting here is that the Judge just a little too conveniently misremembered. That is no pigeon in the sura of the Ant. It is the *hudhud* or hoopoe.)

We went up onto the roof and watched him set his birds loose.

A few minutes later, neighbouring pigeon fanciers arrived, and more coffee was made, suggestive of the Golden Age of which the Judge earlier spoke. The birds flew in the direction of one of the city's most recognisable sites.

'You see over there,' said the Judge, clearly pleased with the spectacle.

We stared at the concrete sandwich that is the presidential palace, recently described by one journalist as 'the Emerald City of Oz, as remodelled by the North Koreans.' I could just make out the circling *v*'s overhead.

'For me the sweetest place for flying birds is above the palace. The police will not dare follow them there.'

§

'Why do you bother with him?' Iman scolded me. 'Stop waiting for him. Go.'

It was the second time this week Abed neglected to show his face. I was pacing back and forth in a rage, avoiding the still wet patches on the stone floor of the hotel courtyard. Delilah the Tunisian's wielding of the mop made for a kind of exquisite, solitary dance. All she wanted was to get home, and here I was, rhapsodising her servitude. Anger was looking for a sedative and she, poor woman, was it. Whatever her story was, doubtless it was a sad one. She was here because she had to be. I could never get close enough to her to ask what probably I wouldn't have dared to ask in any case, although I suspected her reasons for being here were personal rather than political or economic. She had a story which I would not pursue. Was this what the Prophet Muḥammad meant when he said one should go in pursuit of knowledge, as far as China if need be? Would he include in his paradigm this woman with the snub nose? An astute reader of the human heart, surely he would say yes and surely he would say no to the blinkers people set upon themselves. A good Muslim will advise me against seeking to interpret too closely Allāh's motives, Allāh the Unknowable. I must not forget to be polite. Anyway this is how I travel, through people. There's nowhere on the planet anymore one cannot get to, which makes me question endlessly a doubtful literary genre, but people are, and shall always be, for me, the most unexplored areas of the universe. Who shall ever know the atoms of which both Delilah and China are made?

It had just gone on one and Abed was due at twelve.

The receptionist Iman was yet another of my guides to the unfathomable, a touchstone whenever I came to Damascus, a voice of reason which spoke just when I was about to succumb to less sane ones. She could, with a single ironic glance that was both tough and tender, sweep aside the world's nonsense. She could display mockery with her eyes, and I'd seen her do it countless times, especially with tourists about to embark on a ridiculous venture, the gung-ho New Zealander, for example, who indulged in what I can only describe as a species of macho-tourism.

§

I shall digress a little with this absurd figure. Already he had begun to irritate me with 'the facts', which demanded of him that he go to see things with his own eyes, which would be fine if only he did so without so much as a supporting cast in his brain, and all towards no discernible end other than juicing up the postcards he'd write home. We had already got into an argument over some business he'd gone to investigate, and now he proffered a brand new line of enquiry. Sam, let's call him that, was going to find the very spot near Halbūn, about 30 kilometres outside Damascus, where an Israeli missile landed the year before. It was close to an army training camp, which the Israelis claim trained people for other, darker purposes. 'Why do you want to go there?' I asked. 'I want to establish the *facts*,' Sam replied. And the facts would be whatever he chose them to be. I warned him not to compromise Iman or anyone else. A few minutes later, he was asking her directions to the place. 'Why do you want to go there?' she asked. And he mumbled some miserable cliché about doing what a guy's got to do. Iman rolled her eyes. When I saw him again, later that evening, he was in the company of two *mukhābarāt*. 'Meet my new friends,' Sam said to me, with a wink and a smirk, and I pulled away just in time. When I went to the toilet at three in the morning the *mukhābarāt* were still sitting, smoking in the lobby, their guns clearly visible. Quite rightly, next morning the authorities recognised Sam for the idiot he was, and, quite wrongly, they let him go rather than boot him out of the country on his arse. I took against him because all his adventures were at the expense of other people. When later he told me about his arrest and that he'd been taken to a station where he saw a Syrian getting knocked about by the police this struck me as the decadence of those who can watch, tick their mental list of things to experience, and then skedaddle. Would that the Syrian were free to go, which was not something Sam, in his search for 'the facts', would ever pause to countenance. I must confess that here, in the space of this prose, disgust gets the better of me. There were quite a few of these characters, macho tourists, the hapless Japanese, for example, who, against the advice of Iman and her colleagues, went into Iraq only to be separated from his head there. The poor man made the hotel scrapbook in ways he could never have imagined or, rather, because his imagination failed him, an imagination sufficient to be able to see things as they are.

§

If she were less discreet Iman could produce a fool's chronicle, a history of human stupidity, based on her own hotel experiences. I was her fool now but only in the sense that she had affection for me and here I was, wasting my time.

'Go,' she said, 'he won't come.'

'Why does he do this to me?'

'You know better than me. He's *your* friend, not *mine*.'

This was to be the most bitter pill of all, when Abed simply failed to show up for meetings, when I had become overly dependent on his ability to translate. I was up against his despair, which at times was immovable. If I shifted my hours so as to accommodate him more, he would sleep through those as well, and when he was in his bed there was no force in the universe that could shake him awake. We would meet and within minutes he would find some excuse to go home. The truth is, I needed him not so much because of his ability to translate but because he was mad enough to fully comprehend my scheme, to anticipate my next move, such that there were times when things happened quite of their own accord.

Iman was right in a way, to speak of Abed as she did, with acid on her tongue, which is also to say she was wrong in another way, in that she did not allow him sufficient latitude, but from what angle, when the mathematical observes no past tense, could I possibly explain to her what he had meant to me. Abed the Slacker, Abed the God-struck, Oblomov and Prince Mishkin rolled into one, Abed the Street Philosopher and Abed, the Purveyor of Hollywood Romances, Abed who, sooner or later, I would either murder or save. Whatever Abed's finer qualities, they were, just then, as elusive as the shadow Delilah threw over the damp floor, and it was no longer possible to say to Iman that he had such and such in abundance when he had never once made any of those virtues visible to her, and when she, from her side, was perfectly right to demand of men the things a man such as he would always fail to provide. 'What woman would be crazy enough to marry him?' she asked on the flimsiest of evidence, which, of course, in a woman of good sense is the strongest evidence of all, and against this charge I could offer no defence. Abed the Joker, I could have said to her he was funny and then I'd have to say he was nowhere near as funny as he used to be, and, in any case, what is funny in a young man often becomes, in time, the least funny thing about him. Abed the Wise, I could have said he was intelligent, but what intelligence was this that never manifested itself in actions? Abed the Good Citizen, I could have said he was upright, but what was this uprightness when always, in full view of her, he was down on his knees? What about just plain Abed the Good, goodness being of all human attributes the most difficult to describe? The tragedy of such people is when their goodness is bone idle.

When I first met Abed and Sulaymān it was at just the right moment in our respective histories, which is to say it required their being the precise ages they were, when they could still entertain hopes for the future, and my being the age I was, a couple of decades older, when I could see just far enough behind me to fathom there might be difficulties for them in store and so I could tremble for them a little. I could also partake in their youthful dance. The visions of youth, the wilder they are the less supportable, and this is especially true of young people in the Middle East where not much legroom is available. It's not the sun alone that so quickly ages them. Also it required Damascus being at a critical juncture in its history, when there was still such a thing as Arabic Time, when, as yet untroubled by computers, satellite dishes and mobile phones, its mental spaces were sufficient to allow for uninterrupted human discourse. Adjust any of the above and the first book I wrote would not have been possible. The conditions were *just so*. Already certain things I described then as commonplace, such as seeking one's counsel from fools in the street, have become rare. Whither goes the fool one no longer requires? Modernity has done much to embarrass people out of such niceties, and what they felt comfortable with yesterday today becomes fearsome. That my book would soon be somewhat antiquated did not unduly bother me. At least I'd caught the bird in mid-flight, so to speak, before it settled into World Time.

What more can I say on the matter of Arabic Time?

A decade ago, I was wandering through the souq when a young Saudi in pure white called to me from inside a shop, 'Can you tell me the time, please.' I raised my wrist and he laughed out loud, 'Do you call *that* a watch?' Then he showed me his, which was made of solid gold, encrusted with jewels, and probably gave the time on the moon as well as at Fort Worth. Well, I wasn't going to let him get away with such cheek and I said to him, 'So then, do you have more time than me?' The laughter fell from his face, and he rushed over and embraced me. Would such an exchange be still possible? I think not, not now that Damascus has moved from Arabic into World Time. It was in that earlier time frame when, no matter how painful or heavy the 'vicissis*i*tudes' of life were for them, Abed and Sulaymān could still join in the dance. Certainly, as regards their society, they were out of the loop but at the same time they sought to be emblematic of all that was most precious in Damascene life, or, rather, what survived of it, the aristocracy of the broken circle. I never realised just how great the weight of their enterprise would be, but then neither did they. It seemed as though their friendship would lead them through all adversity. 'When I die,' Abed said of Sulaymān, 'amid my bones will be found the gold his friendship gave me.' Sadly it would not so much as endure their living tissue. There would be a parting of the ways for which both were to blame – Abed for his overdependence on Sulaymān, Sulaymān for allowing it.

Young Abed had the ability never to smile at his own jokes. This he described as the genius of English humour and it was something he translated into Arabic discourse. Add to this the elements of irony and play, a finely honed sense of the ridiculous, an immaculate sense of timing, and what you had was something precious, akin to the amethystine ripple one observes fleetingly on the necks of pigeons, which one can never quite capture in word or image. So there too, the avian makes its entrance. And yet even this is not quite enough to explain what I took to be his inner light, which I still do, although one must wait longer and longer for its occasional flashes. Maybe, though, one of the conditions of our friendship was his own solitude, the pain he had to endure throughout most of his life, the rejection by his peers, the slightly crazed look in his face that made him suspect in the eyes of other people, such that quite often I had to explain to them he was above suspicion. What a crazy position I got myself into, justifying Abed to his own compatriots. It could be, of course, that the rank outsider is the only person with whom I could ever really feel free.

All this was, of course, supported by profound religious belief, without which, and in this I do not exaggerate, Abed would not be able to survive. Those prayers which he would never forsake, not even in darkest times, were what kept him afloat, and it was not just belief but the very language which sustained him, the language of the Qur'ān that allows for no slackening in the brain. The claim made several times in my presence by different people that without their faith they'd be nothing is not mere piety, but there is in this cause for both relief and alarm. What happens when, as has been the case in recent times, the Qur'ān is misread in aid of some darker purpose? Should this continue, then Islam will be unrecognisable to itself, and there is even a hadith saying the day will come when holding onto one's faith will be like clutching a piece of burning charcoal. With Abed, however, his belief provided a steady flame. If I may make an important distinction, although I believed him implicitly it does not always mean I believed what he believed. I am not about to put on a turban. I am merely a recorder of what he and other people have said to me. Quite simply, I felt comfortable with him and the greater that sense of freedom the more I was able to gain admittance to a world I would never be able to comprehend otherwise.

So when did that freedom begin to weigh like iron shackles? It was when Abed took increasingly to his bed. There had been a time when he would never *not* show up for an appointment, as if to do so would be to break a bond he had forged between himself and the world. As of late, though, he did not even feel compelled to apologise for his failure to show up. 'What woman would be crazy enough to marry him?' Iman said to me. And here was the crux of his problem. If the women with whom Abed fell in love always rejected him in the end they were not to blame. It got so Abed himself almost needed to be rejected by them, and would utter a sigh of relief when yet another engagement dissolved. I could no longer advise him. There was a time when it was possible to do so, such as when he came to me, saying he desperately required my help, that he didn't know how to kiss a woman, that he'd heard there was a problem with oxygen intake. If there was a time he worked himself into an enthusiastic state it was not because of the promise of a future but because he was after some idea of perfection whereas now, with perfection being the most distant of possibilities, it seemed he was merely going through the motions. I have lost count of his many engagements and now I can only barely absorb the newest one. Any hope now resided only in the recovery of Abed's better qualities. My design was never to take him back to what he was, however, but rather towards what he might become.

§

All came to a head the following evening when finally Abed did come, a complete shambles. We went to visit Yasser where he promptly fell asleep over his cigarette. We went for a bowl of not terribly appetising *ful* and were now wandering through the crowded souq, headed nowhere in particular. Abed swung his arms from side to side, like a giant ape, and, in what seemed a somnambulist's dream of violence, he ploughed his way through the crowd with not a thought for the people he was pushing aside. Acutely embarrassed, I kept my distance. Suddenly there was a child's scream. Abed who was paying no attention slammed into a man carrying a toddler. Clearly the child was hurt. Abed laughed. Then he apologised weakly and the father, not knowing where to set his child down, just stood there in a murderous rage. As we walked away, I could still hear in the distance, above the din of the crowd, the child's screams. At first I was too upset to speak to

Abed, but quietly I concluded there was nothing more I would do to help him out of his malaise.

A few minutes later, he spoke.

'I must go home and get some sleep.'

It was only seven o'clock although, in truth, I was grateful at the prospect of not having to spend the rest of the evening with him.

'You've slept enough.'

'I'm still tired.'

I shot back, aiming at where it would hurt most, the only thing left to him, his religious faith.

'All the prayers in the world will not release you from what you have become.'

One day Abed would have to meet *his* judge.

We parted on the most irresolute of handshakes.

I am not sure if Abed heard me.

Chapter Nine

A Golden Platter of Cherries

A Short History of Pigeons in the Islamic World (3)

Ya'qūb b. Killis (318/380–930/991), a Jew from Baghdad, went with his father to Syria and there, if the dates are to be trusted, aged thirteen, he worked as an agent for various merchants. It is not difficult to imagine him on the streets of present-day Aleppo or Damascus, a boy with a winning smile and a quick turn of phrase, a cash register in his brain, discretion in the blood, and an ability to anticipate the next move. The street is, as it ever was, a school where one acquires acumen. Speed is of the essence, and all begins in servitude: one must first learn to bow in order to be able to rule. The souq is a jungle that civilises, and, where commerce is contingent upon culture, poor is the merchant who does not verbally shine. Thereabouts poetry and business are not mutually exclusive. A man selling olive soap will do so in verse. This, one may conjecture, was the early education of Ya'qūb b. Killis.

In 331/947, apparently unable to repay monies appropriated from several merchants, Ibn Killis fled to Egypt where, as currency exchange broker, he entered the service of Abū 'l-Misk Kāfūr. As regards the vicissitudes of fortune, Kāfūr's story ranks as among the most improbable. A Nubian slave, a eunuch 'of ponderous bulk and misshapen legs', we first hear of him when the Ikhshīdid ruler, Muḥammad b. Tughi, who happened to be passing by the slave market, heard the laughter of the mocking crowd and for eighteen dinars, which even then was a pittance, purchased the object of their ridicule. Kāfūr must have been a most extraordinary youth to be able to rise, without bitterness, above his infirmities: schooled in cruelty, he would show kindness towards even his worst enemies; reared in ignorance, he would feed himself on high culture. Later, playing on his name, his contemporaries would jokingly refer to him as 'Camphor, the father of musk'; in Arabic, just as we might describe someone's character as being lily-white, so camphor is synonymous with *whiteness*. Tughi invested him with increasingly important responsibilities, including the tutoring of his two sons, which, again, is a demonstration of just how quickly Kāfūr must have educated himself. When Tughi died in 946, Kāfūr became regent to each of his sons in turn until, with the death of the second in 966, he declared himself ruler and remained such for the next two years until his own death. Although the four years of his rule, which included his role as caretaker, were, in many respects, a time of discord, they were also a golden age for Arabic culture. A generous patron, he surrounded himself with musicians and poets. One panegyrist composed verses on a recent earthquake, attributing its cause to the dancing of the populace as they delighted in Kāfūr's myriad qualities. The great Arab poet, al-Mutanabbī, was for a while happy enough to receive Kāfūr's favours. 'They went to Kāfūr and neglected all other men,' he wrote, 'for he who seeks the sea despises the rivulets'. Later, when al-Mutanabbī decided Kāfūr's favours were insufficient to his own genius, which is to say he did not get what he had been promised in monies, there was a distinct change in his tone: 'Who can teach noble sentiments to a black castrate?' Sadly, and happily for literature, Kāfūr was to inspire in al-Mutanabbī some of the most brutal satires in the Arabic language.

It might be claimed that Ibn Killis, being a Jew, was at a similar disadvantage but it was then still possible for Jews and Christians of talent to rise above religious prejudice. Ibn Killis became chamberlain and the organiser of court expenditure. Kāfūr, struck by the younger man's honesty and abilities, and desirous of elevating him to a higher position, is reputed to have said, 'Were that man a Muslim he would be fit to be made a vizier.' It is a mute point whether Ibn Killis, presented with this vision of a yet brighter future, decided it would be to his advantage to embrace Islam, which he did in 356/967, or whether he was truly drawn to the faith. There are rumours even that he died in the Jewish faith. A man who embraces a faith will frequently come to believe in it, however, and Ibn Killis, with all the zeal of the convert, studied the Qur'ān in depth and even preached against the iniquities of the faith he is said to have abandoned. Meanwhile, he demonstrated his fine business sense and soon controlled the expenditure for Syria and Egypt. The vizier of the time, Abū 'l-Faḍl Ja'far b. al-Furāt, became increasingly jealous of him and soon after Kāfūr's death, in the same year as Ibn Killis's conversion, had him arrested. Ibn Killis, thanks to interventions on his behalf and bribes, was released. He then set off for North Africa where he entered the service of al'Mu'izz li-Dīn Allāh who was impressed by his abilities. Ibn Killis advised his new master to conquer Egypt and in 362/969 he found himself back in Cairo and in charge of reorganising the financial system. Again Ibn Killis proved himself an invaluable servant of the state.

After al-Mu'izz's death in 365/975, Ibn Killis continued to work for his son al-'Azīz who appointed him vizier in 367/977 and in Ramadan of the following year conferred on him the title of *al-wazīr al-ajall* ('the illustrious vizier'). Ibn Killis was the first vizier of the Fāṭimid dynasty. Certainly he was to prove its greatest. 'What a vizier is contained within that man's sides!' remarked one of his contemporaries. So great was his power that some disgruntled people remarked that his vizierate was a substitute for a caliphate. One poet wrote, 'For Ya'qūb the vizier is the father, while al-'Azīz is the son.' Clearly Ibn Killis preferred panegyric to satire, for he was quick to remove the skull that housed so loose a tongue. Another poet, hearing his patron was suffering from a pain in his hand, was more circumspect: 'The hand of the vizier is the world; if it aches, then everything will suffer from the same pain.' On Thursday evenings Ibn Killis held his own literary salons or sessions (*majālis*) at which he read works of his own composition to an assembly of *qāḍīs*, doctors of Muslim law and other notables, after which poets would advance and recite their eulogies to him. It should not be thought, however, that he merely adorned himself with other men's verses. Ibn Killis was a man of culture. A section of his palace was set apart for writers, each of whom had private apartments and a regular salary. A number of superb *qaṣīdas* may be Ibn Killis's most enduring legacy to the Arabic world. As further evidence of his power Ibn Killis was the first vizier to have had his name appear with that of the caliph's on the *tarrāz* or royal cloth, which normally was reserved for the nobility. Also, and most unusually for the time, Ibn Killis had his own letterhead. The caliph continued to provide him with honours and wealth and it was during his tenure of office that the Fāṭimid empire expanded to its fullest. Whatever interpretation one may place on his bid for power, and his religious conversion, it has to be said he was a brilliant administrator.

The credit for Egypt's prosperity was not his alone. Caliph al-'Azīz (344/955-386/996) was the wisest and most beneficial of all the Fāṭimid caliphs, the peace that followed his investiture being sufficient evidence of this. A man loath to shed blood, he forgave his enemies; he did much to suppress corruption and forbade all bribes and presents, and saw that nothing was spent without a written order. A man tolerant of other faiths, he married a Christian. Some of the greatest architectural triumphs in Cairo – the Golden Palace, the Pearl Pavilion, numerous canals and bridges – were achieved during his reign. Also he had a turn for poetry, and, very much in line with the Fāṭimids and their claim to familiarity with the unknown, he considered himself something of a soothsayer, which raised an occasional smile. If he had but a single fault, it was that his capacity to spend money on others was rivalled only by his ability to spend on himself. What he took he paid for, however. A connoisseur of precious stones, he bejewelled even the housings of his horses. He loved the fine and the rare. A pear-shaped ewer made of rock crystal, with a Kufic inscription bearing his name, and decorated with two seated lions flanking the tree of life, is preserved in the treasury of St. Mark's in Venice. A connoisseur of valuable textiles, he possessed robes so fine they could be passed whole through a finger ring and also he had a collection of turbans many of which were embroidered with gold and were anything up to sixty yards in length. A connoisseur of exotic creatures, he brought to Egypt rare animals, both dead and alive, among them a stuffed rhinoceros that greatly delighted the populace. And now that the scene has been set for the resumption of our avian theme, al-'Azīz, also a connoisseur of what flies up and flutters home, possessed some pretty fine pigeons too.

The vizier's pigeons, however, exceeded even those of the caliph's in excellence.

This was to become a rare source of friction between them. Ibn Killis had already served a short prison sentence for poisoning one of his political enemies, one of the caliph's favourites, but it was pigeons, and the jealousy they engendered, that came close to ruining his career. One day the caliph flew one of his birds against one of his vizier's and lost. Those present remarked the displeasure in his features. A man such as Ibn Killis was bound to have enemies, and some of them saw in this an opportunity to discredit the man they envied. An anonymous note was sent to al-'Azīz: 'That man chooses for himself the best things of every kind and leaves nothing for you except those of inferior quality. It is even so with regard to pigeons.' No words could be better calculated to prey on the mind of a fancier, even in one whose sense of justice was unique for the times. Ibn Killis, quick to spot the danger, addressed 'the Commander of the faithful' with a short verse (whose authorship is still in question). The real winner, according to the poem, was the caliph's bird whereas his own had acted merely as chamberlain, whose task it was to precede the other.

And then came the business that has entered pigeon lore.

One day, al-'Azīz, also a connoisseur of food, having heard about the magnificent cherries that grew near Baalbeck and which were being sold in the streets of Damascus, decided he would go there to sample them. He arranged for the departure of a caravan and was about to leave Cairo when Ibn Killis suddenly came up with a plan to spare the caliph having to make such an arduous voyage. Of the different, extant versions of this story probably the most precise is that given by al-Maqrīzī in his *Historical Geography*, which comes from a lost chronicle, which he admits to not having seen.

> Wanting to go to Syria in the fruit season al-'Azīz ordered Ya'qūb b. Killis to prepare his equipment. 'My master,' replied the vizier, 'for each voyage one needs especially adapted equipment, so what is the purpose of your voyage?' 'I would like to wander through Damascus in order to taste the cherries,' answered the master. 'I hear and I obey,' answered the vizier as he left. He then rounded up all the pigeon owners in order to find out how many birds

> from Cairo were being held in Damascus and the names of those who held them. There were more than one hundred and twenty. Then he asked how many birds from Damascus were being held in Cairo and he ordered them to be brought to him. He then wrote to his lieutenant in Damascus in order to inform him of the number of the birds being held there and the names of those who held them. He told him to order them all to come to his house and to wrap cherries in paper and to attach each one to the birds in order to release them the same day. Only three or four days passed and all the pigeons returned, except ten or thereabouts which went missing, their wings loaded under the weight of cherries. He took the fruits from their papers and placed them in a golden platter, which he covered, and then ordered a eunuch to take it to the caliph. And he went to the caliph and presented his gift with these words, 'O commander of the believers, we have brought these cherries which are here on this platter. If this quantity is satisfactory, good; if not, then we will bring more.' Al-'Azīz marvelled and replied, 'A man like yourself is truly the server of kings.'

All the other sources mention only the Cairo pigeons assembled at Damascus and do not mention the fact that the order was also transmitted by carrier pigeon. According to these other, later versions, 600 pigeons transported 1200 cherries, one cherry attached to each leg of the pigeon and wrapped up in a silk pocket and accompanied by a green leaf.

Ibn Killis died at of the end of 380/February 991. By this point he enjoyed a salary of 100,000 dinars, and left behind him lands, houses, shops, slaves, horses, robes, jewels and pigeons, amounting to a value of four million dinars. He kept a harem of 800 women (which goes rather against the grain of the earlier caliph al'Mu'izz's injunction that for any one man one woman is quite enough), and his personal bodyguard comprised 4000 young men, white and black.

The learned of Cairo lamented his passing for he was highly regarded for his liberality to scholars, jurists, physicians, men of letters and poets, and his concern was to promote learning. The less learned held him in suspicion for showing too much favour to Christians and Jews. The biographers of the time, while not blind to the means by which he attained power, praised him. And none praised him more than his fellow pigeon fancier. His funeral was as sumptuous as his life. His body was shrouded in fifty robes, which, together with the embalming perfumes, were said to have cost 10,000 dinars. The populace assembled in the street leading from the citadel to his house. Caliph al-'Azīz came forth, mounted on a mule, and, contrary to his usual custom when riding out, no parasol was held over him. (The parasol or *miẓalla* was a symbol of majesty and always matched the fabric of the caliph's costume.) Al-'Azīz was heard to say, 'How long shall I grieve for thee, O Vizier!' He wept and prayed over his friend, and with his own hands arranged the body in the grave, and then set the stone to the entrance of the tomb. For the next three days, the caliph would neither eat nor receive guests and for eighteen days the offices of government were closed. The caliph freed all the mamlūks of the deceased and paid his outstanding debts. An extravagance maybe, but then Ibn Killis had shown his brilliance at managing the country's expenses.

The following morning a large number of poets visited the tomb, one hundred of whom recited elegies over it. Slave girls stood beside the tomb with silver cups and spoons, providing wine and sweetmeats to the crowds who came. Doubtless they would have included the poets Ibn Killis gathered round himself and to whom he awarded pensions. It need not be supposed that these were verses of the first order, but they had been provided with an incentive. Poets, then as now, were not averse to obtaining financial reward for their genius.

We hear nothing more of al-'Azīz playing with his pigeons.

The amir al-Mukhtār al-Musabbiḥī describes al-'Azīz thus: 'He had reddish hair, his eyes were large and dark blue, his shoulders broad.' The combination of red hair and blue eyes filled superstitious Arabs with awe. Al-'Azīz won the hearts of the populace not with awe, however, but with magnanimity and a spirit of conciliation. A big spender he may have been, but when he died, aged 41, on 28th Ramadan, 386/October 14, 996, after stepping from his bath, he was clad in only rags and bandages. Shortly before, feeling death close, and mindful of the need to transfer power, he summoned his young son who is remembered to the world as 'Ḥakīm the Mad' and whose brutalities had no precedent in the family genes.

Chapter Ten

Satan's Horn

Abed, Sulaymān and I sat at another outdoor café, again far from the centre of Damascus, at its very edge, as if by choosing these places Sulaymān was deliberately breaking ties with the old city that had been so much his sphere of operations once, and he had become now a frontiersman of suburban possibilities. Would he keep drifting outward bound until he'd reached his ancestral home? We sat at the table furthest away from a sagging line of electric lights, a trio of brooding silhouettes, or so I pictured ourselves. The waiter asked us if we weren't cold, as if the outer dark had made it more so. A song by Umm Kulthūm was playing, her tormented voice in labour, as if giving birth to the night, the whole of it. She was, and remains, Night's voice. A couple of youths revved back and forth on their motorbikes. A dog barked somewhere.

As usual, Sulaymān's folly was leavened with industry and good sense, while Abed's declared intentions to follow a straight line, such as becoming a computer engineer, were all moonshine, random stabs at some ill-considered future. When I asked him if he knew how to switch on a computer, his face became a blank screen. We had been through this routine many times, and I am even less of a job councillor than I ever was a marriage advisor. My success rate with the latter was abysmal enough, although Abed suffered no loss of faith in me. At least romance had a marginally firmer base, be it the workings of a mind crazy with desire. The imagination was Abed's only security, which, oddly enough, seemed insufficient to the requirements of his several fiancées. They always bowed out with an excuse.

Sulaymān, meanwhile, began to speak in a language I'd never heard him use before.

'When an Arab is wounded in his honour or in his dignity he will become harmful. He will consider you his enemy. If you hurt him he'll be sad for five minutes and then move on, but if you humiliate him he will be in a rage forever.'

I wondered if he were addressing some audience behind me. Sulaymān then shifted from the universal to the particular, drawing on his experience of the year before, when he picked up a wrong fare. The scars of that event were something he'd carry for a long time.

'I keep thinking of those people who attacked me. I consider it is righteous to take my revenge on them because they used a gun on me. "If you need money, why not ask me! Why use a gun? This means I must kill you." They are in prison now. If, in twenty years' time, they are released, I will take my revenge on them. I was about to be killed. One of them hit me with the gun. They were military recruits, escapees. I made a mistake because when I saw them I heard a voice saying to me, "You shouldn't let these people in your car." I persuaded myself that maybe this voice was wrong. When they got into the car, all three in the back, I heard that same voice again, telling me one of them had a loaded gun, which he was ready to use. Three times I heard this voice. The last thing it told me was that I should have a gun as well and in order to stay alive I must kill one of them. Many people here find prison better than life on the outside. They commit crimes in order to get into prison! After fifteen years, everything on the outside will have changed. Prison, however, is not just bars and a wall. It is also when you are sitting in a garden surrounded by roses and you can't smell them anymore. What is the point of roses if you can't smell them? We Damascenes no longer smell the roses.'

Stone walls do not a prison make nor iron bars a cage.

Sulaymān seemed to have entered a wholly new mode. This was the man who, when I first knew him, had sat for more than an hour in front of Ibn al-'Arabī's grave, speechless with love. Anger, all of it justifiable, had carved at least some of those creases in his face. Something, though, told me that this anger would never putrefy into hate.

'Would you say this is merely a historical phase?'

'*Inshallāh*. We shall have salvation, either that or we die. There are no other alternatives, so it's either salvation or death. It used to be when someone was killed in some part of the world it was considered shameful to put such a thing on television. Now the media shows these things all in the name of truth, but in doing so it makes a bad mistake. Six billion people all over the world watch the death of a single person on television. In the true etiquette of Islam if you have a sheep which you have raised our *sharī'a* law says it may be slaughtered, yes, but, according to Abraham, in all politeness you should not slaughter it yourself because *you* were the one who raised it, *you* alone fed this creature. You should appoint somebody else to do it and step away from the scene. So how can you consider yourselves world leaders when you feed your own nations and then slaughter them? Logically speaking, it just doesn't make sense. Maybe those elders are on drugs and they are not aware of what they are doing. This is not human nature. We have reached the stage where we kill everything. They attack us from behind, and not face to face, just like those people in my taxi. This is not chivalrous. They will greet you and then seize their chance. Don't ever think they'll come face to face with you.'

'Who are *they*?'

Sulaymān hesitated as if waiting for what he was about to say to settle.

'They are people who consider themselves righteous. They manufacture ideas, brainwash a person with them and afterwards try to use him. They claim to be clerics and other such types. They exploit the common people at grassroots level. They win their sympathy first and then they start planting ideas. The result is what we see now, sectarianism. Previously they used their tongues only, but now they begin to hurt by any means possible. I am from one of the Bedouin tribes, but the Arabs do not understand me. They are lost and they are suffering and I try to address them. The Americans should come in order to rescue a lost people and not to make them feel more lost than ever before. We used to invest a lot of hope in them. We used to imagine them riding white horses, coming to save us, but instead of saving us they have pushed us into an even deeper chasm. This has produced a sharp reaction. America does not know the way whereby it might save the Arabs. Saddam utilised force, but now he is gone and the Americans are employing the same methods. There is something mysterious going on in Iraq. It is like a mental asylum gone out of control. Very soon each sect there will claim that it alone is right. It's the first time in my life I have witnessed such chaos.'

Abed then added his piece.

'There is a famous hadith in which the Prophet Muḥammad, blessed be his name, praises both Damascus and Yemen. When one of his followers asked "What about us?" he replied, "It is from Najd that al-Shayṭān's horn will rise." The Wahhābī get very angry when reminded of this, especially if the words are spoken by Sufis, whom they consider bad Muslims.'

'*Al-Shayṭān?*'

'Satan.'

'Osama bin Laden?'

Abed shrugged. This was not a subject he wished to pursue.

The hadith to which he referred, whose actual wording is 'There will occur earthquakes, trials and tribulations and there will appear the horn of Satan', is for many Muslims a vexing one, and there is dispute even as to where Najd is, or where it was during the Prophet's lifetime. Najd is commonly taken to be the region in central Saudi Arabia which is home to its capital Riyadh, and which was the birthplace of Muḥammad ibn 'Abd al Wahhāb, founder of the Wahhābī movement. Such is the controversy surrounding him in certain quarters that it would be foolish to even try to enter the debate. Suffice to say there are those who believe his religious movement is the heresy of which the Prophet warned. Osama bin Laden is, or rather was, Wahhābī. The Wahhābī, meanwhile, think of themselves as the protectors of Islam in its purest form. Also there have been arguments put forth saying that what was really meant by Najd was Iraq, which might just a bit too conveniently shift the centre of blame. What cannot be disputed, however, is the sense of dread that arises from this hadith. It made the dark we sat in that much darker.

Sulaymān said, 'Let's go. I want to show you something.'

§

Sulaymān drove us to another area on the outskirts of Damascus, where all the brothels and nightclubs are. They seemed pretty tame from the outside, although who knows what shenanigans took place inside. Apparently the dancers were mostly gypsies, which might have been said only in order to hide a deep sense of shame. Yes, *of course* they would be gypsies. Likewise, the pimps were said to be Kurds. And the Arab clients were always from other countries. Syrians will speak about prostitutes, but only to foreigners as a rule. Any discussion of such matters between themselves remains taboo.

'I am going to drive slowly past each one,' Sulaymān told me, 'and you are to tell me what you see.'

We went past several such places, occasionally stopping for a moment to survey the scene. Other than the coloured lights promising an even more colourful nightlife, I could see nothing of significance, quite the opposite, in fact. The car parks were mostly empty and through one window I saw a man pushing what might have been a broom. I asked Sulaymān whether he ferried much by way of clientele.

'I try not to. Once I gave a Saudi a ride here. I pleaded with him, telling him that as a Muslim who'd been to Mecca he ought not to be going to such places. The Saudi insisted, and when we arrived I had a brainwave. I told him to stay put on the street while I checked to see if I could arrange a girl for him. The Saudi agreed, and got out of the car while I remained inside. I ran him over.'

'What, you killed him!'

'No, no. I did it very gently, just enough to give him a good bruising. The Saudi screamed and shouted at me.'

Sulaymān smiled and I saw then, as of old, the mad frenzy in his eyes.

'So what did you see?' he asked me.

'Well, quite honestly, nothing.'

'Exactly! All the prostitutes, fearing an al-Qaeda attack, have fled Damascus.'

I remembered then what a journalist told me once: 'If you wish to find out what next week's news is going to be or the dollar exchange, speak first to a prostitute.'

§

We drove back to the café. There was a growing chill in the air. Umm Kulthūm was still playing, the birth pangs in her voice deepening with every note. *Ya habibi, ya habibi.* Certain things one need never translate. Although this woman was already some years in her grave, every night millions of Arabs worldwide still follow the coffin of sound she made. She makes them comprehensible to themselves. She remains a more than willing sacrifice, and she is loved all the more for it. Against the background of her mournful voice, the time had come for me to broach a delicate subject. I informed Abed that I couldn't see how our friendship could continue. While saying this, I knew it would not be the case, but I needed to shock him awake. All night long I'd been tormented by the question of whether friendship with him was still possible. I wanted to push him away as far as possible and yet, in truth, the prospect of doing so made me ache still more. Abed could ill afford solitude deeper than what he already had to endure. I had to remember what drew me to him in the first place. It was just harder to see what it was I had always seen in him. The best, when disfigured, when obscured, so easily becomes the worst. The occasional flashes of the old Abed were almost worth the price, and they were all I had left to build my hopes upon. It was now or never. Sulaymān, whose instincts were always sure, remained in silence.

'Why?' Abed asked. A terrible panic was in his eyes.

I told him it was because of the incident of the night before, not because I believed he had meant to hurt the child but rather because he did not sufficiently care enough to take notice. Abed squirmed for a while.

'Yes, you're right.'

At last I found cause to ask him if my suspicions were true, that he was on psychiatric medication.

'Yes, these are the troubles of which I have told you nothing. My mother told me not to tell anyone because if people knew they would have nothing more to do with me. Already what she said has come true. Mental illness is a terrible stigma here. My friends have drifted away from me one by one. Sulaymān, too. Over these past few days I felt in my heart that I was losing you as well. This made me suffer terribly. Now I think that perhaps I haven't lost you. Most people, if I told them about this, would never speak to me again. You are my last friend.'

'Do you have any idea how crippling these drugs can be?'

'A shrink, the very best in Damascus, prescribed them. After you left me in 1999, the following year I had a fit. I was hospitalised for three days. I was diagnosed with an irreversible mental disorder that would stay with me for the rest of my life. The doctors said the problem was inside me, that I born with it, and it was not due to circumstance. I completely lost my self-esteem, which, of course, is the oxygen of life. My friends rejected me. The doctor saved me with this medicine. These are the terrible things of which I haven't been able to speak. It began with the fall I had in Turkey in 1998, when I fell three floors down an empty lift shaft. Six months later, I met and married the French girl. She left me. In 2000, I met Zeinab from Turkey. It was planned by destiny. I really believe this. She spoke English. As you know, my cup of tea is to find an Oriental girl with an English tongue. I began to ascribe certain powers to her, one of these being her ability to steal my sperm.'

'What, when she was not there!'

'Yes, I don't know how she did this. And then I was afraid she would become pregnant by remote. I thought the French girl stole my ID, my internal identity. I thought she was a saint and Zeinab a prophetess. And then I told the doctor Zeinab was a snake. I was completely mad at the time. A snake feeds on eggs. The Arabic word for "eggs" and "balls" is the same – *bayḍ*. The doctor told me my delusions were crazy ones and that I was going to be mad for the rest of my life. Also he said the snake was the reincarnation of a djinn, but later I realised that maybe Allāh was hinting to me that it was my ego and *not* Zeinab that was the snake. The hadiths say that one's worst enemy is oneself. So it was quite possible that I had misinterpreted God's hints. These delusions, the doctor said, would sooner or later break me. Also my childhood was to blame, my parents, my father in particular. There is no warmth in him. He saw me as a competitor to his manhood. Spiritually and physically he annihilated my character and my dignity, pulverised, suffocated me. At school the other children spat at me. All this, my being jobless, single and divorced, has contributed to my condition.'

'And if you were to work?'

'The doctor told me that if I were to get a job it will be like taking one tablet, therefore reducing by one the chemical dosage.'

Sulaymān rejoined the conversation, saying he did not think Abed was mentally ill at all, and that what he needed was to haul himself out of the depths which he himself had made. What was extraordinary was that Sulaymān who spoke not a word of English had, as so often before, divined our conversation. Suddenly the breach that appeared between them when we spoke earlier of djinns was that much more explicable. Abed had gone the way of modern medicine; Sulaymān still believed certain demons could be exorcised. Abed translated for me a line from Umm Kulthūm's song called *The Thousandth Night*, which the following morning I'd purchase. It plays as I write. It helps me recreate that scene. The words Abed translated could not have been more apt.

'Inshallāh we will not drink the wine of departure.'

§

With only a week to go before my return to London, I went to see Waseem one last time. I found him in his usual spot, negotiating some deal whose beginning and end would be forever unknown to me.

'I've been looking for you,' he said. 'I've got a story for you.'

It concerned a member of the al-Sawwāḥ family, a weapons smuggler of dark repute, a man not to be crossed, ever. As well as being a gunrunner, al-Sawwāh kept pigeons. The pigeons, it would seem, were his idyll in an otherwise turbulent life. When al-Sawwāh went to Latakia for a few days his neighbour, with whom he had been having a dispute, took the opportunity of his absence to complain about his pigeons to the authorities. The police did then what they wouldn't dare have done had al-Sawwāh been in town and raided his ḥouse, seized all the pigeons, and broke down the dovecotes. It really was tantamount to putting one's hand into the mouth of a Doberman pinscher. Al-Sawwāh returned from Latakia, and, finding his birds gone, visited the mayor of his municipality, challenging him to explain why this had happened and who had authorised the police to enter his house.

'Why didn't you wait? Don't you know who I am?' The mayor pleaded innocence, and told him that the neighbour had connections with security and it was the latter who'd given him backing. Al-Sawwāh felt sufficiently emboldened to pay his neighbour a visit, not forgetting to take with him a Kalashnikov, or, in Damascene underworld parlance, 'a Russian'. The conversation that took place, or, rather, the few words that are remembered of it, was chilling.

'The police took my birds. Their equivalent is your children. My birds are every bit as precious to me as your children are to you.'

The neighbour, realising the implications of this, panicked and ran for his gun. Al-Sawwāh, when he saw he was about to be challenged, took his Kalashnikov and fired seventeen bullets into the first child, killing him outright, wounded a second child, and then shot the father in the legs, after which he made his escape on a motorcycle. After eight months on the run, he surrendered to the police. He went to court and there an astounding verdict was reached. Al-Sawwāh was sentenced to only five years imprisonment. Why only five years, when ten years was the minimum for far lesser crimes? The judge, in his wisdom, considered the case to be on a par with a prostitute's murder. It might even be classified as a *crime passionnel* because, after all, the man loved his pigeons. They had been as children to him. Was there ever a judge so solicitous of a pigeon fancier's feelings? Also he criticised police procedure, saying they hadn't been given the proper authority to remove the pigeons, that they were required to give advance warning and that after taking the birds they did all sorts of damage. The neighbour, meanwhile, was at fault for having employed all the wrong connections. The judge took all these matters into consideration and concluded that a sentence of five years was quite enough to fit the crime.

Clearly there were gaping holes in the story, and although it seemed unlikely I'd ever be able to unearth some underworld connection between al-Sawwāh and the judge, surely there was more to add to the picture. Obviously there were pressures that could be exerted, which were not, strictly speaking, illegal, and that had their roots in a much older way of life, when deals could be struck between warring families. What was a child's life worth? What I wanted more than any lesson in Arabic jurisprudence, however, was to get into the mind of someone who could kill a child over pigeons. This story would serve as a lynchpin to a much bigger one. I asked Waseem what the chances were of my being able to make contact with people close to the case to which he replied that he would arrange everything for me.

The way was open to another trip to Damascus. Anything seemed possible, and nobody was better connected than Waseem, a man who could be in several places at the same time. Waseem was the conduit between the world above and the world below, between the good guys and the bad guys, and, as fixer, his movements were invisible. I suspect that even the cabs which he preferred to buses were invisible. Waseem was a protected species, so suave nothing could ever touch him.

§

If pigeons bear messages, and indeed, when got up as doves, are often seen as auguries, and if, according to ancient lore, whores are doves, and if doves are pigeons and pigeons doves, then what Sulaymān said, with regard to the disappearance of Damascus's prostitutes, became uncomfortably true. On April 27th, 2004, there were explosions and a gun battle in the wealthy Mazzeh area of the city, the first major violence in Damascus in almost a decade, and significantly it was where most of the embassies are. According to the TV news a couple of terrorists with probable links to al-Qaeda had been shot dead; a policeman and a woman bystander also died. An empty building that recently housed UN offices had been set alight. There had also been minor damage to the Canadian embassy. Later, a cache of weapons and explosives was found in a village south of Damascus.

All this could have been in another part of the world altogether. Where I was, only a couple of miles away, there were no police, no sirens, ambulances or anything else. I caught not so much as a flicker in the reactions of people, which could be interpreted as being either deep fear or total indifference. Also, the media are always treated with a certain disregard, which may serve to explain the relative mental health of the populace. What one heard the following day on the street, always a thoroughfare for both true and false, is that the whole affair was a bit of theatre put on by the government in order to demonstrate to the rest of the world that it stood firm against terrorism. Clearly, though, people had died. Somebody else told me it had to do with the drug trade and, with the leading protagonists dead, it was convenient to shift blame onto militant Islamicists. A day or two later, nobody said anything at all and the news was equally mum. I did later walk through the Mazzeh area and there were still plenty of security men in suits, wearing ties too, and with machine guns dangling from around from their necks. One of them, semi-hidden behind a tree, blew me a kiss.

§

A couple of days later, I saw on the front pages of several newspapers some photographic images that simply failed to make sense. There was a surreal one of a hooded figure, draped in a dark cloth of some kind, standing on a box, his arms stretched to either side, with what appeared to be electrical wiring dangling from his hands. The image was strangely iconic. Another photograph showed a dwarfish female in army fatigues, a pageboy haircut, with something approaching mock sadness in her profile, and with a leash in her hand attached to the neck of a naked man lying on the floor. I was too puzzled to be able to register the full horror of those images. I wanted for the Arabic script to straighten out into something that might provide some hint of their meaning. Those images seemed to belong not to the endless file of atrocities, which is the history of our species, but rather to a sick pantomime. When I got back to the hotel, curious to know what they were, I found a group of men watching the news on television, which contained the same scenes and further horrors, one of which was of naked men, hooded with green bags, piled up like logs, with a couple of smiling figures, a man and a woman, posing behind them. 'What is this?' I asked someone. He didn't answer. Came then the weak face of the world's most powerful man making his personal apologies, at which point, in perfect unison, the people watching this burst into spontaneous laughter. All I could think of were Sulaymān's words of a few days before. *These people would be in a rage forever.* America might have removed the Devil, but Hell's acreage was greater than it ever was.

What I couldn't get out of my head was the laughter.

'Yasser, if I could interpret the meaning of that response, which followed President Bush's apology, I think I may understand everything about this place. What was it? Bitterness, cynicism?'

'Every time we hear this arsehole, when he comes on TV to apologise for using the word "Crusader", for example, our response is "Are you kidding us?" There is a big gulf between any two cultures when they meet, which is obvious in their literature or in the way their diplomats talk. It's true of both sides. Each thinks the other a fool or that the other doesn't understand him or else he says to himself, "Does this man really think he can fool me?" The more powerful, of course, have the greater confidence. So when people know *you* have ordered this and then you apologise, the response is, "Are you kidding me?" This is what that laughter meant.'

'I don't mean to cause offence,' I replied, 'but when such crimes are perpetuated by the Americans, say, it hits the Arab soul unbelievably hard but what about this fatal streak in the Arabic mind that allows for leaders like Saddam to keep on and on, crushing them every day? Surely what he did in his prisons was much worse. Saddam killed children in their mothers' arms. There would appear to be this fatal flaw in the Arab character, which is a respect for the strong man.'

'I do not agree with the notion that anyone respected Saddam. Look, I might hit you and the first time you will take it, maybe even a second or third time, but there will come a point when, no matter how patient you are, you will say enough is enough. The mistake America made in Iraq is that here you had this man who had been hitting you for years and years and then someone else comes along, removes him, and so *he* hits you. "What, you too?" is your response. "You also want to hit me! You have become so familiar with me!" This thing with the Arab regimes, how long has it lasted? History here is not measured by years or even decades. During the Umayyad period there were good leaders and bad leaders, history went in ups and downs. Sometimes things got better, sometimes worse. With these Arab regimes over hundreds of years, people here became more patient, more adaptable. If this tells you anything it is not that these people are backward but that they are able to adapt because they have lived through this for centuries. So adapting to a system and trying to survive is something that came to us by degrees. America is not old enough to understand this.'

'What about language, though? Consider how Arabs have always addressed each other poetically, whether it be Nasser, or, for that matter, Saddam and Osama bin Laden whose Arabic rhetoric is said to be beautiful. What happens when a people who can speak of "collateral damage", for example, clashes with another whose language and poetic are inseparable from that of the Qur'ān?'

'There is a book I bought in London, *Metaphors We Live By*, which I have yet to read but the reason I got it was because I was drawn to the title. Actually everyone lives in the metaphors of his own language. We say *ahlan wa-sahlan*, which is the polite Arabic phrase for "welcome". If I analyse the English word I might say you are *coming well*, but if you look closely at the Arabic you'll see how much more is meant. It is in fact a contraction of the sentence, "Consider us your family and your level plane". I don't mean to fall into the trap of comparing English to Arabic. All I want to do is compare the way Arabic and English speakers think. We allow much more time for things to happen, and then we elaborate and sophisticate them, whereas English speakers come to the point immediately. You say Saddam spoke a poetic, a language which an American coming from thousands of miles away with a gun would never be able to understand. Saddam spoke to the people of their tribes, their families. When you are a leader, you are actually talking to sheep and this is how you survive. Some people you can give a bone, other people you give a lump of flesh.'

§

It had been an intense week: Sulaymān's dark forebodings, Abed's confession, the fugitive whores, a shoot-out in the smart part of town, the breaking of the Abu Ghraib scandal – all seem to fit into some dark, premeditated, Satanic scheme and then came Waseem's story, as if the pigeon world, too, had taken a dive. It was time to sit back and analyse. There was another person I'd go to see every so often, Subhī, who maybe is the most sardonic figure in Damascus – not for him the handicap of philosophy, no hadiths either – sooner the clenched fist than the lyrical tongue. A cool businessman with a hot temper, bluntness was his instrument, although always he handled it with intelligence. The worse the news, the bigger his laugh; and the bigger the laugh the deeper the scorn that filled his eyes. Subhī was probably closer to the hypothetical 'man in the street' than anyone else I knew. If one needed to know which way public opinion blew or what it would cost them, he was the man to speak to. I'd go to him, carrying an abacus and a weathervane.

'America and the West,' he began, in response to some question whose formulation now escapes me, 'maybe they don't mean to or maybe they do, maybe they are stupid or maybe they're not, but they complain endlessly about the lack of understanding from

Muslim countries. They talk in this strange way, saying we are a most difficult people to understand. All they have to do is read our history. You don't have to speak to me. Ours is a great culture, with a long history, and I am honoured and happy to be Muslim even though I'm not a particularly good one. I am happy to be Arab *and* Syrian, and I like the way we live with each other, Muslim, Christian and Jew. Usually we don't have any problems, but now we have certain viruses, which I'm sorry to say come always from the West. The first virus is Israel, and I do not mean Israelis as a people, that *they* are viruses, no, not at all, because, after all, there is a new generation who were born there and who had no choice in the matter. I am speaking of the virus which came from the West, via the British, which resulted in our now having many other viruses, the most recent being Iraq. The West compares the dictatorship of Saddam to the democracy they would like to put in its place, and if I have to make any comparison between the two and choose, well, with all that's happened there, I would have chosen Saddam. We, in Syria, were working towards our own form of democracy, our own political path, but what they wanted to do is to replace this with their own fake democracy. Now look! We are forced to protect our regime!'

Subhī burst into a wild, scornful laughter.

'I do not always agree with our government, but I don't want to see what happened in Iraq happen here. So what I am saying to you is *leave us alone*. We never went to America or Europe to create problems and yet they talk about terrorism. Oh my God, it's like we are talking about a child here. First of all let's ask, "What is terrorism?" If we describe what happened on September 11th as terrorism, then I agree, but if we talk about a Palestinian child throwing small stones, then I can't agree. So first let's distinguish between terrorism and resistance. Is it logical with all that is happening here, in this area, with Americans in Iraq killing people, and with Israelis in Palestine, that there shouldn't be any resistance? Tell me, is that *logical*? In America, they resisted the British; in France, they resisted the Germans. Wherever there is an illegal occupation, the normal thing is for there to be resistance. So why is resistance against Israelis in Palestine forbidden? And against American troops in Iraq? It was considered right to resist the

Soviets in Afghanistan, so why is it that these same people who fought the Soviets, and were supported by the Americans with money and arms, are now called terrorists? The pressure on people here, especially with the Americans in Iraq, has been terrible. It's like our heads are in a vice that's getting tighter and tighter. *What's happening here?* Why, if they are bringing all their problems here, do they complain about us taking ours there? What we are giving them is our reaction and what they give us is that which creates that reaction. If you shout at a wall, the sound will come back at you. It's the same with light. I will give you one small, personal example. In the nineteen-seventies and eighties women in Syria were freer than they are now. For each covered woman there were three or four uncovered. My mother was one of them. She went to dances and didn't wear a headscarf, but now it has got all very strange and there has been this reaction. Okay, they say the Americans have spent billions and billions of dollars in Iraq, but they can afford it. They can spend even more on their strategies. When a stupid guy like George Bush says this is a Christian war against a terrorist Islam somebody like me, a poor Muslim who doesn't pray, who maybe drinks a little or goes to a dance and has a bit of sex too, when he hears Bush talking like this he'll become *very* Muslim. This is a reaction and it is a major problem. So here we are, in the 21st century, and we have more fundamentalism than ever before. They say Bush is crazy and his foreign policy stupid. No, no, there is a big plan afoot and the Americans are achieving it perfectly. They do not want Muslims to follow the Malaysian example. They prefer the Saudi model, they prefer to be in bigger circles. They won't say this, of course. They say the opposite because they know Muslims hate them and whatever they say should be done Muslims will go and do the exact opposite. If they say "Go left", we go to the right. They say they want democracy in Saudi Arabia and that women should be freer, but they already know it is the centre of fundamentalism and that those people will never allow for such changes. If America said they support the political system in Saudi Arabia, then everyone there would go in the opposite direction. I'm sorry, but *who* is paying here? It's not the politicians or the American government – it's the American people, the European people, and these people are poor, not financially, but poor in *mind*.

They are highly educated and it all goes nowhere. They believe in liberty and equality, but they can't change anything. Why couldn't the British stop Blair from going to war? Why couldn't the Spanish when 83% of them were against the war? *Where* is your democracy? There is liberty, yes, but where is democracy? Everything is run by money. The British military is no longer a military, they are merely professionals working for money, and the politicos, they work for money too; everyone works for money. There is no Churchill or de Gaulle. There are only unlimited companies, and even elections are run by the media and they have to present their political candidates as if they were Hollywood stars otherwise they'd lose. The Syrian people, to be honest, are scared. They don't trust anyone anymore. After what they have seen in Iraq, they have moved closer to our government than ever before. They had enough problems to attend to on the inside, but at least they weren't confused whereas now their vision is not so clear anymore. Nobody knows what is going to happen tomorrow or next year.'

I decided to put Subhī to the test.

'I want to read you something: "You may think my words are free and often I go against the opinions of many fellow Syrians, yes, but in the end you must remember mine is an Oriental mind and however much I might complain I will resign myself to this fate." Do you remember who said this?'

'Yes, me!'

'That was ten years ago. Are things still the same?'

'Yes, I believe so. We are Orientals. I can't change my mind nor can I change my base. I can't *grow* in this community and its traditions. I like democracy and liberty and freedom, but *which* kind of freedom? Animals are free, but should I live like them? My freedom should stop exactly where it begins to hurt you. So before freedom, there should be respect. When I respect you and you respect me, then this is a nice instance of freedom, but freedom doesn't mean I should walk naked or drink in the street or my wife go out with someone else. These are not freedoms. Freedom is respect. I respect what my wife says, but that doesn't mean I have to agree with her. There should be dialogue – maybe she's right, maybe I'm right – but there are red lines one has to observe and I agree with the existence of those red lines.'

'You are one of the old Damascene families. You spoke once about what is happening to the old Damascene families, and how their traditions have been attacked from the inside. Since then, in the space of only a decade, we have seen the biggest revolution in the history of the human race – computers, mobile phones – such that the very idea of time itself has changed. What has happened to those traditions?'

'I'll tell you a funny story. I always had a problem with my father and probably it's because I have the same mentality as him. Our voices, our smiles, our feelings about women, our sense of honour with regard to family, all are exactly the same. The only problem I have with him is that he is still on old time and I am trying to be more modern. What I say to everyone is that we should be *modernised* examples of our fathers and families. They are not bad, they have something good, but we have to add something else to this goodness in them, and not to destroy everything in the process. My father was a merchant and I am a merchant. I am not talking about this. I am talking about something different, about mentality and tradition, yes, but about how to continue it in a modern way.'

'So how do you modernise tradition?'

'This is the big war we are having now between the old and the new generations. According to the hadith, "As you are, so your leader will be", so if you are a bad people then your leader will be bad because he comes from the people. And if you are good, it follows that your leader will be good. So if we have a dictator, it's because we have something of a dictator's mentality in ourselves. The son must do as I do, as I want, and this is a kind of dictatorship which I hate. I want to give my son lessons in life, but I do not want to oblige him to do exactly as I do. He has to lead his life as he sees fit. This is a problem to which we were trying to find a solution but, as I've told you already, this virus from the West has come and destroyed everything. I told you I have a problem with my father because he is always trying to analyse my friends and classify them and quantify the good and the bad in them. Always he wants to share everything, his problems too, but many of these are problems which he created for himself. Why should I be involved? For example, he married four times. It is not my field. I have one wife.

He must face this problem himself, but he wants me to share this, to carry a big part of the responsibility. He wants me to share the responsibility because then he won't have any bad feelings about himself. He will not have to face the fact of his own failures.'

'You also spoke about the old families as if they were a kind of nobility once and how this has been broken down.'

'Where's the nobility in London or Paris? This is a problem we face everywhere. Maybe we preserve bits of this nobility more than the West does, but the problem I have with my friends is that they are always looking with one eye and I am telling them to look with both eyes. Only then do you see where your responsibility lies. Only then do you see whether you did well or poorly and you can see, too, how the others behave towards you.'

Subhī concluded with something he saw on television during the Afghan War. An old man was standing beside the rubble of his mud house. When they told him that the missile that destroyed his house cost one million dollars, he replied, 'Why didn't they ask me? I would have knocked it down for five thousand!'

§

A mosque can be wherever you like.

I was sitting with Abed in the Hejaz Café, waiting to catch my plane. Sulaymān, for the first and only time, didn't show. A year later I would discover there had been a misunderstanding with regard to time and place, and all the while he had been looking for us elsewhere. This, then, was to be half a goodbye.

A signal was made and the men got up from their tables, Abed too, and dragged plastic mats from various directions and placed them edge to edge, and, forming three rows of seven, they got down on their knees, the waiter leading them in prayer. As soon as the prayers were done, each man returned to his table.

'While praying,' Abed told me, 'I had this message: "If you keep going the way you are going now, you will end up in prison, whereas if you repent and change your ways, you will not." If I stay rooted in my corruption, Allāh will create the cause for my imprisonment. I recently had a vision in which I was offered one final chance.'

'. . . do not a prison make . . .'

I didn't ask Abed whether his prison would be a literal or a metaphorical one.

Interlude, with Brown Dog

On Boxing Day 2005, the day of the Asian tsunami, I bit into a piece of frozen chocolate and shattered the bridge in my upper row of teeth. While I ought not to attach so slight a matter to the fates of hapless tens of thousands of people, it did seem to me that with powerful seismic forces at play this might have been a distant, maybe sympathetic, response. We would do well to note even the slightest flutter of the needle. After all, dogs do. Sulaymān told me not just dogs but fools as well are the first to detect earthquakes. Somewhere in my notes, if only I could decipher them, he cites the name of one famous in his time, who alerted the populace to an earthquake. Who, nowadays, will give a fool credence? A fool cries, and, caught skimpily between utilitarianism and purposelessness, the revellers on the beach pay him no heed. We've gone from reading signs too many to signs too few. A crack in the earth's surface would also result in my older daughter being shunted several longitudes eastward, from Moscow, where she worked for the Red Cross, to Colombo where she still operates. Those were strange and urgent days. One might even have developed a metaphysic if only there were sufficient truths to disturb, deeply held beliefs to rattle, but with the world's brain clogged with cost-effective prose, or with what the philosopher Jacques Maritain calls 'the finality of the useful', all one could do was write a cheque to the charity of one's choice. The world, rightly, threw its purse at this misfortune; wrongly, it would ignore others. Meanwhile, involuntarily, I worked at the sharp ridge in my mouth until a red blister formed at the tip of my tongue.

The breaking of a tooth produces in me deeply superstitious feelings and whenever it happens, which it has done several times, it is usually at a period of crisis in my life. As to whether it is a harbinger of things to come or a consequence of what has just been or a reaction to what is currently taking place, I've never been quite sure. There is a whole negative symbolism attached to the loss of teeth that may apply equally to false ones. It ranges from the fear of castration to a sense of complete failure, and even, according to Hans Leisegang, author of *Die Gnosis*, to the battlements guarding one's inner self having been breached. Why not simplify and look upon one's own teeth as broken tombstones? If I may pedestrianise things a little, I did have a dread of what this would cost me, which was confirmed for me a few days later when my regular dentist produced a stratospheric figure. I almost bit his little mirror in two, saying I'd need time to consider the matter.

A Syrian friend of mine living in London visited me, and, thrusting his mobile phone in my face, he said 'Smile!', took an image of my mouth, which he then e-mailed to his dentist in Aleppo who, within a couple of days, came back to him with a quotation of less than a hundred American dollars. The way I calculated things, which is to tease at figures until they become justifiable, all I needed to do was estimate the cost of the trip, subtract what I'd owe in dental fees, a mere fraction of what I'd have to pay otherwise, and then add up what I'd save by being there and not here. After a cursory glance at my friend's teeth, which seemed infinitely better than mine, I planned, sooner than I might have, amid whispered accusations of dental tourism, my next visit to Syria. I would fly to Aleppo where I'd be fitted with a temporary bridge, then go to Damascus to make further avian enquiries, and then I'd head back to Aleppo for my permanent fixture. I would do so to the alarm of friends to whom I had shown the dentist's business card, which my Syrian friend had given me.

The editor of a magazine asked me whether I might be prepared to produce an article on my Syrian dental experiences, an invitation that could only have been framed in the anticipation of some calamity. Sadly for him, luckily for me, there was nothing to write. Dr Z—, despite his card, was a serious man, and, besides, dental practice in Syria is on a par with the rest of the world. The only query I have is with regard to an additional crown he gave me, which, although perfectly functional, and quite well hidden from the public gaze, resembles a transplanted camel's tooth, otherwise all I can relate is that I sat in a padded chair that tilted backwards, opened my mouth and squinted into the dentist's lamp above me. I spat when told to.

After I had my temporary bridge fitted, I took a bus to Damascus. It stopped midway at a roadside restaurant, a huge cavern of a place close to Homs, where one might stuff a kebab in one's face, take a pee, and consider the extent of Lipton's empire. As I sat outside, in the sunshine, with my Lipton's tea, adding sugar which I never do at home, I noticed at a garage next door a brown dog, a mongrel of some kind but a handsome enough creature. It didn't have the cowering aspect that one so often associates with its fellows in the Arab world. This was a dog secure in the affection of whoever its master was, although, as Byron wrote of his beloved Newfoundland, finally he would be 'denied in heaven the soul he held on earth.' Good on it, I thought. *Bow wow*.

The very idea of a dog (*kalb*) is anathema to most Arabs. It is not enough that in the *sūra* of the Cave (*al-Kahf*) there is a precise and tender observation of a dog, traditionally known as Qitmīr, that stretches his paws at the threshold of the cave, and which, quite clearly, is a friend to the Prophet and his Companions who are taking refuge there. The utterance of this verse, incidentally, is said to be a ward against a dog when one is about to be attacked by one. It is not enough that Maymūna, one of the wives of the Prophet, had a dog called Mismār that accompanied her when she went on pilgrimage so as to guard her baggage and that when Mismār died she wept for him. It is not enough that in the *sūra* of the Table Spread (*al Mā'ida*) it is said one may consume whatever a trained hound catches. It is not enough that whenever the poet Abū Nuwās mentions dogs it is in order to sing their praises. It is not enough that Muslims are enjoined to be solicitous of God's creations. 'Whoever is kind to creatures of God is kind to himself,' said the Prophet Muḥammad, according to al-Bukhārī who quotes 'Abdallāh bin 'Amru. It is quite true that the Prophet ordered a mass culling of dogs at Medina, but this was aimed at strays infected with rabies and other dangerous diseases. When he learned that his Companions were killing dogs indiscriminately he ordered them to stop, saying only the dangerous ones were to be eliminated. There is even a tradition, also found in al-Bukhārī, in which the Prophet Muḥammad speaks of a man who for the sake of a thirsty dog lowers his shoe to the bottom of a deep well and fills it with water and on account of this act, the Prophet says, the man's sins will be forgiven. The ninth-century author of prose and satire, Al-Jāhiz, in his *Kitāb al-Hayawān* (*Book of Animals*) writes, 'If you were to visit every single Bedouin tent in the world, looking for one which did not contain one dog or more, you will not find it! Thus were the Bedouin before and after Islam.' A Mu'tazilite, al-Jāhiz chose to praise dogs precisely *because* they were considered unclean and could therefore show God's justice and mercy in the least of creatures. The Bedouins allowed dogs to sit by their sides. These would have been mostly salukis which, on account of their hunting abilities, were especially valued. Al-Jāhiz relates an extraordinary story of a baby who alone of all his family survived the plague because it was suckled by a bitch. Also there is a tenth-century collection of poems and anecdotes put together by the Iraqi scholar, Ibn al-Marzuban called *The Book of the Superiority of Dogs over Many of Those who wear Clothes*. The title speaks for itself.

The books of Islamic law contain several passages with respect to contact with dogs. Because the saliva of a dog is considered unclean anyone licked by one should perform purification, a sensible enough precaution where once rabies was a serious threat, and also because of the climate it is not considered hygienic to keep a dog in the house. It should be remembered too that in times past there'd have been very little water available for ablutions. According to one hadith, anything a dog touches must be washed seven times, the final time in dust. Also the Prophet was highly sensitive to bad odours. The tradition that no angel will go near a house that has a dog in it has its origins in the visit the angel Gabriel makes to the Prophet, which is cut short when he discovers there's a puppy in the room. *What was that puppy doing there?* Some religious traditions hold that if a dog passes in front of a man preparing to pray it pollutes his purity and negates his prayer. Such things have been written of dogs, true, and indeed they have served as a simile for unbelievers and apostates, but nowhere is there any justification for their abuse. On the contrary, Islamic laws pertaining to the welfare of animals were, for many centuries, the most progressive in existence. All said and done, given the attitude towards dogs in this part of the world, it always struck me as unusual to see one in domestic circumstances. I finished my tea, and, satisfied to see this creature had made an inroad into prejudice, I got back on the bus to Damascus.

§

As soon I got there my temporary bridge promptly fell out, which is what often happens with temporary bridges, so this is not a reflection on the abilities of my dentist in Aleppo. Thereafter I had to keep shoving it back in place. Moreover, I had to avoid speaking any word beginning with an 'F' because this had the effect of firing the bridge from my mouth at whoever I was speaking to. One day I was walking through modern Damascus when a man came up to me and kissed me on the mouth. I stood there too startled to speak when he proceeded to explain he was a masseur from Beirut and that he would be very pleased to treat me for free on his premises.

'Fine!' I said.

The man turned on his heels and fled. Abed said it was an invitation I had been wise to decline. My temporary bridge spoke for me. I made a mistake when I called out 'Hello, Fatina!' Graciously the Queen of the Souq feigned not to notice. While I was in Damascus I did more of what Sulaymān calls my 'foraging' and met with further adventures, which I shall relate soon enough, where there is call for them, but this, coming where it does, just a little artificially, perhaps, at what will be the centre of this book, is the record of a dark interlude.

§

A week later, on the return journey to Aleppo, the bus stopped at the same spot. I got myself a cup of tea, and, sitting in the same place, in the sunshine, I noticed the dog from the week before. Good, good. It was wagging its tail at someone. Al-Aḥnaf b. Qays (d. 69/688) said, 'If your dog wags his tail at you, then you can be sure his tail-wagging is genuine. But do not trust in the tail-wagging of people.' I went back to scrawling in my notebook. I was not a little bleary from sleeplessness and also, after being caught unawares by one of those treacherous winds that blow in from the desert, I was running a slight temperature. Those sudden winds strike one to the very bone. Just before I left Damascus, I visited a chemist and got from him some syrup for my sore throat and, as an afterthought almost, I asked him if he could give me a few sleeping pills. The pill I took when I got into Aleppo that night was to be the cause of an accidental drug overdose. A brilliant doctor, after quizzing me, worked out the cough syrup contained an antihistamine that boosted the power of the sleeping pill up to ten times. *Caveat viator.* Meanwhile, some hours in advance of my near demise, I shivered in the sunshine, scribbling notes.

Suddenly I heard a cracking sound and an unearthly scream, a cry so acute, so piercing it made me see white. I looked up and saw a burly man, a stupid frown on his face, clutching an iron bar which a second before he had brought down upon the middle of the friendly dog's spine. The dog was spinning in circles and then it collapsed, delirium filling its eyes. The man leaned down a little, hands on his knees, and watched with mock interest, his head tilted a little. The dog, now half-paralysed, dragged itself forward by its front feet. It was hard to tell whether it felt pain anymore, or if the pain was so terrible it stifled any further cries. A group of people congregated, all of them watching impassively to see what would happen next. A couple of youths smiled the idiotic smile of those whom brutality takes by surprise. The man then picked the dog up by the collar and, dangling it by the neck, slowly turned it in a semi-circle to his gathered audience. There was extraordinary strength in that arm of his. Steadily he raised the dog high and then dropped it and I observed him watching with almost scientific detachment as the dog crawled some more and then collapsed again, its two front legs stretched in front as if at prayer, its rear ones splayed, deadened appendages.

Whoever this man was, there was one thing indisputable – he had the authority to do as he liked with this creature. Any challenge to him would have had serious consequences. It was, in short, a dangerous situation. I hoped the dog would die quickly. What if it didn't die? Who would apply the *coup de grâce*? It would not be this man whose physique was remarkably similar to that of a recently deposed tyrant, right down to the killer eyebrows and moustache. Any satisfaction he got came not from slaughtering an innocent creature but from inflicting as much pain as possible, which made me think he was no amateur in matters of torture. Something I had been told only a few days before in Damascus came back to me – a specially constructed chair made entirely of steel, with a low back against which its occupant would be pushed backwards until he suffered agony, and if still he didn't talk, then a crack to his spine. The complete stranger who told me this shook all the while. Clearly the victim to whom he referred in the third person was himself. And now I was looking at a dog sprawled in the dust of a bleak landscape, its once charmed existence snapped in two. A signal was made to get back on the bus. As I turned away from this scene, I wished I had a gun and two bullets. I wouldn't require more.

§

Abed spoke always of *occurrences*, those events which, coming when they do, demand of us that we interpret them. It was what made him a street philosopher par excellence. The world becomes, when one allows *signs* to guide one, a place of wonders and also a place of terrors. What happened that day on the road from Damascus to Aleppo, why had it been reserved for me? What were the chances of my coming back just in the nick of time to witness an act so vile? Synchronicity is one of my themes: the air is full of connections simply waiting to be made. If sufficiently attuned, one might even produce a decent simile. There are times, though, when it seems something more, akin to what Schiller meant when he wrote, 'There is no such thing as chance, and what seems to us merest accident springs from the deepest source of destiny.' I know what Abed and Sulaymān would say – what *all* good Muslims say – that God is the cause of all things. I'm not equipped with those certainties. The random is for me a surer guide. It wouldn't have been quite the same had I not seen the dog the first time round, horrible, yes, but I wouldn't have felt as if I'd been implicated in a demonic cycle. It was almost as if what took place required my presence. A broken bridge in my mouth took me there. What would I take from this? What lessons here for a student of the human condition? Such were the thoughts that ran through my head on the bus to Aleppo, and then, quite unbidden, another image came to me, which, some years earlier, had been the focus of my poetical enquiries.

At the British Museum, in the Assyrian section, there are several rooms of bas-relief carvings taken from the palace of Ashurbanipal, at Nineveh, in what is now Iraq. They did not seem then of such appropriate provenance. Those carvings, separated as they are, into panels, may comprise the earliest cartoon-strip – the action that begins in one panel continues through into the next or sometimes even two or three panels further on, and nowhere is this more vividly conveyed than in the section devoted to the royal lion hunt. One may watch its progression from the beginning, when a naked slave boy perched on the roof of the lions' cage, pulling up a trapdoor, releases them into what will be sure death. Flanks of bearded soldiers with shields create a moving field blocking their escape, while a couple of horsemen with spears prick the lions towards the chariot that carries the king with his terrible beard, Ashurbanipal, who was the last of his line, apparently the first to be able to read and write. A civilisation he may have helped to make, but it was not one that I could ever love. What strikes me is the sameness of the human figures, characterless, most of them functionaries. And then there was the action itself, which is rendered with some brilliance. If one closes one's eyes a little, one feels the adrenalin whoosh of the chase. One hears the rumble of the chariot's wheels, the *wheest*, *wheest* of the arrows' release. A single arrow flies seemingly forever through stone, although in the next panel we find what surely is the same arrow lodged in a lioness's spine. She drags herself forward, her body arched in the air, her paralysed rear legs pulled behind her.

Another voice spoke to me through the cold Assyrian stone. Whoever sculpted this figure pays more attention to anatomical detail here than to anywhere else in the sequence. Moreover, the dying lioness is individualised in a way never accorded any of the human figures, the king included, and, in this respect, in the placing of visual truth above all else, there is surely in the artist's mind something subversive happening, which keeps him separate. 'The sculptor faithful to what he sees,' I wrote, 'will always be at a distance from what he serves.' Here, in a world too soaked with blood to revere, one finds a small but welcome escape.

My Syrian friend in London asks that I not repeat the story of the dog. After all, he says, what purpose would it serve? Surely people are dying in Iraq and Palestine, many of them children, he says, and here I'd be, lamenting a dog's fate. All it would do is reinforce the prejudice many people feel towards a country about which already they know far too little. Against his arguments, fair though they are, I set Abed's injunction: *Are not certain things revealed to one?* Should we not, therefore, seek to interpret them? What do we bury of ourselves, if we consign revelation to silence? And what is revelation but a clock set to the hour when one awakes? The anonymous artist who carved upon stone a lioness's dying agonies placed himself at the service of artistic truth; what surely he did as well was to show that one thing begets another, and that cruelty doesn't stop at one level only when there are others to explore. Maybe he didn't think this at all, but felt it rather, or maybe it wasn't so much feeling as making sure that what he sculpted was accurate. The morality of the chisel sometimes exceeds that of the pen. And now somebody will tell me of a mass murderer who was kindly towards animals and painted scenes from nature. And I'll begin to wobble a little, fearing it's an argument I might lose. No, I'll steady my nerve: it was never kindness at all but sentiment and sentiment's a sweetener that rots the moral fibre. What I saw on the road to Aleppo might have left a scar in my psyche, and it may well be true that Syria was showing me its dark side. Although this may be unfair of me, it would signal a change in my feelings about a country I had hitherto unreservedly loved, such that from now on any such love would be of a wholly conditional nature.

I should never have fallen for generalities. That is the end of the lesson. So where's the cure? Or, as my Syrian friend with better teeth than mine says, *Where's the wisdom*? I have tried many times since to undo the damage, to reason to myself that this could have happened anywhere, and, of course, cruelty and kindness are universals both, the urge to destroy and the need to preserve, yet doesn't my friend's request for silence signify what he and his compatriots would rather not countenance, that they would sooner blame outside pressures, anything other than look to themselves? So many times I had been told by Syrians they felt their country is falling through space. They speak of the neighbouring war and of their own culture in decline. An image from some old high school textbook depicts the letting go, inside a perfect vacuum, of a feather and a cannonball, and how each, subject to the pull of gravity, falls at the same rate. What these worried faces might have seen on the road to Aleppo is their predicament writ large: the devil within needs to be fought before one can ever fight the devil outside.

Chapter Eleven

Portents

Sometimes Damascus seems like a mighty graph upon which there are inscribed a certain number of fixed points, constellations of faces, by whose lights one can navigate almost. Turn left at the Ottoman moustache, right at the blind man's cane. There are people I never speak to, but with whom I might exchange a smile – the chubby man in the red fez who plays oud outside his shop, for example. When I stop to listen to him, enervated by an audience he strikes the strings with added verve. And then, overreaching himself, he fumbles and the tune he's playing all but collapses. A Syrian journalist wrote that there is only one person left in the country who knows the secret of cleaning and ironing the fez and that he is soon to retire. Does my oud-player realise his already near-obsolete headgear's days are numbered? There's the man who sells old textiles, who never quite knows their provenance, or their age, or even of what they're made, or when he might strike lucky with me. All he has is my face to go by and what I try to do is to keep as much of it hidden from him as possible. And there's the scowling man who sells pastries. Why are the purveyors of joy universally miserable? The scowling man's chocolate éclairs, along with everything else he makes, are quite the best in Damascus. I think his scowl is because I buy only one at a time. I join the queue, rifling through my pockets for that rarest of commodities, small change. And there's the stocky figure who sells religious texts opposite the mosque (I will not say which one), who used to invite me to drink tea with him, but this year he feigns not to know me, and I wonder if I have Mr Blair to thank for this. And there's the man with the ashen face, whose lips are blue, who puffs at the nargileh from morning to night and looks as though he himself might go up in smoke. Already, the day barely on the go, his eyes are dead behind his glasses and his mouth droops a little. There's a baby's behind his sucking mouth, and he's so far gone you could wave a Kalashnikov in his face and he wouldn't notice. And then, of course, on a Street called Straight, there's Abū Walīd peddling his crooked histories. Amin, who is fed up with him, tells me lies fill every crease of Abū Walīd's face and that even the lies have creases in which there are still more lies. Surely, though, the whole point of Abū Walīd is his lies. Shall I stop here? These faces, although not set down here in their proper astronomical sequence, have been fixed in their firmament ever since my first visit to Syria and only death, or a passing comet, or a stray missile, will remove them.

When I got back to Damascus, in the spring of 2006, the face I wanted most to be upon this graph was not there. Waseem was not on any of his usual perches, not in the spice market which was a favourite haunt of his, nor was he at his favourite café. Where was Waseem, for Allāh's sake? I kept expecting to see the light bouncing off his shiny bald dome. I explored every corner of the souq, thinking he might have switched venue, although, as I said, people in Damascus rarely move from their self-appointed places. When I enquired after him, people merely shrugged their shoulders, saying he must be away on business somewhere. Admittedly I began to panic a little. Waseem was my fixer, the only man in Damascus who seemed to give not a fig for any repercussions that might come of telling me things other fanciers preferred to keep to themselves. Waseem was going to take me to a gun-toting judge; Waseem was going to reveal to me a thousand secrets of the pigeon trade; above all, Waseem was going to help me get more on al-Sawwāh who gunned down his neighbour's children. It was imperative that at least one story be as complete as possible. What did al-Sawwāh look like? What was his defence? And could one dip into that murky zone where death and obsession embrace? Waseem, whom nothing could touch, who was free to go as he likes, would be my most excellent guide.

I retraced my steps to his house in the Mohajarine area and pressed several times at the buzzer, but there was no answer. It felt empty inside. What is it about a place which has not been occupied for some time that it emits those particular vibes? What is it about a telephone that rings into an empty room that it tells you nobody will be answering it in the foreseeable future? When I stepped into a little shop next door to ask after his whereabouts the proprietor, clearly nervous, told me he knew nothing but that if I were to walk several streets further I'd find a tiny confectionary where most days, if the weather was fine, Waseem's father sat outside.

When I got there I found an old man in a wheelchair or, rather, it was a metal chair with four miniscule wheels. Slowly he lifted his hand for me to shake, and it seemed to both swell and dissolve in mine. I felt and then saw the stained bandages in which both hands were wrapped; there were also running sores on his feet that were swollen and bare.

'Waseem's in prison,' he told me. 'I may not live to see him again.'

I looked for some combination of words that would not necessitate my having to ask him directly what his son's crime was, or, more delicately, the charge brought against him.

'We know nothing. We have appealed many times. We have written letters. We have no idea why he is in prison. It's been six months already. And we don't know how long he'll be there.'

There was nothing for me to do but to leave, and after I made my farewells I asked him one last question, trying to make it sound like an afterthought.

'And the pigeons, what about them?'

'*Khaffouone!*'

The word is Damascene demotic slang meaning to take someone or something to an unknown place. It comes from *khaffā* 'to conceal, make hidden'. Etymology aside, it is a strong word whose meaning is clear to speaker and listener, which frees either from having to elaborate. During the 1980s especially, when there were many arrests, it was often used to describe the fate of people, 'the hidden' (*khāfūn*), who'd disappeared without trace. There was a terrible finality in that word, a wall beyond which one could go no further, whose mere utterance seemed to absorb whatever strength was left to this man sitting in dappled sunlight, staring into his lap, slowly consumed by disease.

§

Something else would dramatically alter the picture, a stain that went deeply into certain people's souls, so deeply it would signal in a certain quarter the death of pleasure. In 1997, in Hong Kong, a falcated teal was discovered to be carrying a strain of avian flu, subtype H5N1. Mike Davis in his book, *The Monster at Our Door: The Global Threat of Avian Flu* (2005), grimly jokes this single teal might one day be dubbed 'the duck of the apocalypse'. A child of three died soon after, apparently of the same virus, although at the time this was thought to be an isolated case. It wasn't long before domesticated fowl were infected in other parts of China. Other human deaths followed. The most recent human fatalities, almost always resulting from close contact with poultry, occurred in their largest numbers in South East Asia but have since spread to Azerbaijan, Iraq, Turkey and Egypt. A stain had moved clean across Asia and was now seeping up the slopes of Mount Qāsiyūn. If ever H5N1 mutates into a human pandemic form, and scientists say it is only a matter of time before it does, then this could result in the loss of many tens of millions of lives. Meanwhile, we clutch our binoculars, nervously watching for more signs. Three swans perished on the island of Rügen off the Baltic coast. The corpse of another was located in some estuary in Romania.

A parrot was found dead in British quarantine.

The spectacle of a dead bird impresses that part of us inclined towards a belief in astral influence. There's nothing stiller than a bird that no longer flies. It is like a small planet stopped in its orbit. I was in the middle of writing this passage when an acquaintance informed me that yesterday all the birds in downtown Austin, Texas died en masse. And the question that first springs to mind is not *why?* but *what does it mean?* In ancient times priests and soothsayers sought portents in the entrails of birds. And where have London's sparrows gone? If, as the Romans believed, sparrows are psychopomps guiding the souls of the dead to their final resting place, what will become of ours? Will they amalgamate with the traffic fumes? To get back to bird flu and the sober language of statistics, the last great pandemic, in 1918, killed almost 40 million people. Mankind, which is already half in love with the idea of apocalypse, such that barely a week passes before some fresh horror is announced, may do well to stock up on vaccine. And where vaccine is in short supply, the choice will be between prayer and booze.

Although there had been no reports of pigeons carrying the disease, the flying of them in Damascus was now banned. It is not a little tempting to read into this a troubling alliance of common-sense and ancient prejudice. There were even rumours of grounded birds being arrested in their cages. Whole flocks were confiscated, and while some people said the pigeons were thrown alive into fire or else buried still twitching in the sacks into which the police stuffed them, others said they were donated to old age homes and orphanages, either as food or as company, a questionable solution if ever there was one, and still others claimed the police, some of them fanciers themselves, were reselling them on the black market, which begs the question *Who polices the police*?

Still people flew their birds in defiance of the ban, and, towards evening, standing in central Damascus, one could look up at the mountain suburb of Ṣāliḥiyya and detect amassed pinpricks of darkness circling and swooping against reddening skies. The police had difficulties tracing them to the houses from whence they came, but they could often depend on the good citizenship of neighbours who had old scores to settle. They had another source, though, far deadlier than anything activated by a spurious concern for the public good. The vast majority of informants came not from neighbours but from fanciers themselves who were driven by jealousy and spite. One fancier I spoke to admitted that he himself had gone to the police although, as one might expect of a snitch, he argued the law was on his side. The stain had seeped into him as well. The wealthier fanciers, thinking themselves untouchable, were either powerful enough to avoid censure or else, much as Londoners during wartime sent their children into the counties, they sent their birds into the countryside where they would not be so closely scrutinised.

What it meant, of course, was that fanciers were now more sensitive than ever to strangers poking their noses into their activities. The greater number of them refused to speak to me. Would they have spoken to me at the best of times? Damascus, for the first time ever, had begun to close its gates to me. The pigeon fanciers had good cause. A Japanese journalist had written an article that resulted in his informants' birds being seized and this was two years *before* the ban. Others said they'd talk for money, but I have always made it a firm principle never to pay for stories. The stories one has to pay for are not the stories one really wants. And then some did speak to me, but getting information from them was like trying to pick stones out of camels' hooves. A fear of pandemic was, quite naturally, coupled in people's minds with other kinds of worries. Quite often, those fears manifested themselves in absurd theories. The Americans were to blame. They cultivated viruses which they then set loose in the countries they did not like. SARS, for example, was Canada's punishment for not joining its neighbour in the war on Iraq. An even wilder theory involved the mafia who were controlling the prices of red and white meat. Mad Cow Disease had been used by them to destroy the red meat market so they could increase the prices for poultry and now, with avian flu, we were witnessing the reverse. On the other hand those of patriotic leaning who, in truth, comprise the majority of the Syrian populace, did not want to speak of anything that might be interpreted in such a way as to produce still another negative image of their country.

'We do not kill each other over pigeons,' one fancier said to me, scornful of any implication that he and his fellows might be savages.

'I can't kill a bird,' said another. 'How much more difficult is it to kill a man?'

'And the police call us terrorists!'

'In any case, the murders are rarely over pigeons themselves.'

Strictly speaking this may have been true. Those murders were, rather, the consequence of bad feelings generated by indiscipline – a rude gesture, or a slighting remark about another man's wife. What begins as play, when too much adrenalin is released without anywhere to go, ends up as a matter of honour. Would that it were really so because honour and pride, when misplaced, are merely excrescences of a warped intelligence. The disputes are mostly pointless and the more pointless they are the more violent they become. The birds become mere ciphers for what people would prefer not to articulate. When words fail, fists fly. Here, I was told, was an analogy as good as any for the Middle East and its troubles. And then, of course, and this probably applies to the majority of fanciers, there were plenty who were not prepared to talk in any case, although, paradoxically enough, their very obmutescence would produce a clear enough picture. Others were simply inarticulate, or else, in their ignorance, were just smart enough not to pander to my enquiries. What they all had in common – bright, dim and obstinate – was that they were quick to accuse interlopers who weren't playing by the rules. It was always the *other*. Yes, I asked, but would this be the case were it not for a breakdown in the code?

The code? You speak of a code?

It was then that a nostalgic mist would settle over their eyes, or maybe it was just a gaseous discharge from a slag heap of scuppered hopes. They would speak of some golden age when every player was a gentleman, when flying pigeons was considered an 'introduction game', and when every bird was clean and pure. One could almost hear the thunder of a thoroughbred's hooves or see the flash of a scimitar in detoxed sunlight.

§

The Syrians are a gentle people. This surprises people who have never been there, whose minds have been stuffed with journalistic images. I do not think it is too much of a contradiction to say they are also a fierce people. After all, gentleness calls to its opposite. There lies between the two extremes an unpredictable strain, which others would do well not to encourage. There are continual eruptions at the surface. I had witnessed one such on the road to Aleppo. What is inescapable, however, is that in times of trouble people will swallow foul medicine. They will support even what they most despise in order that they preserve what they most love. Syria, maybe more than any other Arab country, clings to the idea of nationhood, and, in order to ensure its survival, seeming opposites will join forces. It goes without saying that interference breeds monsters and they grow quickest in an atmosphere of pressure. The word one hears more than any other is *pressure*. Tempers explode. This year saw not just the continuation of Iraq's troubles but also, after the assassination of the Lebanese ex-prime minister Rafic Hariri, the humiliation that came of having to quit Lebanon. A man pulling up his sweater showed me wounds he had acquired while fighting the Israelis in southern Lebanon, crying aloud that he'd fought on behalf of a people who were now jeering at him. 'They dare to speak to me like this? I fought for them. I ask you, who *are* these people?' Aside from the question of who really fights for who, whether for others or for themselves, there were as many explanations for Hariri's death as there were people willing to discuss it, but only rarely was the Syrian regime held to blame. A people perpetually criticised tends towards silence. Or maybe, as the Arabic proverb has it, *Silence is the ornament of the wise person and the veil of the fool.*

§

On March 29th 2006, there was a full eclipse of the sun. Yasser was too solid a Muslim to go barking after auguries. I was beginning to see nothing but. We were in his shop, deep in conversation, while gradually the street dimmed outside.

'Have you noticed anything different this year?'

Always, never.

'The preparations for the Prophet's birthday are greater than ever before. They are huge, at least ten times greater than last year, and for the first time in my life I've even seen signs in English. It's as if people are pushing back towards something they've lost. They are, of course, using the Danish business.'

After the publication of cartoons offensive to the memory of the Prophet in a Danish newspaper a few months before, and which only recently had grabbed the headlines, there were signs in café and shop windows, saying Danes were not welcome.

'It was considered *ḥarām* to do so, but there used to be something sweet about telling foreigners of all the bad things that happen here, whereas now all this is going into reverse. Mr Bush helped, of course, and now comes this latest attack on our very symbols. It is making people more and more paranoid. People, who used to complain only about what happens here, now complain about what is happening on the outside as well. There is a kind of dismay, of not knowing anymore where to turn to, a feeling of having failed everywhere and of having been betrayed both from inside and outside.'

'So would you say there has been a closing of doors? There is also this whole issue of fear. Would you relate this to recent events? Things here are not as bad as they were a few years ago, but the fear seems just that much greater.'

'It is a different fear now. We talk about things now we would have been too frightened to discuss even a decade ago. The mere question would have alarmed me. It is more relaxed now. You hear more opposition. You turn on the satellite channel and you see what crimes are committed by which governments against their own people. As I said, our fear is of a different hue. It is the fear of everything you have, which you hold sacred, being attacked and exploited. We do not want anyone to come and take still more things and exploit them. Even if it is only about pigeons, we do not want someone to come and find still more shortcomings in us and then criticise them. Enough's enough. You have criticised everything, whether mentally or by means of force, and now you turn on even our most religious symbols. So what else do we have to endure? We have a word called *qaraf* which means something like "disgust". People are just plain *disgusted*. It is not fear of the authorities anymore. You cannot erase thirty years of fear, of course. You will need another generation to erase that which has been implanted in our souls for three decades, but the fear of which I am speaking is of people insulting what little is left to us.'

'Although this feeling may be justifiable,' I argued, 'it is also an incredible overreaction on the part of Arabs. Anything, however slight, in whatever place, however remote, is seen as a major attack. After all, if one looks at what happened in Denmark and puts it in perspective, what you have here is a country that hardly ever gets into the news. What is Denmark to the rest of the world? What is this newspaper? Who are these five or six people who decided to commit this stupid act? Meanwhile, nine people get killed in Libya. What kind of reaction is this? Surely there ought to be some kind of perspective.'

'We have a saying here, "The smallest birds become eagles." You can reverse this, make it ironic even. What's this tiny newspaper in a tiny country that insults the Prophet and then the whole world stands by it? We are weak now. You have to understand the straw that broke the camel's back. It is an accumulation of all the insults and humiliations we have had to endure. If one were to think a bit objectively, the West is treating this part of the world, especially Palestine, with double standards. They demanded democracy and so democracy came. The people voted for a fundamentalist government, and quite aside from whether it is any good or not, isn't democracy what the majority wants? The majority wanted *this*. It was the same with Egypt and the Muslim Brotherhood. They went to elections and won seats, but America did not like this particular democracy. So there you have a double standard. When it comes down to us here the world wants to punish Syria for the assassination of Hariri. A resolution was taken in just five minutes, and Syria is supposed to cooperate otherwise the world might turn its forces against it. What about all the resolutions to do with Syria and the Golan Heights? Do those people in New York or at the UN think we are *that* stupid?'

'I don't think they think about what people think.'

'That's it! This accumulation has been going on for years. When did Israel take the Golan Heights?'

'Yes, but in the West this is already ancient history.'

'There is still a resolution, however, and then along comes America and Israel boasting about how they can target Hamas leaders. All countries do this kind of targeting. I don't need to take you back to Lawrence of Arabia or to how the English betrayed the Arabs or to the French and what they did. We are speaking of the very near future. There's been an accumulation and now a cockroach-sized country brings something like this to the world, boasting about it. You take a mind already attuned to conspiracy theories, and consider this: it took only five days for a legal measure to be taken against a British historian because he said something about the Holocaust. It is big news here. How do you expect people to react?'

'Yes, okay, but the waters are getting a bit muddied here. The world did not come to the side of Denmark. The general feeling was that a bad mistake had been made, but only by a handful of irresponsible people. So why blame all Danes?'

'Well, then, let me remind you of something. When in Saudi Arabia economical measures were taken against the import of Danish products, at that same moment France, Norway and then Germany reprinted the cartoons. They were published in *six* European countries. And then there's George Bush whose government is spending billions on brightening America's image in the Arab world. Abdullah, son of King Hussein of Jordan, meets with George Bush in the White House. What does Bush do? He criticises the way the Arab world has reacted to the cartoons, this without a single criticism of the Danes. You have an Arab king sitting next to you, so, hey, what about a bit of respect?'

'But let's look at it from another perspective,' I argue. 'Islam is superior to the ridiculous posturing of a little newspaper, so why should it feel so threatened? After all, *Allāh is greaṭ*, is he not?'

'The answer is simple. When you are strong these things don't matter, but when you are falling and everyone throws even the smallest knives at you then it hurts. We have this story about how, after he destroyed all his father's pagan statues, the prophet Abraham was thrown into the fire. A little frog came and filled its mouth with water, which it spat onto the fire, hoping to quench the flames, and then a white gecko came and started puffing at the flames in order to make them bigger. A prophet was put into the fire and ever since then people chase away these geckos and let the frog be. They say that although the frog couldn't extinguish the fire and the gecko couldn't make it bigger, each showed what it had inside. And this hurt Abraham because at that moment he was falling. We are a whole nation that's falling. You are not speaking of when Islam was great. You are talking of a civilisation that is now on its knees.'

As the eclipse entered its final phase, we could hear raised voices outside.

§

The death of the Prophet Muḥammad's infant son, Ibrāhīm, on 29th Shawwal 10 H/27th January 632, was marked by a solar eclipse. It must have appeared to people as a condolence from heaven. According to the hadith found in Bukhārī, the Prophet led the people in prayer during the actual period of the eclipse, telling them not to interpret this as a sign of heavenly mourning. 'The Sun and the Moon are two of the Signs (*āyāt*) of Allāh: they do not darken for the death or birth of any person, but Allāh strikes fear into His servants by means of them. So when you see them darken, remember and mention Allāh, declare His Greatness, offer prayer, give in charity, and supplicate to Him and seek His forgiveness.'

A false prophet would surely have taken advantage of such an event whereas the Prophet Muḥammad, in his humility, knew he could not worship Allāh by worshipping creation because to see heavenly bodies as having an influence over one's personal fortune would be to ascribe partners to Him. 'And among His Signs are the night and the day, the sun and the moon. Prostrate neither to the sun nor to the moon, but prostrate to Allāh who created them, if it is truly Him you worship.' (*Sūrat Fuṣṣilat* or The Signs Explained). An eclipse, as understood by proper Muslims, is a reminder of the Day of Judgement, when the sun and the moon and the stars will lose their light. 'When the sight is dazed, and the moon is buried in darkness, and the sun and moon are joined together: Man will say on that day, *Where is the refuge?*' (*Sūrat al-Qiyāma* or The Resurrection). The actual period of the eclipse is therefore a time for prayer, remembrance and charitable acts. There is even a special prayer (*ṣalāt al-kusūf*) that is recited during the actual period of eclipse.

Although the Qur'ān is absolutely clear in condemning the notion of an impersonal fate because this is to put God into second place, and although it does not condone soothsayers, it does, on the other hand, say we must heed signs, especially those found in nature. Portents, which are often enough natural phenomena, remind us of God's power and to ignore them, or worse to reject them, is to risk divine wrath. We must interpret what a sign (*āya*) truly signifies. In a beautiful passage in the Qur'ān, (41:13) God proclaims that he will show people his signs on the furthest horizons as well as deep within themselves.

If astrology is condemned in Islam, this does not stop people from seeking to divine the future. A journalist I spoke to, a man who to all appearances was a man of our times, white shirt and tie, a slinger of two mobile phones, when I mentioned the eclipse of a couple of days earlier, he shook his head, saying he was worried. Selim and I were having a morning coffee in al-Ra'īs Restaurant, a favourite haunt of journalists, not least because one can get a drink there. *Ra'īs*, Selim told me, means the captain of a small ship, although in Egypt it is often used as slang for 'president'. The name and place could not be more appropriate. This restaurant was, in its heyday, a birthplace of conspiracies. Selim pointed to a table in the corner, saying this was where the older Asad, in the days before he was president, planned his revolution. At the table diagonally opposite sat an occasional visitor to Damascus, a handsome young man, another plotter by the name of Saddam Hussein, and there, at another table, was where another military coup was planned, I forget which one. Were there tables enough to cover all the Middle East's political intrigues? We occupied a small island in the middle, a sparkling white tablecloth spotted with just a couple of drops of coffee. The staining of so big a cloth seemed an extravagance. The restaurant was dark and dingy and, if a negative can be said to point to a positive, a reminder of better times, along the edges of a ceiling there was a row of sagging balloons, a thin layer of dust showing up their wrinkles.

'You were saying about the eclipse of the sun?'

This may have been one conversation Selim regretted having started.

'It is believed, and inherited in the thinking of the Middle Eastern peoples, that natural phenomena can be explained on a psychological and spiritual basis. You will find a theological basis for this, especially with respect to the prophet Daniel or what is here called "the Daniel wisdom". There are two kinds of eclipse, the solar and the lunar, and each has its own significance. While the solar represents the first level of government, which is to say the president himself, the lunar represents his ministers or councillors. If a solar eclipse comes in January the implications are quite different than if it were to come in March, which is what we are looking at here. So I went to my books, and what they said is that there will be death in groups, disasters such as earthquakes, sinking ships, planes and so forth. Well, these things actually happened. An earthquake, although it wasn't too serious, hit the Mediterranean the day after the eclipse, and then a ship sank in Bahrain with a loss of many lives. And the books say that the ruler of Egypt will die before the year is out. We expect this. There'll be a lot of bloodshed and it is even said that the leader of Greater Syria will face problems from his own inner circle, in particular his own relatives. They will try to topple him. It means also the harvest will be good, but that with it will come plenty of diseases.'

'Avian flu?'

Selim hedged a little.

'You have chosen a dangerous subject.'

'What, pigeons?'

'Well, let's just say I think you're looking for analogies.'

'And if I were, what would you advise?'

'I'd say you're onto a good theme.'

§

A few days later, another portent: the sky turned a rotten pink, with smudges of brown here and there, and then it began to rain a rare combination of water and sand, which left a thin layer of reddish sand over everything. I was told that if one were in Palmyra it would be even worse and one wouldn't be able to breathe. The wind itself is called *rīḥ al-khamsīn* ('the wind of the fifty') because, at its source, in the Sahara, it often lasts over a period of fifty days. W.W. Lane, in his *Modern Manners of the Egyptians* (1834), describes the rituals that marked this meteorological event: 'A custom termed "Shemm en-Nessem" (or the Smelling of the Zephyr) is observed on the first day of the Khamaseen. Early in the morning of this day, many persons, especially women, break an onion, and smell it; and in the course of the forenoon many of the citizens of Cairo ride or walk a little way into the country, or go in boats, generally northward, to take the air, or, as they term it, smell the air, which on that day they believe to have a wonderfully beneficial effect.' The celebration dates backs to pre-Islamic times, to at least 2700 BC, the word 'shemm' having its origins in the Egyptian harvest season called 'Shamo', which means 'renewal of life'. During Coptic times this became 'shamm', which translates as 'smelling' or 'breathing', and then was added 'nessem' or 'breeze'. Damascenes, though, were not inclined towards such a favourable interpretation. The sky was angry, they said, about what was happening down here on earth.

Sulaymān, too, was troubled.

'The pink you saw was the shed blood of nations whose citizens have been unjustly killed. My wife said to me, "This is the blood of martyrs everywhere." There is to be a change, but what this change will be we don't know. I felt uncomfortable. I went into the open and started saying, "There is no God but Allāh", and then I made a supplication. May God help us!'

Sulaymān then said he would take me to see a pigeon fancier, a man of forty years' experience, who lived in Baramke, an area not far from the centre of Damascus. It was Sulaymān's understanding that the police had only recently removed this man's pigeons. I was warned he was in a terrible mental state, and that he was crying all the time. Admittedly I was uneasy about this, not least because the appointment was set for ten o'clock at night when his wife said we would be able find him at home. She was, apparently, at her wit's end, saying maybe our visit would distract him a little. I argued against this, saying surely I wouldn't be welcome, while at the same time with a story like this I knew I would be able to plug another hole in my narrative. This might be my only opportunity to speak with someone whose birds had been confiscated. Coldly, if such an approach were achievable, I might even learn about the police procedure.

'Do you know him well?'

'I was seven years old when he last saw me.'

'So you don't know him!'

'I know him *very* well,' he said cryptically, 'but he doesn't know me.'

Sulaymān told me not to worry, that he knew the combination of words that would gain us certain admittance. There were, he assured me, old family ties. Sulaymān was indeed a man with a thousand keys, only a few of which he ever made visible. When we got there, Sulaymān pointed out a jar lying on it side in front of the house, which held grain once.

'There is no earth, no heaven for him,' he said. 'I already know this without his having to tell me.'

Sulaymān went in first to clear the path, so to speak, and then, a few minutes later, Abed and I were signalled inside. On the way in I saw through a divide between two short curtains a woman whom I took to be his wife huddled together with their children who had runny noses. I shouldn't have looked – it was not polite. Already I wanted badly out of this house of sorrow. We found the man sitting on the edge of his bed in a narrow room, the life drained from his face. The questions I asked him, even as I spoke them, sounded callous even though I intended the opposite. When I asked him about his future, he said life without his birds would be meaningless. What about his family, I thought, but it wasn't for me to tell him where hope lies.

'Are they all gone?'

'Mostly,' he replied. 'There are just a few left and soon they'll be gone too.'

'The police took all the others and left these?'

The man looked startled as if we had slipped onto a wholly different track. After he exchanged a few words with Sulaymān, Abed whispered we ought to leave. This time I knew it wasn't because he was bored. Something had been said that made him want to get out of there, and, besides, I really didn't want to further penetrate this man's sorrow. When we got back outside, grateful for our release, I learned the truth of the situation. The police had *not* come. There hadn't been any intimation that they *would* come. There had *never* been any police. It was the *fear* of them coming that so obsessed this poor wretch that rather than see his pigeons doomed to an uncertain fate he started eating them one by one. This man's bed was perched on the rim of whatever circle it was that Dante chose not to put into verse.

'They are my children,' he'd said to Sulaymān, tears welling up in his eyes.

Small wonder Abed wanted to escape.

Chapter Twelve

Armageddon at the Qaboon Pigeon Café

I met through the friend of a friend of a friend a pigeon fancier who'd finally speak to me. Mahmood was a poet among fanciers, which doesn't mean he prettified or embellished but that he was imbued, one might even say *sickened*, with love. Such people carry their ardour in their faces, and it is all they can do to stop it from spilling over and making an awful mess. Whenever Mahmood spoke of his birds it was with a swooning voice. Actually there was something in the register of that voice, a peculiar slur too, which reminded me of Anthony Quinn in *Requiem for a Heavyweight*, a tough who at the same time is fatally gentle. It came as no surprise to learn that in his youth Mahmood had been an amateur wrestler. A boxer garners all the poetry as a rule, but Mahmood's story certainly rates a verse or two. Certainly he'd been floored more than once in his life. Mahmood's friend, Amin, laughed at him. And Mahmood laughed at himself, although his laughter, unlike Amin's, was a defence against capitulation to sorrow. A story would be told the memory of which might bring him close to tears but he would laugh all the same.

'You have chosen the right guy to speak to,' said Amin who spoke with a curious American twang he'd picked up somewhere. 'First of all, this son-of-a-bitch has a good sense of humour, and, although I wish he'd come to his senses, he's been my friend since we were, like, sixteen. The first time we saw each other was when we were six or seven but we didn't talk then. And now he's the guy with whom I spend most of my evenings. I don't give a fuck about pigeons, and I won't go anywhere near them, but I love the stories he tells about them. And he's got so many stories, believe me, you'll never get out of here.'

We were sitting in the Rawda Café, whose clientele was a curious mix of trendy and conservative, writers, musicians and other such types in one area, smart young men who wore their hair long together with smart young women, devastators most of them, in another, and the meek and the dubious where we were. It was a place to be seen and not to be seen, which in fact made for quite a happy balance. It had *buzz*. This was to be my only opportunity to talk with Mahmood because early next morning he was flying to Saudi Arabia where he worked.

'What about your pigeons?' I asked.

'I pay somebody here to look after them.'

'When did you start with this?'

'A cousin of mine, he's a dentist now, gave me a pair of pigeons. It is like smoking. You begin with just one cigarette. I took care of those two pigeons little realising what was behind the door. The moment I discovered what was there was when I spent a whole night inside this little shed with not two but *twelve* birds of mine. I was at a critical age.'

'Yeah,' interjected Amin, 'when his cock began to rise.'

So then, it would appear two powerful forces had been set loose in young Mahmood's brain, and, between the fluttering of wings and the fluttering of eyelashes, it was not difficult to see which possessed him more. Although he was married now and with children, and by his account happily so, by his own admission it was his pigeons he misses most when he goes into working exile. It is them and not his family that make him pine. Yes, Mahmood was a *majnūn*, which is to say 'a fool for love'.

'You dream about them when you're away?'

'Yes, every night and I think about them all the time too. When I close my eyes, I remember every single pigeon I have ever had. I can tell you their names, what each one looked like, where they were when I made sketches of them. We have an old house, which has been in my family for three hundred years. We still live there, in Ṣāliḥiyya, and the greatest pleasure in life for me is when it's semi-winter, and the rain falls and then stops. The atmosphere feels so much cleaner then, after it rains, and the smell is so nice. I have my tea, Umm Kulthūm is singing, and I set my birds free. They are more active in winter because in summer we cut their wings. They are at their most active in the cooler weather, whereas summer is too hot. I sit with my tea and watch them. This is a pleasure greater than making love. I listen to Umm Kulthūm singing *al-Aṭlāl* ("The Ruins"), which is about memory. It is not a song for young people but for old men. I never much liked it before, but now it means so much to me.

> Give me my freedom,
> Set my hands free.
> I gave freely, I held back nothing.
> Ah, your chains have made my wrist bleed.

The meaning of that song goes deep. Pigeon fanciers smoke hashish and they listen to the songs of Umm Kulthūm for their meaning.'

'Many people say keeping pigeons is unIslamic.'

'This is true of anything that makes you forget your prayers, which amuses you to the extent that you ignore family and work too, and which makes you lose your will, and which sometimes even forces you to tell lies.'

'Is your son interested in pigeons?'

'I keep my activities secret from him. I don't want him to become addicted to this.'

'What is your worst nightmare?'

'Which do you mean, dream or reality?'

I hadn't really expected this.

'When I was eighteen and still living at home, I went on a school trip to Palmyra. As a rule pigeons are fed once a day, after sunset, and there I was, watching the sun going down over the ruins, and all I could think of was feeding time, and that it would be another twenty-four hours before I'd be back home with my pigeons. I was so happy to be going home, but when I got there some kids were outside my house, laughing and making fun of me. I knew something was wrong. I rushed upstairs and found my father and his cousin at the table, at dinner. My father's cousin was smiling, and then he said to me they were eating my pigeons. I rushed up onto the roof and found all the cages broken down, all the birds gone. I was so upset and angry I wanted to throw myself down from the roof. My father wanted me to pursue my studies and was unhappy with my results, so he had the throats of my pigeons cut. But because it was too high for him to climb to the roof he asked his cousin to butcher them. They were eating my pigeons! Was this for real? "Why did you do this?" I cried. I respect my father and I had never said anything bad to him, but now I was screaming at him, "This is as if you had killed my own children. How would you like it if somebody killed me, my brothers and sisters?" My pigeons, I spent a couple of years training them, it wasn't easy either, and they knew me. At a single movement of my hand they'd change direction in the air. Even now, speaking about this, I want to cry.'

Mahmood smiled away the pain in his face.

'It's the worst single thing that's ever happened to me. What I did next was go back upstairs. I had hidden a single female. We had this TV antenna, a barrel of cement holding it in place, and underneath it there was a hollow where I had hidden the female so as not to let the cats get at it. She was a professional, what we call in the trade a "hooker" or a "bitch". Some female pigeons are trained as prostitutes in order to attract males. You have to work really hard to get a bird to this stage, when she is able to seduce any number of males. First, she has to be isolated from the rest of the group for four or five days and then when you bring a male from outside, you use the bitch to make him feel this place is truly remarkable.'

'Now I'm getting excited!'

Amin roared with laughter, 'Yeah, me too!'

'This bitch is very important to the story. All one's hopes are pinned on her because she can bring back a whole flock with her. So the first thing I did was to push back the cement barrel to see if she was still there. She was. I was so relieved I swore to God right there and then that I'd rebuild my flock. This time I'd have *forty* pigeons. I would defy my father and everyone in the world. And even now I defy them, my beloved wife too, because she hates this. She says to me, "Don't carry on with this madness." She doesn't know that much really. I buy birds and keep them elsewhere, a pair of birds here and a pair of birds there. An opposition grew within me at that time, or, as my friend says here, when my cock began to rise, and it was between my love of girls and my love of birds. I went to my cousin who originally taught me this hobby. That same evening we went into town. My cousin was proud of me because of my physical strength and because nobody would dare come near us. He stole some money from his father, and together we went to the pigeon café, which once upon a time was a caravanserai for olive oil, and the birds we bought were not from Damascus but from Aleppo, so they weren't familiar with the skies. They would not easily escape. Between our house and the house opposite, where my cousin lived, there's a little alley two metres wide. We brought back the pigeons in a huge sack and in order to fool my father my cousin threw it from his roof onto mine. At night, I turned on the light on the roof and put each bird in a cage on its own, so as to familiarise him with the place. There was a danger that if they were kept together they'd fly off somewhere. I started to put this hooker with each of them for half an hour or so. I was the pimp, you see. All night long, I moved her from cage to cage. They were nervous because of this female. At six in the morning – I had not slept yet – I grabbed the pigeons and with a needle and thread I started to sew their wing feathers together, locking them in place, so they couldn't fly away. After finishing with each one, I'd throw it onto the floor and send the female after him. And then I'd see if this male pigeon was attracted to the whore or not. He should attack her. If he goes after her, then I know he'll stay. If not, then he might try to escape and so I'd put him two metres above the floor, spend a couple of days teaching him to jump this distance, and sometimes I'd keep his wings sewn for up to ten days or until he mated with the whore. After this, I could fly him a little, not in the morning when he might leave but at sunset when he knew darkness was on the way and he'd be hungry and there's somewhere to go back to. Then, for three or four days I'd fly him in a single circle, bringing him back by holding the female up so he could see her. This is how it's done. If he doesn't see her, he won't return. After a few days you set him free at around noon and when you feel sure he knows the place you ask another pigeon fancier nearby to set his birds free. You let him steal your bird by mixing mine with his and by now the pigeon should know the place well enough to fly home.

You should try this only with your friend at first. Then you put out the hooker. They will only want to fuck and eat.'

'Do you steal your neighbours' pigeons?'

'Whenever I get angry with another pigeon man, I say to him, "Set your pigeons free, so I can show you how strong mine are." This is a challenge to do battle in the sky – *kashsh al-ḥamām*. If a group is strong enough, it will bring back pigeons from the other.'

'Yes, but do you steal your neighbour's pigeons?'

'I was like a pirate, young and strong, and didn't care about anything else. I had nothing else to do.'

Amin shook his head.

'I am sorry you're my friend, to be honest,' he muttered.

'I had to set them free quickly otherwise my father would hear the fluttering of wings. All this time I was keeping them in secret. They attract mosquitoes and other insects that are not good for people. Now our government is seizing them and the pigeon men are having heart attacks.'

Mahmood was still being evasive.

'Okay, then, are you involved in pigeon wars?'

This spurred him into giving a response.

'I'm one of the main ones! I challenge everyone! People wake me in the middle of the night, asking if I'd stolen their birds. We fight with knives sometimes. There was an older man who, if he were alive now, would be over seventy. He died ten years ago. This man's house was very small, like a lunchbox, the area upstairs on the roof was small too, and I could see directly from my roof onto his. There was a deep courtyard. One time he was flying his pigeons and watching them and he moved a bit too quickly. I remember he had a funny-shaped head where he was wounded once. I will not tell you his name because Allāh asks of us that we respect the dead. He was a fireman. One time he invited me, was seemingly kind to me and then he opened a suitcase to show me something. "Do you see this?" he said, waving a pistol at me. I always made fun of him and, worse still, I'd catch his pigeons and not give them back. He would get furious but he didn't dare attack me because of my size. Anyway he said, "I'm going to kill you with this." I wasn't afraid of him though. And then, later, he fell to his death because of the pigeons.'

Amin nodded thoughtfully.

'So Allāh took care of this guy.'

Mahmood's neighbour was not the first to take such a plunge.

'Umar Shaykh Mirzā was, briefly, king of Ferghana, in what is now Uzbekistan. Grandson of Tamerlane, father of the great Baber who founded the Mughal dynasty, he had neither the prowess of the grandfather nor the deep culture of the son. Baber describes his father as 'short and stout, round-bearded and of fleshy face' and another account, written by someone with a yellow journalistic eye, describes how he would breathe in deeply in order to fasten his sash only for it to burst open as soon as he relaxed. 'Umar gets barely a mention in the annals and this was because he spent most of his life, in his great fortress of Akhsi, playing with his pigeons. According to Turkic shamanistic tradition, in 899/1494, shortly after his thirty-ninth birthday, 'Umar disappeared and took on the form of a gyrfalcon. This somewhat picturesque account of his death conceals an altogether more unseemly end. Under the influence of drugs which, in later years, took precedence over an earlier passion for alcohol, he seemed to have fallen under the impression that he had grown wings and was thereby divinely equipped to follow his birds. Although he did indeed take off from the battlements it was only to plunge a tremendous distance into the Syr Darya (Iaxartes), the great river of central Asia, which ran along the foot of the fortress. It could be, of course, the shamans were right and he really did become a bird of another feather. The story was still doing the rounds among pigeon fanciers throughout the Mughal Empire a century after his death. Corpulence and pigeons: 'Umar is remembered for little else.

Mahmood continued with his story.

'Another man shot at me twice. Now he was really bad. One of his pigeons landed on my roof. It was a poor quality bird, missing feathers. I thought this man didn't care about it, maybe because it was worthless to him, but he shouted to me, "Set him free." "What?" I replied, "I'm not going to set it free." So he started shooting at me.

'Did he miss?'

'Bad people live a long time. Fate somehow leaves them alone.'

'Are you a bad or good man?'

'Well, if I capture anything, I won't return it.'

'What happens if someone steals from you?'

'If he is a true pigeon man, I won't ask him to return it, although in some cases, especially if the bird is a rare and expensive one, I might negotiate or I might even kiss the arses of others to act as middlemen.'

'And if still he doesn't negotiate?'

'It depends on how serious the game is. If we decide beforehand that it is "hunting" between us – we call it *tomas* – then it's a challenge to be more serious. "This is yours and this is mine," we say. "So let's start from this point. If I capture a bird or if you capture mine, we will not ask for its return." There are all kinds of agreements between fanciers, another being that if I catch one of your birds I will break its neck or cut its throat.'

'Everything you say suggests you are following a code of behaviour, yet people say this code is breaking down.'

'No, it's more like rules. They will not vanish. It works now as it did a hundred years ago.'

'What about the ones who do not follow rules?'

'We don't care about them. Rules are rules. You get to respect the game more with time. These others are poor or from the lower classes. There are millionaires here who have people on monthly salaries just to take care of their pigeons.'

'Why are there murders over pigeons if people are following rules?'

'Those people are impolite, from the lower classes. They lack aim and education. It's the same with normal people, not just fanciers. There are people with evil inside them, which they will take out on others. They'll fight with everyone they see. If somebody on the street looks at them in the wrong way they'll want to fight. What are you going to say if you look at someone by chance?'

Amin burst in, guns blazing.

'An American soldier in Iraq, when someone looks at him, will say to him, "Why are you looking at me? You want to fight, asshole?"'

'So what about avian flu? Is the government using this as an excuse to clamp down on fanciers?'

'No, the government is serious about this. The flu travels with birds from other places.'

'But three years ago, before any of this started, they were chasing after fanciers.'

'This is because of the social problems that keeping pigeons creates.'

'What happens to the birds the police confiscate?'

'They take them and sell them. Some of the police know about pigeons. But they won't stop us. It won't change, this tradition, because it is our heritage. It's in our blood.'

'Sometimes people's lives are destroyed. Can you give me examples?'

'I told you about this man who fell off the roof, leaving behind a wife and children, and you want more! Can stories get any worse? I will not open the bad books for other people to read, only the good ones. Okay, some of these people, to be honest, are not good. There was someone who lived not far from here, a baker who made cheap quality cakes. I was very young and one day he asked me if I'd like to go to his place to see the pigeons. He tried to abuse me. Some of these fanciers chase boys too. This is the worst part of their lives. A lot of them smoke hashish. I left the cake and made my escape.'

'Do you live in fear of the police? Would you fight them for the sake of your pigeons?'

'No, no, there is no joking with them.'

'And if you lost your birds, would you start over again?'

'Of course! My dream is to make a fortune, and buy a house and keep only the very best pigeons. I'd spend all my time with them. I have stories about how pigeons came back from other countries. Once I sold a group of pigeons to a Lebanese man. A year later, I went to Beirut. I was walking somewhere. You know, pigeon fanciers always look up in the air all the time. We get all these bruises from bumping into walls. I saw a pigeon flying above. "Look," I said to my friend, "this *Babarisī* in the sky is mine!" "How do you know? After a year, how can this be? I need something connected to reality before I can believe this. After all, there are many birds of the same breed." "Okay," I said, "let's go up, knock at the door, and see who owns this bird." This Lebanese guy comes to the door. "We are from Damascus and would like to see your birds," I said. The man welcomed us inside. When I spotted the *Babarisī*, I cried, "*da, da, da*!" ("Come, come, come"). Directly the pigeon landed on my shoulder, and then I asked the man, "Would you sell this to me? Where did you get it from?" "I bought the bird from somebody who got it in Damascus. When I set the group free that pigeon flew for three days non-stop and landed only in the dark of night when it was exhausted and hungry." He said he wouldn't sell it to me. And so I whispered to the pigeon, "I'll be waiting for you in Damascus." When we got home to Damascus, I found the pigeon there waiting for me.'

§

My researches had led me into surreal situations and places. Most bizarre, perhaps, were the pigeon cafés one finds in various parts of Damascus, which are clandestine in atmosphere. I went to one in the relatively poor area of Qaboon on the outskirts of Damascus.

There was nothing to indicate there was a café here, no sign on the crazy patchwork of wood and cardboard that was a door, and the building itself was something a child might devise. A skeleton of steel pipes joined together supported three walls and ceiling, which were made of whatever scrap material was available – sheets of corrugated iron, an old carpet, and scraps of wood and cardboard.

Men sat at small tables, drinking tea and playing cards, the plaintive songs of Umm Kulthūm playing in the background. The inner sanctum of this makeshift temple comprised three walls of pigeons, their cages large enough to step inside. This was the pigeon fancier's equivalent of a busman's holiday: the men present were taking a break from their birds in order to look at more birds, sometimes to buy and sell them, but, most importantly, to talk pigeon talk with their fellow fanciers.

Clearly I was an intruder in a world of whose existence not even most Damascenes are aware. Abed stared in amazement, saying he never knew life in his city could be so strange. We sat at one of the rickety tables, waiting to be approached rather than make a direct move. *Shuwayya, shuwayya* ('slowly, slowly') is one of the most commonly heard Arabic phrases. The owner of the café brought us tea and then asked the purpose of our visit. I was after stories, I said, tragedies, comedies, anything relating to pigeons and to the pigeon wars in particular.

'I don't know anything.'

'Yes, but maybe people here do.'

'I can tell you plenty about pigeons, but it is all very technical.'

I said I was more interested in the people who kept pigeons than in the pigeons themselves. What were these stories one heard about people killing each other over birds and to this he replied that there may have been the occasional bit of violence but that other people were to blame.

'They are not serious pigeon people,' he argued. 'They are punks and thieves, all of them of a younger generation that doesn't play by the rules.'

Another man joined us at the table. Smartly dressed in a silvery suit, maybe he was a businessman.

'Who are these people?' he asked the café owner.

'A man from London wants to know about our pigeons.'

'A journalist?'

'He says he is writing a book about pigeons.'

'You shouldn't say anything to him. Our country has already had enough criticism from outside.'

The café owner, obviously swayed by the man's disapproval, tried to say it was not the best time to follow my subject because ever since the government clampdown business was slow and fanciers had lost their enthusiasm.

'Avian flu comes from the West,' our intruder muttered.

'On the contrary,' I replied, 'it comes from the East.'

'No,' he snarled, 'it comes from the West and your moral corruption. Very soon avian flu will kill all the Americans. It will be Allāh's punishment for what they are doing in Iraq.'

'So why, in that case, should avian flu come here?'

'It won't! There's no flu here. And there won't be. We are a protected people.'

Abed was anxious we should leave. I said no, we'd play this out to the bitter end. I told my accuser he had no right to judge me any more than I had to judge him on account of the insurgents' terrorist activities.

'We are not terrorists,' he exploded. 'We want peace, but if forced to we will fight for that peace. I come from a family of revolutionaries. You are in Qaboon, which, in 1925, was the scene of the most powerful resistance against the French. We have produced heroes and we have produced saints here as well and the waters of the river that runs through here are famous for their healing properties.'

'So if you want peace so badly, why do you reject the offer of mine?'

'Alright then, follow me.'

Abed was reluctant but at the same time he was badly in need of some fresh adventure. We followed our interrogator through dark and twisting alleys until we found ourselves in a wondrous place, what was, in effect, a shrine to the Resistance, the walls adorned with guns and photographs of heroes, and, most thrillingly for me, because I'd never seen any outside the Azem Palace, several paintings on glass by the artist al-Tanawī.

Abū Subhī al-Tanawī (1888-1973) is considered by some people to be the first modern Syrian artist although I think it is more accurate to describe him as the country's foremost folk artist. The most common theme in this group of paintings was that of Antar, which was appropriate given the setting. Antar personifies the most courageous of Arab warriors and his love 'Ablā embodies beauty and virtue. As a young boy al-Tanawī would have been familiar with these stories, which were the common stock of the storytellers in the cafés and also in the shadow theatre. There is a story which is told about him, that when he was asked by a Western journalist if he knew Picasso because in his paintings he would, for example, paint a horse with both its eyes on one side of the face, al-Tanawi thought for a moment and replied, 'I don't remember anyone of that name buying anything from me.'

Our enemy turned host brought us fresh orange juice, followed by coffee, and when finally we took our leave, turning down an invitation to stay the night, he embraced and kissed me, saying I'd always be welcome.

CHAPTER THIRTEEN

War Doves

A Short History of Pigeons in the Islamic World (4)

When did pigeons go legitimate? When did the men who loved them camouflage their love with a pious cause? A tweaking of the law here, a shift in attitude there, and a negative became a positive: the Arabs developed the world's most sophisticated postal system employing carrier pigeons. At last a distinction could be made between birds that were kept for idle pleasure and those that provided for the public good. A message, if delivered in time, could save a romance. It could also save an empire. The public use of homing pigeons to carry messages was not new, of course – it is as old as Solomon. The Egyptians, in 2900 BC, would send pigeons from incoming ships to announce their arrival and the army employed them for its manoeuvres, and they'd be used to report on flood levels on the Nile. Later, the Greeks, always on the ball, had them announce the winners of the Olympic Games. Also the Romans and the Jews used them for carrying messages, but as a system – an actual ministry, in fact – it was resurrected, and perfected, by the Arabs. If all this sounds a bit antiquarian in tone, it should be remembered the pigeon post was the most rapid means of communication in the world and remained so until the invention of the electric telegraph in 1844.

A smart fancier might be able to play both sides.

Sometimes, though, the façade broke. The first Abbasid caliph to employ 'messengers of the skies' was Abū 'Abdu'llāh Muḥammad-b-i'l Mansūr or, more simply 'the Mahdī'. One of his most notable achievements, which points to a refined sensibility, was to have transported, by means of camel, snow to Mecca so that there his drink and dessert might be served cool. Although he was a man of faith, and indeed his name translates as 'made victorious', he took great pleasure in pigeon games. Once, when he was playing with one of his pigeons, he invited his *qāḍī* Ghiyath ibn Ibrāhīm to recite from the hadiths whereupon it was related to him that the Prophet Muḥammad decreed 'there shall be no wager except on a hoof or an arrow or lance head.' (The only prizes allowable were those for skills useful in warfare.) The *qāḍī*, aware of the Mahdī's love of pigeons, surreptitiously added 'or a wing' to the sentence, passing off those last three words as the Prophet's own. This is often cited as an example of a forged hadith (*mawḍū'*). The Mahdī, not a man to embrace white lies, ordered that the *qāḍī* be given 10,000 dirhams, after which he informed him, 'I declare that the nape of your neck is as the nape of the neck of a liar. Surely you have interpolated this.' He then gave orders that the throats of his pigeons be cut, which seems rough justice for creatures that never asked to be anyone's playthings. The story almost exactly duplicates one told later of the Mahdī's son, Hārūn ar-Rashīd, except that rather than blame the *qāḍī* the caliph blamed the pigeon.

Strange things, meanwhile, were going on in the provinces.

The world has seen false prophets aplenty, and their successes, brief though they are, have been largely dependant on the means of communication available to them. Only rarely, though, have they been posthumously made founders of sects they never actually founded. This is precisely what happened in 938 when Ibn al-Nadīm produced his *al-Fihrist* ("The Catalogue"), an anthology based on earlier Arabic sources, which, in part, recapitulates Ibn Rizām's polemic, the original of which has been lost, against Ismā'īlism. Whether through error or design, more probably the latter, the founder of Ismā'īlism was said to have been one 'Abd Allāh b. Maymūn al-Qaddāḥ who lived in the second half of the eighth-century near Ahwāz in Hūzistān. This falsehood was allowed to survive, especially among those who were critical of the Ismā'īlīs, until the middle of the twentieth century. The spurious 'secret doctrine', which was supposed to have comprised seven stages, culminating in atheism and libertinism, crept even into the writings of Casanova who might well have found the subject attractive. The true al-Qaddāḥ, a false prophet if ever there was one, whose name means 'oculist' and who claimed to be able to cure diseases of the eye and other maladies, was also good at conjuring tricks the most dramatic of which was one involving pigeons. The pigeon post, in the area where he lived, was still a largely unknown quantity. Carrier pigeons would bring him news from his disciples who were scattered throughout the region and al-Qaddāḥ, pretending that the earth, rolling at the speed of light, transported him to faraway places and back again, would present the bits of information which the pigeons brought him as instances of divine revelation. For several years al-Qaddāh was able to trick the more gullible people of the area into joining his sect. After being exposed as an impostor he fled first to Baṣra and then to Salamīya in the northwest of Syria where he stayed in hiding until his death circa 261/874. Al-Qaddāḥ, a cad more like, rates not even a mention in early Ismā'īlī sources.

The public use of carrier pigeons during the Madhī's time was still quite rare. There wasn't yet an adequate return system. Most of the correspondence went in one direction only although there were a few pigeon keepers who'd exchange captive birds, and, in any case, the system was restricted to the main cities, with Baghdad as the main centre. Carrier pigeons were often used to conduct love affairs, some of them illicit, memory traces of which can be found in the poems of Rabī'a Raqqī and Abū Nuwās. An Arab lover sending his pigeon would await hers. The Western poet, by comparison, has been a bungler in thinking his bird will take a message to a loved one and bring back an answer. Carrier pigeons do not take messages *both* ways. Gradually the pigeon post came into more common usage, and as early as the ninth century the pious *qāḍī* Bakkār b. Qutayba was able to import, without legal or religious censure, pigeons from Basra to Fusṭāṭ, then capital of Egypt.

Pigeons began to prove themselves invaluable.

§

The doves of peace were also war doves.

One of the most famous messages ever sent by pigeon was that which announced the death, in 329/940, on the approach to Rayy, of the Daylamite rebel chief, Mākān b. Kākī: 'As for Mākān, he has become his name' (*ammā Mākān fa-ṣāra ka-ismihī*). The secretary responsible for this note, Iskāfī, created a brilliant play of words on the name of the rebel, giving him, in Arabic, a definition that was slightly different from the meaning of his name in his own language. When split in two, '*Mā*' denotes negation and '*kān*' the verb 'to be', which results in the expression *he is not* or, in other words, 'He is no more'. The Samanid amir at Bokhara was so happy with this message he offered Iskāfī a pension, saying, 'Such a bright mind no longer has to worry itself over domestic problems.'

God help the man whose pigeon misbehaved or was insufficiently trained. One particularly unlucky figure, a secretary of Bagkam, a traitor, tried to send a pigeon with a message warning the enemy of his army's advance. The pigeon, rather than fly off, settled on the back of the boat they were in. The hapless secretary was savagely executed and thrown into the Tigris.

By the end of the Abassid period the postal system (*barīd*) was so sophisticated the Caliph an-Nāṣir was able to use it to maintain a surveillance system that would have done any modern dictator proud. Surviving records of the *barīd* offer us a glimpse of the hierarchy that existed at any one of these pigeon stations. There would be the chief of the dovecote (*ṣāḥib al-burğ*) who sometimes, if given authority, would actually send the messages. Beneath him was the guardian (*barrāğ*) who was entrusted with pigeons' maintenance and would watch the horizon for returning flights. The first pigeon to appear would be referred to as 'the blessed bird' (*al-ṭa'ir al-maymūn*), a phrase that is still applied to the safe arrival of air passengers; the second bird to arrive was called *rafiq* or the first one's 'distant shadow'. And then there were people who'd take the captive birds to the outposts, and beneath them the servants (*huddām*) who'd clean the cages. They were allowed to keep the bird droppings which they would then sell as fertilizer to local farmers. A secretary (*baṭṭāq*) would compose the messages and then the *mubaṭṭaq* whose job it was to tie the message to the bird and then release it. The people who looked after these stations did so for life, and it was monotonous work for much of the time. And there were different sorts of stations, among which would be the main pigeon centre (*marākiz al-ḥamām*) or message centre (*marakiz al-bata'iq*) or release points (*masāriḥ al-ḥamām*) or places for the take-off of pigeons (*maṭārāt al-ḥamām*), which, once again, in modern Arabic, has been applied to modern usage: *maṭārāt* means 'airport'.

With the decline of the Abbasid there was a parallel decline with the pigeon post and under the Seljuk dynasty it all but disappeared. The sultan, Alp Arslān, at the behest of his Persian vizier Niẓām al-Mulk, suppressed the postal system altogether. The dovecotes were demolished. Meanwhile, their use had spread to Damascus and east to Transoxiana.

The Fāṭimid, the next great dynasty, used pigeons for short distances, from Damascus to Aleppo or Cairo. A bird of good fortune was quite often honoured in public, one such instance being the Fāṭimid conquest of Syria, in 382/992, when the bird which brought back the good news was carried in triumph though the streets of Fusṭāṭ and Cairo in a cage covered with brocade. It is said the bird found this a particularly stressful occasion, given all the people shouting at it. What was being celebrated was not just the victory but also the exploits of the messenger itself. At that time no other bird had returned from so distant a place.

§

It was not until the Ayubbids that the system reached anything approaching its former glory. Saladin, founder of the Ayubbid dynasty, recognised the importance of carrier pigeons, which alerted him to the movements of the Crusaders. It was in fact the Crusaders who, following the Arab example, reintroduced the system to medieval Europe where it had been out of use since the fall of the Roman Empire. Arnold, Bishop of Lubeck, wrote in his history of the Crusade under Henry VI, in 1196, that 'the Infidels are more highly gifted than the children of light.' After the fall of Beirut in 1197, Bohemond, Prince of Antioch, announced the good tidings to his subjects by despatching a pigeon. The Arabs had an extensive network in Syria with lines of communication between Damascus and Hama, Bosra and Homs, Homs and Aleppo, although there was no direct service between Aleppo and Damascus which were too far apart from each other. There is much information in Arabic sources about the use of pigeons. For example, during the lengthy siege at Acre, which the Crusaders were trying to recapture from Saladin, pigeons were the sole means of communication with the outside world.

Saladin's secretary, Qāḍī Fāḍil, who died in 596/1200, called carrier pigeons 'prophet birds' or, more literally, 'prophets of the birds' (*anbiyā' al-ṭayr*). They were the preachers of the bird population perching on their branches in the same way as preachers on their minbars and because they served sovereigns first and foremost they were also called 'angels of the kings' (*malā'ikat al-mulūk*) even though sometimes they were sinister and brought bad luck. They would descend from the sky to the sovereigns as did spiritual beings to the prophets.

An intercepted carrier pigeon could be used as a form of counter-intelligence. A particularly famous instance of this took place earlier, in 518/1124, during the Zengid period, when the Frankish army lay siege to the city of Tyre, which had hitherto proved invincible. William of Tyre describes Tyre as 'a matchless bulwark, an incomparable tower of strength, without an equal in the entire region.' Finally, though, the walls of the city were breached and the defence towers crumbled under the power of the war machines. The townspeople sent a message to Ẓāhir al-Din Ṭuġtakīn, *atabeg* of Damascus, begging him for assistance. A message was sent back to Tyre, saying, 'Within several days I will arrive with a large army, so take courage and stay strong. Do not be discouraged.' The bird delivering the message fell into the Crusader camp by mistake and there the message was switched with a false one. 'Sons of Tyre,' it read, 'you have asked us to come to your rescue. We must let you know we are unable to come and we do not have at present an army capable of standing against the one assembled against you. Please do not expect anything from us. Say prayers for the safety of your lives and give yourselves up.' With the arrival of this message all hope evaporated and the starving populace, already badly reduced by disease, opened the doors of the ancient capital, one towards the land and the other towards the sea. In fact, it is unlikely the *atabeg* would have come to their rescue in time. A river of citizens flowed from the town towards exile. One thing on which both Arab and Frankish sources agree is that the victors were magnanimous in this instance. According to William of Tyre, 'the townspeople, worn out by the long siege, emerged from the city and hastened to our camp. They were eager to relieve their weariness and to see what manner of men these Christians might be . . . It gave them great delight to examine the form of the machines, to gaze at the height of the moveable towers and the variety of weapons; they admired the position of the camp and even desired to know the names of the leaders.' The Christians, from their side, 'had only praise for the resolute perseverance of the citizens who, despite the pressure of terrible famine and the scarcity of supplies, had been able to ward off surrender for so long.' Some of the citizens of Tyre made it to Damascus, which opened its doors to them, while others were dispersed throughout the country. The siege, which began in winter, on February 15th, ended in summer, on July 7th. Although less than five months in duration, the agonies it imposed were such that the citizens imagined they had been under siege for almost seven months.

§

The Mamlūks were probably the most proficient when it came to running a pigeon service. Sultan Quṭuz provided the citadel at Aleppo with a magnificent dovecote in 658/1260 to replace the Ayyūbid one that had been destroyed by Hulagu. When the Mongols returned a year later they once again reduced the dovecote to ashes. It has been suggested that the presence of the dovecote so irritated them, maybe because of the spirit of revival it represented, that they destroyed much of the rest of the city. More likely, though, is that they knew precisely its strategic value.

It was Sultan Baybars, whose rule lasted between 1259 and 1278, who did the most to establish the *barīd*, especially in Cairo which is where he spent the greater part of his time. Syria was also under his control and to make sure both countries were under control he reformed the postal system so that it extended not just to carrier pigeons but also to horses. Royal pigeons, almost 2,000 of them, had special markings on their beaks or feet and any message they carried could be opened only by Baybars himself. Whenever a despatch arrived he would interrupt his sleep or his meal, once even coming naked from his bed, to read the mail. The system was perfected to such a degree that Baybars was at all times able to check his enemies, both foreign and domestic. By this point the value of a pair of prize carriers could sell for 1,000 gold pieces.

One of the earliest European accounts of the Mamlūk system was made, c.1425, by the German soldier of fortune Johan Schiltberger:

> It is also to be noted, that the king-sultan also sends letters by pigeons, because he has many enemies, and is afraid that they might stop his messengers. They are sent mostly from Archey to Tamasgen, between which places is a great desert. It is also to be noted, how the pigeons are sent to any city to which the king-sultan wishes to have them sent. Two pigeons must be put together, and sugar must be put into their food, and they are not allowed to fly; and when they know each other well, the hen-pigeon is taken to the king, and he keeps it, and marks the cock-pigeon that it may be known from which city it is; it is then put into a separate place that is prepared, and the hen-pigeon is no longer allowed inside. They no longer give him so much to eat, and no more sugar as he used to have; this is done that he may wish to return as soon as possible to the place where he was before, and where he was trained. When they wish to despatch him, the letter is tied under a wing and he flies away straight for the house where he was trained. There he is caught and the letter taken from him, and they send it to whomsoever it belongs.

Sometimes pigeons were physically transformed to become, as it were, messages in themselves. They would arrive in their altered states, which signified either bad or good news. The mere sight of one could be enough to alert a populace to a disaster elsewhere. Such birds were spoken of as 'birds of bad omen' and one writer with a poetic bent referred to them as *ḥamām al-ḥimām* or 'birds of death'. These particular specimens had all the feathers plucked from their heads in order to indicate distress from a town that was currently under siege. The Mamlūks, when announcing a defeat, would sometimes darken the plumage with soot, a symbol more potent and less humiliating than having to put into words what they did not have the stomach to write. During the Crusades, a bird with a red string around its neck would be a sign of bad news, signifying the death of a leader or massive bloodshed. Bearers of good news were called, obviously enough, 'birds of good fortune' (*uṭyār al-bašā'ir*) and would sometimes be dyed with a yellow or reddish hue. Also they might be covered in scent – saffron, musk, or essence of rose or sandalwood – and could often, especially if it were raining, be smelled before they landed.

Very few specimens of the messages they carried survive. Obviously the writing had to be extremely condensed so they could fit on small pieces of paper. They were, in a sense, the text messages of their time. A new kind of writing, attributed to the famous calligrapher Aḥwal, was devised in order to save space. The messages were written on a very fine paper especially made for the purpose, called 'bird-paper' (*waraq al-ṭayr*) and if the news was good the messages would come with a whiff of perfume. The messages did not have margins and only the day and month were mentioned, never the year, and the usual preambles praising Allāh were dropped for fear of the messages falling into infidel hands. There would be no indication of the address either. Any Muslim chancing upon such a message was obliged to attend to the pigeon's needs and then send it on its way with a note explaining what he'd done.

Pigeons would be used to announce the imminent arrival of an important person. A man's importance, though, is not equal to his moral stature. In 711/1311 the Mamlūk amịr Sayf al-Dīn Argūn arrived in Damascus without any advance warning. A clearly obnoxious figure, he claimed to have sent a pigeon in advance when in fact he hadn't done so. The amir, when he was brought food and drink, proceeded to vomit into the bowl, blaming the guardian of the Damascus dovecote for being inattentive. The poor man was duly punished.

The reputation of the Mamlūk *barīd* was so widespread that it is mentioned in Ariosto's *Orlando Furioso*:

> As soon as the warden of Damietta had established the Orrilo was dead, he released a dove with a letter tied beneath its wing. The dove flew to Cairo, where another

dove was released for the next destination, as was the custom in those parts. Thus in a matters of hours Orrilo's death was known throughout Egypt.

§

Carrier pigeons also proved their worth in business.

The wily traders of Aleppo employed pigeons to get advance notice of ships arriving at the coast of Syria. They would learn what goods were on board on these ships, which would be most profitable, and the number of camels required for their transport. An accidentally or purposely felled pigeon might provide valuable information. One trader shot down a pigeon that bore a message enquiring after the price of walnuts. Their value had suddenly shot up in England and so, at the expense of the merchant to whom the message was originally directed, he was able to make a killing. Pigeons were also used by caravans travelling across the desert, which were otherwise reduced to radio silence. A desert sovereign might have several days' notice of an approaching caravan.

Sadly, though, many of these pigeons could not endure the desert heat and dropped to the ground 'like glowing embers', which is how one observer described it. Sometimes travellers would find them where they fell, just barely alive. We shall close on this melancholy note, a pigeon sprawled on its back, its message undelivered, beak wide open, waiting for the morning dew that may or may not come.

Chapter Fourteen

An Occidentalist Goes to Leighton House

Constantin François de Chasseboeuf Volney, *savant*, in his preface to *Voyage en Egypte et en Syrie*, writes: 'I have endeavoured to maintain the spirit with which I conducted my researches into facts; that is, an impartial love of truth. I have restrained myself from indulging any sallies of the imagination, though I am no stranger to the power of such illusion over the generality of readers; but I am of the opinion that travels belong to the department of history, and not that of romance. I have not therefore described countries as more beautiful than they appeared to me. I have not represented their inhabitants more virtuous, not more wicked than I have found them, and I have perhaps been enabled to see them such as they really are, since I have never received from them either benefits or injuries.' What is especially striking, although maybe it ought not to be, is the date of publication: 1787.

Understanding is not modern.

One might take exception to the certainty of *such as they really are*, which is both philosophically and critically unsound. Do we ever see anything as it really is? We can be certain only of our uncertainties. This said, Volney's must be judged not just by his good intention but also by the result. Writing of this same preface, Edward Said, in *Orientalism*, says only that Volney came into some family money making it possible for him to voyage east in 1783; he makes no mention of the above passage, and then goes on to say that the text which follows served as a crib for Napoleon's imperialistic ventures. This is disingenuous to say the least. Why not blame the cartographers too? Said did considerable good – this he demonstrated in many instances – but the academic machine he helped create is making peculiar, stuttering noises. It is beginning to shuffle across the floor of its own accord, leaving behind it a wide trail of grease. The oily precipitates have seeped through the whole of academe. Students parrot him endlessly, unthinkingly, accepting what he has to say about the authors he criticises but without actually going to the original texts. Worse still, it has fed the Arabs' own sense of grievance.

The writers Said deals with, if he's to be believed, seem all of them either suspect or else deserving of blame. Granted he chose his moment well, or, rather, the moment chose him. Collective guilt is the most marketable of commodities. Guilt is modern. One may conclude from Said and his disciples, from the latter even more so than from the former, that a dispassionate observer of the Orient has got to get it wrong sooner or later, which is to say he does wrong even when he thinks he does right, that is, *he is doomed to failure*. An assumption of failure is not the best attitude with which to mount a camel or a horse. If, on the other hand, one consequence of Said's thesis is that writers become just a shade more responsible then his book will have served some purpose.

Another passage Said ignores is that relating to Volney's experiences among the Bedouins, and one hopes it is not because Said found it too inconvenient to draw attention to in his book. 'The Arabs,' Volney writes (meaning here the Bedouins), 'have often been reproached with this spirit of rapine, but, without wishing to defend it, we may observe, that one circumstance has not been sufficiently attended to, which is, that it only takes place towards reputed enemies, and is consequently founded on the acknowledged law of almost all nations. Among themselves they are remarkable for a good faith, a disinterestedness, a generosity which would do honour to the most civilized people. What is there more noble than that right of asylum so respected among all the tribes? A stranger, nay, even an enemy, touches the tent of the Bedouin, and, from that instant, his person becomes inviolable. It would be reckoned a disgraceful meanness, an indelible shame, to satisfy even a just vengeance at the expense of hospitality. Has the Bedouin consented to eat bread and salt with his guest, nothing in the world can induce him to betray him. The power of the Sultan himself would not be able to force a refugee from the protection of a tribe, but by its total extermination. The Bedouin, so rapacious without his camp, has no sooner set his foot within it, than he becomes liberal and generous. What little he possesses he is ever ready to divide.'

What Volney describes here is what Bedouins, understandably proud of their ancestry, have related to me. So, maybe he did see *some things* as they really are. Could one wish for a more enlightened view on a people about whom Europeans of that time knew so very little? Could there be a clearer line running between what Volney relates and what Sulaymān is proud to describe as his ancestors' finer qualities? Volney was driven by a hunger for knowledge and that he did so without the comforts of modern travel and a pocket guide ought to speak in his favour. Certainly he is innocent of the outrageous slur Said makes when he speaks of travellers such as Volney and those who came after him as going to places that were principally *in their minds*.

In 1791, Volney published one of the most widely read philosophical treatises of the age, *Les Ruines, ou, méditations sur les révolutions des empires*, a work that has its roots in his visit to the ruins of Palmyra. 'The dusk increased,' he writes, 'and already I could distinguish nothing more than the pale phantoms of walls and columns.' This, for anyone who has ever walked through Palmyra at that hour, is precisely what those ruins become, *pale phantoms*. Soon Volney falls into a reverie, or so he says because maybe he doesn't do so at all, maybe it is a literary device, and in this state, that is, *very much in his mind*, he is approached by an apparition that speaks to him, Ozymandius-like. Although empires fall, as fall they must, benign self-interest is what makes them rise. Volney's other prediction is that the world's religions would unite because of the common truth underlying them, which equally sounds like a recipe for no religion at all. The first English translation of *Les Ruines* was an anonymous one made by Thomas Jefferson. Jefferson, perhaps mindful of his electoral prospects, left the translation of the final chapters on religion to someone else. His version, although printed in Paris, did well in America. Abraham Lincoln read it. There have been no similar presidential sightings of late.

What has been going on in the department of history then? If travel literature has become suspect, it is so to the degree that it has become romance. At what point, exactly, did the labels on library shelves switch from topography to travel literature? If there is no going back to that earlier phase it is because travel, as it used to be, is no longer possible. After all, barring war and disease, there is nowhere we can't get to. If I have failed to meet Volney's exacting standards it is that I have been all too often the happy receiver of benefits. Such injuries as I have suffered are mere grazes. One of the greatest benefits for any traveller to the Middle East, especially if he journeys, as I do, *through people*, is that there can be few places in the world where one might better confabulate. The talk is rarely less than good.

§

Yasser and I were having one of our debates, this time on the matter of Orientalism. I had just thrown Volney at him, which he caught with good grace; Burton we had already done, Lawrence was in the wings, and he came back at me with memories of when he was last in London and I had taken him to see the Arab Hall at Leighton House. I had corrupted him, he said, with a mischievous smile. *Was it the nudes?* We'd looked at the paintings too. Yasser admitted to having a special affection for images of women's bare backs, the exposed shoulder, a running of the eyes down the spine's curvature.

The Arab Hall, which Lord Leighton modelled on the banqueting hall of the thirteenth-century Moorish palace of La Zisa 'Palace of Delights' in Palermo, stands as the very epitome of the vogue for Orientalism in nineteenth-century Europe, and, with its pulling together of materials from places thousands of miles apart – a tile panel and stained glass from Damascus; figurative tiles from Persia; an Iznik tile from Turkey; pierced windows from Cairo; and then various English additions, a fountain designed by George Aitchison, a mosaic frieze by Walter Crane, and tiles by William de Morgan (made to replace Syrian ones broken in transit and done with such skill it is not easy to spot the difference) – it might have been truly appalling were it not all rendered with such exquisite taste. The magnificent calligraphic tiles are said to have been collected by Leighton's friend, Richard Burton, and may have come from as far away as Pakistan. Their wording is taken from the

Qur'ān, *sūra* 54, 1-6: 'In the name of the merciful and long-suffering God, The Merciful hath taught the Koran. He has created man and taught him speech. (He has set) the sun and the moon in a certain course, Both the moon and the stars are in subjection (unto him).' Yasser noted that one of the calligraphic tiles had been positioned in the wrong order, a mistake that would give rise to the conversation we were about to have.

'You corrupted me.'

'Yes, I have been worrying about your descent into western culture.'

We had each adopted the other's cultural position. My Occidentalist friend poured some milk into his tea, while I who in London always add milk took mine clear.

'It is one thing to read or think about something and quite another to *feel* about it,' Yasser continued. 'When I go looking at houses, the first thing I want to discover is whether such and such a place has a good feeling about it. Two things happened that day. When you told me you were going to show me Leighton House, on the way there I thought to myself, "So here you are, Marius the Orientalist!", and then came what I took to be a supportive sign when some woman on the street handed you a business card with a belly dancer on it for a Persian restaurant. I thought to myself, "This is really coming together!" Anyway I was curious about this man practicing his Orientalism on me. We walked into the house, and, as you can imagine, the first thing I looked at were the rugs and then the architecture. You cannot look at one and not be interested in the other. After all, a prayer rug is the reflection of the *miḥrab* inside a mosque. The central medallion in a rug is like the dome. Then we looked at some of the paintings and when I got out of there it was with two powerful impressions. There was love in this house and there was ostentation, but it was not ostentation of a negative kind. It was a demonstration of pride and of the fact that the owner had good taste and a fine eye.'

'So why did you come out feeling like this?'

'I had read *Orientalism* and for me the best idea in Said's book was that there were some honest people who were abused or, rather, they were *used* but not in the way they meant themselves to be used. They were genuine about what they were doing, but there was a machine there, which pushed everything in the direction it was going in – colonialism, for example – and whoever the people behind it were, at that moment in time, they were directing the actions of some of these honest people. You can use the Qur'ān or the Holy Bible in a corrupt way; equally you can use them in the right way. You can use the law to kill someone and you can use it to save someone. This, despite my occasional objections, is the best side of Said's book, and then I read his *Culture and Imperialism*, which ruined everything for me. It sent me back into the dismay or the haze I was in before reading *Orientalism*. I really wanted to believe that there were people who were *not* working for the colonialist governments in France or Britain. I wanted to believe Lawrence of Arabia was honest and that he was betrayed by his own government, although the Syrian side of me says this was a conspiracy right from the start. I had a school friend called Muḥammad Lawrence. His father was a great admirer of Lawrence and they are of a religious family! And then there are those who say Lawrence was the biggest betrayer in Arab history, that he was put there as a means to selling out the Arabs. Said says these authors who wrote about other parts of the world had conspiracy in the backs of their minds, and that they were never really honest.'

'And then he writes about Conrad's *Heart of Darkness*, basically accusing him as well.'

'Excuse me, but at university I studied that book! Our professor told us Conrad wrote out of bitterness, and that people then were using religion for material purposes against people who didn't want this thing brought to them. So along comes Said who tells me something different, that Conrad already had this attitude. This is why I say you corrupted me. I came out of Leighton House with this love/hate relationship in me, but I have always trusted my feelings for place. When I go to a mosque to pray, if I don't have a good feeling I will never go back there again. After all, if this is supposed to be the house of Allāh it should be open for me. So this is how I came out of Leighton House, with a combined sense of love and ostentation, which was very positive. Say you were British at that time and had never been to the Middle East. You enter Leighton's house. When you leave, what is your impression? You would want to have the experiences he had and to go to the places he'd been to. Is that good or bad? You might be evil and want to use it in a wrong way but you might be good and want to have these experiences. I didn't find anything false in that house. As always, and I have to think of myself too, we love our culture and what informs it, but, however careful we are, we still make mistakes, and in Leighton's case we saw a couple of tiles with the religious inscription spread over them placed in the wrong order. I always used to tell my students, "You are learning a foreign language, so use it; open a window to another culture." The majority of them would reply, "We are afraid of making mistakes." My spontaneous response was, "Aren't we always making mistakes in our own language, especially when we get excited. When we are happy, we make mistakes." We have this strong hadith. This man, a Believer, is in the desert and he has lost his horse, which bore his food and water, and he thinks to himself that he is dying and there is no way out of this mess. He looks for his horse everywhere and finally gives up, puts his head down, and sleeps a bit and then wakes up to see the horse has returned. Immediately, in his excitement, he cries, "Oh Allāh, I am your God and you are my slave!" Out of happiness, you see, he made a mistake. I always use this as an argument. You might make a mistake in another language. So what? People might laugh at you or they may even correct you. We do the same thing in Arabic. So this Leighton, who, after all, had been so excited by the Orient, when he went back and constructed his house he might very well have made mistakes. Why do we always have to interpret things in a negative way? You could take ten Muslims into that house. You will find among them someone who will say that Leighton did this on purpose in order to insult the Qur'ān. According to our faith – and it is in our books, although unfortunately it is no longer adhered to, and in fact it has become more of a Western principle – a man tells the truth unless it is proven otherwise. A man is not a deceiver unless proven otherwise. So these Orientalists who came and made mistakes, why should we say they were full of malice?'

'This is also a demonstration of just how unforgiving these critics of Orientalism are. They go looking for a mistake and make of it an entire picture. Your hadith stands as a corrective for this kind of thinking.'

'The hadith actually has another purpose, which is to demonstrate how happy Allāh is when somebody returns to him. Allāh would be happier than that man who would reverse the whole thing, who, in a moment of absolute happiness, made the most terrible mistake. If we want to write about the evils of Orientalism we can attack endlessly. I could drag this still further, but then I would be condemned in this society. As to those who criticise Islam or the way we treat women, for example, it doesn't necessarily mean they are evil. They have been raised in a different culture and they wish for our culture to incorporate certain of their values. But if I were to say this publicly, I would be told to shut up. I fell into Said's trap for a long time, and I am not exaggerating when I say this, that our visit to Leighton's house, to the home of someone whom I took to be a major Orientalist, with all the faults Said describes, put a full-stop at the end of the sentence. Why should calling someone an Orientalist have a negative connotation?'

'What happens, though, when faiths collide?'

'I am not a conservative Muslim, but I am a Believer and I pray five times a day. I am not one of these Islamic revivalists. My boss was such a traditionalist that if anything edible was given to us by a foreigner he would tell us it should be thrown away. We were told to thank the foreigner so as to demonstrate our appreciation and then to quietly throw it in the bin. This is how conservative my own family was. I worked there for nineteen years. I worked with more than a hundred people, almost all of whom inherited this line of thinking. If my boss told them something, they did it. They would never dream of betraying him, even in his absence. I was the only one who, when a foreigner gave me something, would hide it away. When my boss was not there, I would eat it, finding in this forbidden fruit much exquisite pleasure. Maybe he was right and that's why I'm corrupt now and maybe that's why I put milk in my tea. I am telling you about Syria as it was in the seventies and eighties. We were kids from a poor family who had never seen nicely wrapped chocolates. I am sure some of our customers really felt badly for us. We'd be sweating in the summer heat, working all day. They would bring us chocolates from abroad. It was so painful to have to throw them away.'

'You reveal something deep in the frustrations of modern people. You are a good, traditional Muslim and yet there is this hunger for a slice of the West. To what degree is this true of you?'

'I am of that school that is never much spoken about here, a school of thinking among Arab authors, shaykhs and thinkers that is rarely revealed or materialised but which is there all the same, and which even you gave voice to when you described the movement, via the troubadours, of Arab culture into Europe. This school believes that during the Renaissance the West took on certain Islamic values. This is not a matter for shame. It is not something of which we should boast nor is it something of which you should be ashamed. Islamic culture, after all, has taken a lot from the West, and from the Persians and the Chinese, and all this we managed to assimilate and make into something great. One civilisation rises to the top – we do not really see it at the time, not for hundreds of years sometimes – and then another civilisation comes and this one goes to the bottom. We are the ones who are losing now, ever since the fall of Islamic civilisation. I do not believe in a *pure* Arab civilisation of any kind, by the way, because there isn't any such thing – the greatest doctors and authors were from India and Iran. Anyway Islamic civilisation has been falling for a long time. We can still see some of our values swimming there. It is nice to be able to see some of yours as well, so when I talk about these things it is not from the perspective of those kids selling carpets down the street from here, who ask foreigners to tell them whether or not they look Italian. I know who I am and although what the majority of Arabs are doing disappoints me, I still know where the good things are and I aspire for those things that reflect on me as a human being. So if I go to England for the first time and discover that English tea with milk is really good, it doesn't matter to me whose tradition it is, I will take it. These are principles in our own religion. A believer's lost treasure – the Holy Grail of any true believer – is wisdom and this is something he takes literally. Wherever he finds it, he will take it. If I think it is good for me, I will take it.'

'You say Muslim culture is in decline and Western is on the ascent. I would suggest to you that western democracy is ill and

Islam is ill, and when pundits talk about a clash of civilisations what they really should be talking about is a clash of two illnesses. Walking through Old Damascus, one sees signs of that illness everywhere, the trashy imitations of the West, which find their expression in the architecture, this aluminium door across the street from here, for example. Whatever was there a hundred years ago had to have been better than this, but people here seem to prefer our junk culture. I'd say you are unique among Arabs I've met. Arabs will speak with love of their culture, but only rarely do they see anything in ours. When do they ever listen to Johann Sebastian Bach? What about the incredible productions of Western culture? They back away, saying they see nothing in them or else Islam makes it all irrelevant. You are an exception. I watched you looking at the paintings in Leighton House. When we talk about Orientalism what we are looking at is a tremendous revival of interest in the East. Go into any bookshop in London and there will be books on Moorish architecture, but when one comes here does one see any genuine interest in Western culture? It would appear to be a one-way road. Young Arabs in particular seem to want only our rubbish. This is where you have done something with your hunger in that you've been looking in this other direction.'

'I want to point out one thing. As languages differ, so too does the way people express their interests. You express your interest in things here firstly as a Westerner and secondly as someone deeply into books, especially when you begin to talk about this "one-way street". I will tell you something that is very deep and very shallow at the same time. This aluminium door you are talking about, it is one of the things, which, when compared to what you see in a book on Moorish architecture, you describe as the trash of your civilisation, and I agree with you, but not many people here would agree. They think this is much more practical than wood and that its maintenance is much cheaper. You talk to many people here, but very few Arab intellectuals will say to you what they say to me. They say to me these Westerners come to the Umayyad Mosque and what they see is an architectural treasure, an illustration of human genius, but then these same Arab intellectuals will also say they have not actually seen the whole truth or that only part of it is true. They say what these visitors have taken from us is only the shell and that they have not gone deep inside. So you come here and find this aluminium door. You say we have taken your rubbish.'

I had a feeling this door was not going to go away and I could detect an edge of disapproval in Yasser's voice.

'A cousin of mine,' he continued, 'who is a real Sufi, spent years wanting to go to Medina, which is Wahhābī and where they stick closely to rules. I don't want to criticise the Wahhābīs who do have some really good things, but then so do the Sufis. This cousin of mine was dying to visit the Prophet's tomb. The moment came and he knelt down and kissed the marble of the tomb. This Wahhābī brother, a *ḥarām* policeman, came with a stick and hit him on the head, saying, "You are kissing Italian marble." My cousin replied, "Praise be to God who blinded you to what is behind this marble." There is a kind of sarcasm in his response, which is also mixed with empathy. You are bitter because the other side does not see what you see. Getting back to where we were, there is soul in our culture. There is no shame in trying to capture it or even in seeing it in the wrong way. You may know the following story about Moses. Moses was in the desert and he saw this simple Bedouin praying to God, saying, "Oh my God, if you were here now, I would comb your hair, remove the lice, and wash your feet in hot water." Moses who thought he knew more than anyone else cried, "What are you talking about? You think you know your God? He is not like this. He is like nothing you imagine." As well as being a prophet Moses was huge and this man ran away. Then Allāh spoke to Moses – he was the only prophet to whom God spoke directly, that is without the intercession of an angel. "You have ruined one of the best prayers. This man was seeing his God the way he understands him. I was enjoying his prayers and so was he." So Moses ran everywhere, trying to find this man in order to apologise to him. After a while he found him, and said, "I am very sorry to have ruined your prayer. Go back to where you were." The man answered, "You have ruined something that can never be repaired because now I no longer know what my God looks like." Now, whether you want to cast this in the modern way of Orientalism or Occidentalism or whatever, this man took an ugly shape for his door, which for him may have been a wonderful thing. It serves many purposes, it is easy to clean. It may have depth even, and for an Orientalist who comes to the Middle East and finds great architectural monuments because, after all, he has been raised in a culture where he is taught to appreciate beauty, for him to say I should see things the way he sees them, and really there is nothing wrong about me seeing something you don't see, this is a very cheap, arrogant attitude.'

Yasser was never a man to mince words.

'I hate it when I go with educated friends into a simple Damascene house, which the family living there has ruined. We say to ourselves, "Look what they've done with this place." This is so arrogant, so inhuman. It is one thing to tell these people how they might improve their place and another to criticise them for how they live. I should be talking about appreciating old things because, after all, I love them too, but this intellectual arrogance is cruel and inhuman, so very bitter sometimes. I came from a family which was poor. I was lucky. My father was educated and my mother appreciated things and we lived in a poor neighbourhood that has now become trendy. The minute someone talks like this about someone's house, right away I go back twenty-five or thirty years ago to my childhood and you could be talking about my next door neighbours. I love them and to this day I think they may be the best people in my history. This is a simple example. We are so arrogant today, in that each one of us thinks he is different, but we are *all* different in a way that makes us similar. So when dealing with Orientalism or Occidentalism, with the arrogance that you know everything, who are you? You will live for a few years and then the whole world will forget about you.

'I was reading in Robert Fisk's book [*The Great War for Civilisation: the conquest of the Middle East* (2005)] his chapter on "the Shah of Shahs" and this big birthday party which he held in Persepolis, all this greatness, and Fisk writes how in his last days nobody would give the Shah political asylum and he ended up in Egypt. Fisk puts this in a way that reminds me of Shelley's "Ozymandius". He went looking for the Shah's tomb. He found himself in this modest place, where he meets the keeper who cries, "Baksheesh, baksheesh!" and Fisk gives him fifty piastres, the equivalent of forty cents maybe. So it cost him only forty cents to sit at the foot of "the Shah of Shahs". Who are you to sit there with all your arrogance? Orientalism, Occidentalism, classifying all these people? Who am I? We will disappear and life will continue and within seconds, unless we are lucky enough to have accomplished something, we will be completely forgotten. People coming here take away not even a tiny bit of the Umayyad mosque. I have personal experience of this. I shall draw another parallel from my own life. We were school kids. Those were difficult times. We were really bankrupt. This friend of ours had a birthday party. It is a comparatively new thing here to celebrate birthdays with parties. So this friend of ours had a party and we were laughing, saying, "Can this be really true?" We went and got some old, dried parsley and made a nice box for it. We took it to his place. "You brought me a present!" he said. And then we ran away from the house. So to continue this argument of people just seeing what is outside and not inside, I heard an Egyptian shaykh give a talk. He said people look at the pyramids and the Suez Canal as symbols of the greatness of ancient and modern Egypt, but that really they ought to be symbols of enslavement. How many people died for a pyramid in which to store a single corpse and how many people died to make a canal to allow some colonial ships to pass through? Religious people here are disillusioned with Westerners who come and judge by appearances only, who point to our women, for example, saying they must be unhappy because they are covered. Some women are much happier when covered. They have always lived like this. If you removed their scarves, they would feel naked, they would never be comfortable. Just because you have been raised in an environment where you were not covered means you are happy and she is not? This is arrogance.'

'You've been on a roll, Yasser!'

Yasser, the pasha of Badreddin al-Ḥasani Lane, perched on his pile of kilims, knew it.

Thereafter, each time I passed it, I would look upon that door with a kindlier eye. Aluminium, symbol *Al*, number 13 in the periodic table. Pliny the Elder, in his *Historia Naturalis*, relates a story that may point to its early discovery. We can't be absolutely sure. Also Pliny often relied on hearsay. A Roman goldsmith brought the Emperor Tiberius a dinner plate made of a new metal that was very light and almost as shiny as silver, and which he claimed was made from ordinary clay, adding that only he and the gods knew the secret of its manufacture. The wily Emperor was shrewd enough to realise that if this were true, and this wonder metal could be so cheaply made, then his treasure of gold and silver would decline in value, so rather than risk a slump in market values he promptly had the goldsmith beheaded. Genius, poorly timed, often has fatal consequences. It would be another 2,000 years before aluminium reappeared on the scene. And when it did, in the 1850s, the aluminium of that door in old Damascus would have been worth considerably more than the house itself. Aluminium was, for a while, the rarest of metals. Scarcity, not beauty, is the true measure of things. Napoleon III's favourite cutlery was made of aluminium and such few settings as were available were used at a banquet to welcome the King of Siam while at the far end of the same table the lesser folk had to make do with gold. The figure of Eros in Piccadilly Circus was one of the first statues to be cast in aluminium. The message containers attached to carrier pigeons' legs during both World War One and World War Two were made of aluminium, it being, as far as we are concerned, never mind the pigeons, at an atomic weight of 26.981539 amu, close to weightless.

Chapter Fifteen

The Father of Skulls

Promises, promises – a word which, when repeated, becomes a negative – a fool might have guessed from the largesse, the ease with which they were made, they were none of them realisable. Still they did make the blood race. Most thrilling of all was a promise of access to police and court files. Al-Sawwāḥ, surely, was in one of those files. There, at last, a stenographer's hieroglyphic might reveal chance remarks that would light up the whole stadium at once, which would lay bare the mind of a man who killed his neighbour's child for the sake of some confiscated birds. A mug shot would show what he looked like. Who knows, and this really had been put to me as a possibility, I might even be able to meet him wherever it was that he was incarcerated, although this would require my having to adopt a whole other mode, not one in which I would feel comfortable. I figured anything less than a journey into the darkest recesses of a killer's mind would be a mawkish exercise. A prison visit would not allow for any such depth and where there is no depth there'd be only damage to one's own soul and a compromised soul is no place from which to write. No, it was best to stick to the files, and to construct from them a picture that might go some way towards validating everything else.

This became the goal that temporarily blinded me to all other possibilities. I was shunted from office to office, from face to face. Deep in some newspaper archive, somebody translated an article for me, which called for a better understanding of pigeon people, with psychiatric support if need be, and squads of social workers too, so they might be freed of their terrible addiction. Were any of them ready, I wondered, for so much state benevolence? The search went on. A message would come, instructing me to be at such and such a place at such and such an hour and when I got there, always in plenty of time, it was only to find myself at yet another social gathering where still more promises were made, either that or I'd be presented with things I already knew and then I'd have to make a show of gratitude but not too big a one for fear that my informant would think his mission complete. The people who made those promises did so either because they were genuinely amused or because in their amusement they were genuine. Tactics were never of the moment. Tactics were for later. Now was a time for promises. At al-Ra'īs Restaurant the journalist Selim had whispered to me, 'Those people at the table over there, when they see us talking like this they assume we are forging peace for the Middle East. And here we are, talking pigeon wars!'

All those avenues, if they ever existed in the first place, would lead nowhere. This is not to say I had been lied to, but that I'd entered a conundrum that can be summed up thus: never say *no*, even when *yes* is out of the question. An Arab is reluctant to proffer a negative for fear of seeming impolite. This, as anyone who has ever conducted business in the Middle East can tell you, makes for countless misunderstandings. If there was one thing in me that failed to adapt to life there, it was the unreasonable expectation that a thing said was a thing done. The closest I ever got to a concrete response to my enquiries was one that would sadly diminish my hopes: al-Sawwāḥ was a name as common as 'Smith' and more details were required if we were to pinpoint his file. The man who could have provided them was himself in prison and I knew not where to find the judge from the year before, and if any of the pigeon fanciers I met knew, and it seemed impossible that at least some of them didn't, nobody among them was going to tell me.

§

There was one week in particular when it seemed as though I'd entered a labyrinth whose every turning brought me to the beginning of yet another tale, only there was no single thread whereby I might connect it to the previous one. This, perhaps, is the illusory nature of Damascus, in that the closer one thinks one is to one's quarry the greater the actual distance. A carefully devised plan gets one nowhere. What one must do is to surrender oneself to circumstance. There was a danger too of forcing analogies into places where they wouldn't go, and, in this respect, emptyheadedness of a kind several degrees short of stupidity was often the better course. As I would realise later, it could be several months sometimes before the value of certain experiences became apparent, when it was at last possible to impose a pattern upon them.

There were times even when I found myself in the chandeliered halls of power, when there was no making sense of my presence there. These were situations I had been led into, mainly because of the enthusiasm of one Kosay Mustafa who I met when he was second secretary at the Syrian Embassy in London. A witty man, when he said my book ought to be translated into Arabic and I asked him what the chances were of Syrians reading it, he replied, 'We will give them a choice – either they buy your book or they join the Party.' Whatever his politics, and he was a Baathist to the core, Kosay was intelligent and passionate. A skilled player, he flew just so high above the political game, sometimes only barely skimming the surface. There is nobody quite so liberal as he who is separated from its opposite by a single degree.

And there was nothing he loved more than running me past his associates, Muḥsen Bilāl, for example, the elegant white-haired Minister of Information. I had heard it said that people waited five years for an interview with him whereas with me, who sought nothing of the kind, it took only five minutes. We eyed each other as if we had just arrived from opposite ends of the universe. There was an expectant look in his face. Surely I had a question for him because, after all, didn't *all* people have a question for him. The question was never asked because it was never formulated in the first place. I had been taken completely by surprise. A couple of hours earlier, I had seen him at some function, in a grand marbled space, full of echoes, and wherever he walked a comet's tail of journalists and functionaries followed him as if they were metal filings on a sheet of paper beneath which a hidden magnet pulled them to and fro, so hungry they were to be granted just a moment's audience. What did this man with the deeply intelligent face make of it all? Did he thrive on, or was he sickened by, the press of supplicants all crying at once? Once upon a time, actually not so long ago,

Arab kings were obliged to hear out their subjects, which was a mark of deeply civilised values.

One day I found myself seated, sloppily dressed, at a long table of smartly suited men in a fashionable restaurant on the Barada River. I wasn't meant to be there, or, rather, I missed the telephone message cancelling what had been planned as a casual luncheon date for three people. I turned up at the appointed time and place, and, as I realised later, my visibly uncomfortable hosts were too courteous to disinvite me. A few minutes later, I was among some of the most powerful people in the country, seated to the right of me the Minister for Foreign Affairs who had that very morning completed a poem he had been working on and which now he recited, one hand in the air conducting the lines, making them do, perhaps, what they were disinclined to do on the page, *dance*. I'd been in enough poetry circles in my life to be able to detect certain universals, one of which being that a man of power reading his new verses is every bit as naked as a man who has no power at all. Several of the Minister for Foreign Affairs' lines provoked bird-like flutters of delight from both sides of the long table.

Sitting opposite me was a man with cold, slightly bulging eyes, across whose face nothing seemed to move. Almost immediately he began scrutinising me. There was no escaping his gaze.

'What are you doing here in Damascus?'

What would he care about pigeon fanciers and their curious activities? So I told him, abbreviating my aims as much as possible.

'Yes, I understand they have their own judges.'

I said this was true, and that while in the past the judges were selected from only the most honest fanciers they tended now to be recruited from the criminal classes.

'Would you say this is true of judges worldwide or just in Syria?'

'I have yet to decide.'

Admittedly this was not a good response.

'What do you have to say about your country's presence in Iraq?'

I could hardly be considered Blair's representative, and when I told him I was one of many tens of thousands of people who marched in protest against the war he wriggled his nose at me.

'So why don't you write about the plight of the Palestinians?'

'There are writers far more qualified than me to write on the Palestinian issue,' I replied, 'and besides, I thought you might appreciate the fact I am presenting a side of the Syrian people not normally seen from the outside.'

'These charming people you are writing about,' he sneered, 'your policies are going to turn them into human bombs.'

I did what one ought never to do when addressing Arabs and pointed my finger at him.

'Are you trying to teach me?'

At last he smiled faintly, and, picking up his glass of *ayran*, he clinked it against my sitting one. The conversation was closed. I got up and went to the other end of the table where sat the person who'd brought me there.

'Who is that man interrogating me?'

'Well,' he said, 'let's put it this way. He is very high up in Intelligence and the fellow sitting beside him is his second-in-command.'

I had just wagged my finger at a man who made others quake in their shoes. Clearly, though, he could see I was too harmless to pursue. Although it was unfair of him to have made a target of me what he said was, of course, horribly true.

I had been looking in the wrong places. Maybe one reason I had been invited into those high circles was some element of the nostalgic, which took people back to a time when one might contemplate the flight of birds rather than that of missiles. One thing was certain, however: I wasn't fooling anyone. They all knew I was seeking analogies.

§

Any rich pickings were to be found only in low places.

About two miles north of Bāb Sharqī, on Friday mornings, there is the so-called 'Thieves' Market' (*souq al Ḥaramīya*). It occupies a truly bleak area, a sort of wasteland, where for over a mile, on either side of the highway, people gather to sell the unsaleable. There are parts of machines, broken clocks, broken toys, broken radios, an LP with a crack of almost three inches, ragged clothes, nuts and bolts, metal scraps one could never imagine being able to utilize. It is the poor selling to the even poorer. Further on, there is a white city of beds and cupboards and refrigerators and washing machines. There is maybe just a little more hope here, otherwise the area as a whole suffers from a case of bad nerves. It is the most joyless of markets, with nothing to excite one's foraging instincts.

Just before one turns into this avenue of despond, in the middle of a roundabout under perpetual construction, upwards of a hundred people gather to buy and sell pigeons. Men and boys stand pressed close together, holding open plastic feed sacks into which one might peer at the pigeons inside. They are a breed apart from the aforementioned people. The eyes of the sellers of junk maintain a steady gaze, whereas the eyes of the pigeon sellers dart back and forth, suspicion attending their every move. The atmosphere there is at its most furtive because not only are many of the birds stolen but also because the police had been arresting people. Anyone selling pigeons here is of the lowest possible caste. This is the bottom end of the pigeon world. Where emotions are at their most raw, tempers easily explode. Needless to say, a foreigner stood out. Nowhere in Syria, not even in the remotest areas, did people glare at me as they did in that place.

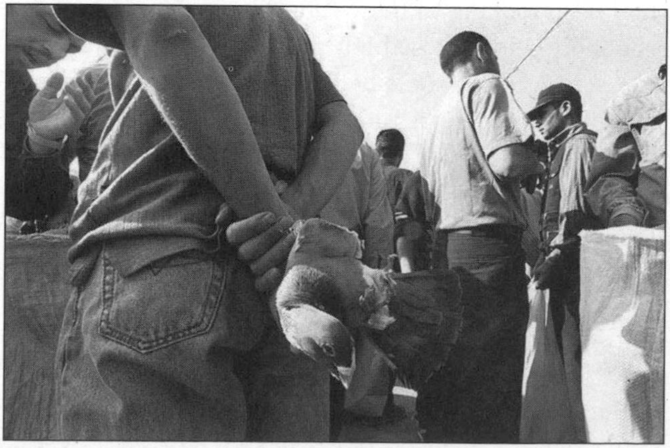

'Where is he from?' a man asked my translator.

'London.'

The man, as tightly wound as a broken clock, eyed me up and down.

'How do I know he is not American?'

There was a look of hate in his face such as I had never encountered in this most hospitable of countries. It was a signal to make our stay as short as possible.

A moment later, there was a cry and people ran in all directions, boys charging through traffic, clutching their swollen bags and making their escape over a wall, the older men running here and there, uniformed men pursuing them. It was as if the crowd itself became a flock of pigeons scattered in all directions. The police arrested one or two people, pushing them into the back of a lorry. After they'd gone, as if from out of nowhere, the crowd reassembled. Clearly there was no shrink's cure for the passion which took over these people's lives. They would continue to fly their birds, flu or no flu. Suddenly, seemingly apropos of nothing, a fist fight broke out between two young men, and it seemed, just then, that what Waseem had said was true. All the problems of the Middle East were concentrated in those two contorted faces.

§

Abed and I visited another pigeon café, which we were politely asked to leave. Actually no, we skedaddled out of there as quickly as possible. Even the pigeons glared at us. A bunch of youths took images of birds on their mobile phones. They spent more time looking at the displays of their phones than they did at the pigeons themselves. Soon the whole world will be at several removes. Our enquiries about al-Sawwāḥ were met with feigned ignorance. Amid hostile laughter and a pressing of bodies, we were given what turned out to be a fake address for another pigeon café. We had only just stepped out onto the street when Abed recognised a figure from his childhood, Samir the Clown, who had once advertised a brand of chewing gum called PARACHUTE. Samir wore a red checked sports jacket, baggy trousers and pointed shoes, an outfit that seemed to be some straight version of a more comical one. Stopping to say hello to him, clearly pleased to meet his childhood hero, Abed spoke of our frustrations and suddenly he turned to me, saying, as he always did, when excited by the workings of chance, 'Are you St George?'

Samir the Clown was of the al-Sawwāḥ family.

It was at such times that Abed shone. There had been signs of improvement in his mental state, although no sooner did I dare to cling to those hopes than they would dissolve, and I'd be left hanging in mid air. Just then, however, he was as vital as when I first knew him, playful, delighted to be in the race. Samir the Clown invited us to his house, and so we leapt, the three of us, into a taxi, stopping, on the way, for sugary cakes. Abed explained my project to him, saying I wanted to get at the truth of the al-Sawwāḥ story. Samir who'd never heard of the case said that his family was a big one, but that the following morning he'd be visiting the head of the family and would ask him. Such matters demanded that permission be given, and, in this respect, daily existence, and, by extension, all family discourse, even in a city as modern as Damascus, was still a tribal one. If I were going to intrude, just once, this would be it. As far as I was concerned, and maybe now I was playing hide-and-seek with my own conscience, al-Sawwāḥ had already put himself beyond the pale. All that was required from Samir the Clown was a full name, one that would lead me to a police or court file.

'Come to see me at three o'clock tomorrow afternoon and I will have results for you. Meanwhile I have another story for you, but first let me tell you your topic is strange, bizarre even. I am looking deeply into your nature and I believe you must have your roots

here because your subject is so completely Arabic in essence. I congratulate you. This is a dangerous subject, but it is an important one.'

When we got to his place, it was as if we had entered a dream, everywhere the props of a clown's trade. Samir introduced Abed and me to his talking parrot, a feathery toy in garish colours, which recorded whatever one said to it and then instantaneously played it back. Such toys are, apparently, widely available, but it was the first time I'd ever seen one.

'I will tell you the story of Aḥmad Sayf,' he said.

I will tell you the story of Aḥmad Sayf, the parrot repeated in a somewhat metallic voice.

Samir borrowed Abed's cigarette, which he dangled from one side of his mouth, and then he picked up the parrot, blew smoke into its face, and began a lengthy mime. Samir groomed the parrot, removing imaginary ticks from it, flattened the feathers again, and, when finished, he kissed it on the beak.

'Aḥmad Sayf was deeply infatuated with pigeons and he spent most of his spare time with them on the roof of the apartment next door. A wicked character, very peevish, he wore a perpetual frown. Aḥmad had dark eyes, straight black hair, and he walked a bully's walk.'

Samir the Clown reproduced Aḥmad's bully's walk.

'All the family walked like this, arrogantly, except, that is, for their father and mother. They were originally Palestinian, but Aḥmad was born here. He was in my class, always sat at the rear, and our teacher was afraid of him. We were all afraid of him. After leaving school, he sold vegetables and dealt in pigeons on the side. I used to watch him. He would talk to his birds as if they were his children and all of them had names.'

Samir the Clown put the toy parrot close to his ear, ostensibly to get the rest of the story from it, listened, gasped, and pulled a sad face.

'One day Aḥmad and one of his friends got into an argument over a pigeon that had flown from his roof. I don't remember the name of the friend. Aḥmad said, "Give me back my bird" and the other man who was really afraid of Aḥmad gave it to him. Aḥmad turned and walked away with his bird and then the other pulled a gun from his jacket and shot him in the back. After three days in intensive care, Aḥmad, aged nineteen, died.'

Samir the Clown laid the parrot to rest and gave back Abed his cigarette.

La commedia è finita!

§

'Would you say honour and revenge come into this?'

'It's good for a man to preserve the honour of his family,' said Samir, 'but I am against crimes committed in its name. There is a woman journalist here who is writing articles on honour killings. She wants to address the laws in our constitution so that they will be made less sympathetic to the men who commit these crimes against women. Our judges tend to give them only short sentences. I will tell you a story. This man was trying to chat up a girl in our neighbourhood. She refused to speak to him, so he became angry with her. Later, he boasted to his friends that he knew this girl and had slept with her, and, as evidence, he said there was a mole on her thigh. Some time before, quite by chance, he had caught sight of this mole when she was walking up some stairs. She was beautiful but very decent and conservative, and here he was bragging, pointing to the existence of a mole. The rumour spread and the girl's brother got wind of it, checked out the mole, and killed her. During the forensic investigation she was discovered to be a virgin. The girl's brother was imprisoned for five years. Those stairs she climbed are steep and ancient ones.'

We then moved on to the matter of adultery, both Abed and Samir reminding me that there is nothing in the Qur'ān to support the stoning of women for adultery. It is specifically written in *sūra* 4:15 that any sexual transgression has to be witnessed by four adult males of proven piety and this does not include circumstantial evidence. Women thus accused are to be confined to the home until death or *until God makes a way for them*, which is to say repentance is possible. In the following verse it says, 'And if they repent and improve, then let them be. Lo! Allāh is Relenting, Merciful.' The Qur'ānic teachings make it practically impossible to bring such a charge in any case. The chances of four people actually witnessing the act of penetration are already remote, if not impossible, add to which it is unlawful to pry into the concealed actions of people. Some commentators go so far as to say that the aforementioned passages are an injunction to people to mind their own business. What is absolutely imperative is that slander be prevented, and even in those cases where the guilty confess their crime, their repentance exonerates them from punishment. A verse in the Qur'ān reminds us that 'man has been created weak' (4:28). The very darkest passage, which may in fact be an abrogation, says that any whosoever brings a charge against an honourable woman be given eighty lashes. The hadiths say otherwise, death by stoning, and between my reading of them and my admittedly weak understanding of the Qur'ān all I can see is an unbridgeable chasm where 'never the twain shall meet.'

'So what are the chances of producing reliable evidence?' Samir continued. 'This is just about impossible, and, in any case, marital betrayals in Damascus are very rare. It happens, of course. A man I know of came home early one day, opened the door to his bedroom and caught his wife with someone else. He was old and ugly and his wife was young and beautiful and here she was, together with a handsome young man, making love. He said nothing to her, but to his wife's lover he said, "I want only one thing from you, a single coin." The young man took a coin from his pocket, gave it to him, and fled. You could say the husband acted wisely. He did not kick his wife out because he had children who needed taking care of. However he took a strange and horrible revenge. Once a day, she never knew when, silently he would take that coin from his pocket and flip it in the air and catch it. With this single gesture, which he made sometimes in front of their children who, of course, were unaware of its meaning, he'd remind her that she was a whore. *Sharmūṭa*. This word is extremely powerful in our culture. This was psychological torture. She stayed with him but was continually reminded of her infidelity, such that she grew thinner and thinner, more and more frail. She would escape to her family sometimes and then return home only for the torture to continue.'

Samir took a coin from his pocket, tossed it in the air, caught it, and slipped it back from where it came. He said he hoped he would be married soon and that this was one of the reasons for his meeting with the head of the al-Sawwāḥ family the following day.

'I was betrayed once.'

Samir stared into some place we could not see.

'A woman called Umm Aḥmad, a *shaykha* who works mostly with djinns visited me. I didn't know her and she didn't know me and certainly she knew nothing of the girl with whom I was in love. She mentioned the colour of the door to my girlfriend's house. She told me the date of her birth too. She then told me my beloved was mocking me, and that she was in love with someone else. She was betraying me with another man and there was even sex between them. I will never speak her name. Only Allāh and I know it. I shivered when Umm Aḥmad told me this. Another time I took her to see a woman called Umm Khālid. Now Umm Khālid had two daughters, one of whom was called Rābi'a. I wanted to marry her, even though I knew she was a divorced woman. When we got there, Rābi'a entered the room. Her mother asked her whether I should be asked to leave. No, she said, I could stay. The *shaykha* Umm Aḥmad asked her, "How many times have you been divorced?" It was then I discovered she'd been divorced three times. Three times! I presumed she was deflowered, of course, but Umm Aḥmad, by means of djinns, knew the truth, which was that she had indeed been married to three men but that none of them had been able to consummate his marriage with her. There was not one among them who could so much as open her legs. She was still a virgin. This, Umm Aḥmad said, was because Rābi'a was already married to a male djinn who was jealous and would not allow her to have sex with any of the three husbands.'

Samir stopped as if interrupted by something invisible.

'I can see from your face that you are not convinced by what I say.'

Surely, though, I had kept well hidden the doubt that was in me.

'It is not that I don't believe you,' I replied, 'but before one accepts the fact of their power doesn't it require one having to believe in djinns in the first place? I am trying to close a gap in my mind. Will you help me?'

'Djinns exist. I am an educated person. There are plenty of djinns in Morocco. There is a house in this neighbourhood that is haunted by them. It's always up for sale. Every time somebody buys it he gets roughed up at night by the djinns who live there. They exist, believe me. Even our government acknowledges their existence. Rābi'a and her mother belong to the upper class. They are educated. They are not primitive people. Rābi'a's mother said to me, "Where did you bring Umm Aḥmad from? How could she possibly know my daughter was married three times? Nobody knows this." Umm Aḥmad said, "I will help you get rid of this djinn so you will be free to marry again." At that point Rābi'a kneeled down and kissed the feet of Umm Aḥmad, this *shaykha* who was now going to rescue her. I was present at the expelling of the djinn from Rābi'a's body although the djinn is visible only to the person who has it. After one week Umm Aḥmad managed to expel it. At one point Rābi'a's mother, Umm Khālid, came into the room. Umm Aḥmad said to her, "Yesterday your husband was stretching his legs towards the stove and said, 'A camel could enter through the door.'" This is a saying we have here. Somehow Umm Aḥmad knew this. She is truthful person. She spoke to us of things known only by God.'

'So it first requires a belief in djinns?'

'Clearly you do not believe me.'

'We are not discrediting you,' interjected Abed, explaining that he too had seen djinns. 'I used to enter isolation, hunger and prayer and I'd see them then. We accept entirely what you are saying.'

I tried to turn the subject back to pigeons.

'Do you see ways in which the pigeon wars are reflected in Damascene life?'

Samir who some minutes before had ceased to be a clown darkened.

'They do not reflect our society. We do not consider them a part of our heritage. The Damascenes are a noble, generous and faithful people, honourable, and they are jealous of their land and wives. When the French were here all our people were like a single heart behind our leader. My ancestor was one of these heroes. There is a street here named after him.'

There was a sudden and rising panic in Samir's voice.

'I am 100% positive that of all those who joined the great Arabic revolution not one of them was a pigeon man. Anyone who says otherwise is wrong. If you write this in your book, it will be rejected by the audience. I am talking facts here. I respected Hafez al-Asad. I looked upon him as a father to me. I remember the October War when we emerged victorious, when we got back part of the Golan Heights. We have been treated unjustly by the Western media, which is controlled by international Zionism and the Jewish lobby. They spend millions, those people.'

I stared at the parrot lying on its side, thinking maybe a djinn was to blame for the deterioration between Samir and myself. It was by no means certain he'd be willing to speak to me again, although when Abed and I left he did say we would meet the following day. I couldn't sleep that night for thinking about the story of the coin. Here, surely, was a tale worthy of Edgar Allan Poe. She would die, yes, presumably from starvation, and what then? Would the husband have sent back the coin to her lover, thereby making the murder weapon his? Or maybe, more appropriately, it would be Scheherazade's final, hitherto unknown, tale whose inclusion would have altered by one the most numerically famous of all titles.

Abed did not turn up.

I phoned twice and his mother said there was nothing she could do to raise him and that he had only gone to bed that morning. All night he had been pacing the floor. She was worried for him. My head swam. I had come as close as I'd ever come to penetrating al-Sawwāḥ's world, and now, at this most critical juncture, Abed had failed me. Samir the Clown was waiting for us. I had just lost the best story I was likely to have. When I saw Abed again, I could barely contain my rage.

'What kind of game do you suppose Samir thinks we are playing at?'

'Who said anything about games?'

'Well, we didn't show up when we said we would.'

Abed hedged a little, and then told me the truth.

'Samir phoned me late last night, saying he had been warned not to speak to us.'

'Why didn't you tell me?'

'I didn't know what to say.'

'So rather than tell me, you left me stranded!'

Then I saw something I hadn't seen before in Abed's face. There was a good reason why he didn't go to bed until morning. He was frightened. I knew then I'd dragged him into a place he'd rather not go, and so, right there and then, I decided this part of our relationship had come to an end. I would ask no more favours of him. I had no right to compromise him. We could go back to being simply friends again. We could go back to discussing the problems of oxygen intake.

'Who warned him?'

I already knew the answer, of course.

'The head of the al-Sawwāḥ family.'

§

Best not to say who took me to see the Father of Skulls because the Father of Skulls could well taint the reputation of any who dares to associate with him, although it has to be said of the people in whose company I found him they did not appear to be overly solicitous of their respective futures, and they were, some of them, by their own admission, in positions of legitimate power, which to say they had some distance to fall, or rather this would be the case were they not of a world in which the laws of gravity could be defied with the wink of an eye. The people among whom the Father of Skulls was most free to move were the very people who could put a stop to his being able to move at all. Clearly he was a protected species. A man of humble origins, the Father of Skulls could stride through the corridors of the elite perfectly visible. As to what enabled him to do so, the answer is sheer nerve or maybe an element of panache. Sweetness attends the rotting apple, and quite honestly I found him sweet, which is not to say his behaviour was excusable. There's something in all of us that inclines towards a reprobate. Obviously there was much he would not tell me, and already I could hear the ellipses in his voice, which he filled with grins that induced titters from his mainly female audience. Working against those silences, however, was a scoundrel's desire to tell an airy tale. Only rarely is the hoodlum a creature of darkness because more than anything he wants to be clothed in powerful light. The sun's not bright enough for him. It needs to be tungsten at least and the shadow he throws as sharply defined as a Samarqand blade. A thug loves hyperbole. If I felt perfectly safe in his company, it was because he struck me as one who observed a code.

A robber would not rob me in his own house.

When later I mentioned him to a couple of people they gasped, saying I had just been in the company of one of the most dangerous figures in Damascus. The streets were full of stories of his gangland activities, and the most recent was of how one of his associates had shot a man in broad daylight, in front of dozens of witnesses, and then calmly got back into an unmarked Mercedes. I did not know any of this, of course, when I met him surrounded by friends and family, among them his fiancée. She would make a perfect crook's wife although her presence, it was explained to me, was a signal that the Father of Skulls was about to mend his ways and settle down into the domesticity of which he had been deprived for most of his life. And it was true, there was a bit of glow about him, such as one finds in converts to a new faith, and several times he told me he was going straight, which probably was one time too many to be able to fully believe. What was surprising was the candour with which he told his stories and, even more so, the delight his fiancée took in them. She clapped her hands at his most outrageous admissions. She had her girlfriends to support her, a squealing chorus of décolleté banshees. They were so incredibly *modern*. Would she who cheered him on now prevent him later from committing acts that would supply him with material for yet more stories of derring-do? Would pushing a pram curb her appetite for further criminal follies? It could be, of course, she was far more subtle and knew precisely where her power lay and that with a good ear one could diffuse even the most dangerous bomb. The Father of Skulls, meanwhile, was not at all pleased with the attention she lavished on me, and my interpreter nudged me, describing him as an extremely jealous man.

After a few minutes, the Father of Skulls relented and said he'd forgiven me, although for what I didn't know because I had in no way encouraged, or responded to, the flirtatious remarks of the woman who kept pouring me powerful coffee. This, too, was highly unusual behaviour in a society where one hardly ever saw the women of the house and where pouring tea or coffee was a man's prerogative. These people were bad enough to be Christians. Any real flirtation, one may presume, was between fiancé and fiancée. She fed his jealousy in ways that would soon enough find their resolution in the bedroom. She would either be strangled or made to climb a gaudily painted vine. This was not a fanciful image. I had caught an earlier glimpse of some such artwork, which went well with the artificial flora. The Father of Skulls announced he was pleased to invite me to come to his wedding on the fifteenth of the following month, to which I said I would be equally pleased if he came to mine on the fourteenth and when he asked who the happy woman was, I nodded in the direction of his fiancée. This broke the ice although equally it might have broken my nose. All applauded, fiancé and fiancée included, and it was then that he agreed to tell me his story or as much of it as was allowable. The Father of Skulls would provide me with no more than the bare bones of his existence.

'Why are you called "the Father of Skulls"?'

'It goes back to when I was eleven and my cousin was studying medicine. One day I overheard him talking to someone else. He was in terrible despair. At the university they told him that he required a human skull in order to pursue his studies. I wanted to do him a favour so later that night, at two in the morning, I went to the Christian cemetery in my town. There was a strong door to the tomb but I broke it, went down some steps where there were layers of coffins. There are still Christians in Syria who do not bury their dead but place them in sarcophagi. I took from one of the drawers a skull and two bones, a thigh and breastbone. When I came out I found myself face to face with two policemen. "So what have you got there?" they said. When they opened my bag they found inside it the skull and two bones. I was taken to the police station. A neighbour of mine happened to be out in the street and accompanied us. I was put into jail. My neighbour said to the police, "I can guarantee he is a good boy, so please set him free, and we will return the skull and bones to their rightful place." I was in prison for three days and they handed over to the judge the skull and bones which were then returned to the grave and I was freed. From that moment on I was called "the Father of Skulls". This story made me famous at a young age.'

'So is that how your life in crime begin?'

My translator said he would rephrase my question, asking instead how it was that his life of *problems* began. Crime, he said, was too indelicate a word, and, besides, he was getting married soon and would be going legitimate.

'As I said, I began to be famous. I'll skip a few years. I started up a phoney company in Romania. My name spread to Interpol who wanted me. In Romania you can take any small shop and call it a company. If you want to create an export/import company you need a specific amount of capital in Syria, real estate, to demonstrate you are a businessman working there. Some of my friends said, "Why don't we form a company?" We worked for only six months under my name. In the fifth month we discovered we would have to pay taxes in Romania. I had never been to Romania, but my friends took my passport and had it stamped to make it look as though I'd been there. Fifteen days later, my friends sold the company to some Iraqis and the company was now put in their name, which meant the Iraqis would be stuck with having to pay the taxes, $25,000 except it didn't quite work that way. They tried to come after me. Later, I really did have to go to Romania but because I couldn't go on my own passport I altered one letter in my name. I stayed for three days in Romania and then they got wind of who I really was. I escaped, by illegal means, through the port. When I got back to Syria because of Interpol my name was already registered with the police. I admit my debt to the Romanian government is $25,000. I do not deny this.'

'You say you were in export/import. What were you dealing in?'

'Chocolates and biscuits.'

'That seems innocent enough.'

The Father of Skulls' fiancée shrieked with laughter.

'Well, not exactly biscuits!'

'Ah, were these *Russian* biscuits then?'

'Okay, then, we'll say biscuits and chocolates, but God knows what was inside them. Something white, apparently. You get what

I mean. You don't have to tell anyone my real name because you don't know my real name.'

The Father of Skulls entered a thoughtful silence.

'Do your stories end there?'

'I've already given you ten years!'

'Ten years?'

'That's what my sentence would be for what I've already told you. I am about to get married and those who are about to get married need money so maybe you'd like to pay me 1000 lira for each story. My stories would fill five books.'

Apparently the Father of Skulls was not going to reveal any more. I thought maybe it was best to return him to somewhere closer to the age of innocence.

'Were you a bit of a wild youth after you stole the skull?'

'I was a smuggler. I smuggled tobacco. I considered smuggling a normal job. Everyone did it here. I no longer have problems.'

The Father of Skulls then told me the story closest to his heart.

'I used to have a dog, Marjan was his name. Marjan used to help me in my smuggling activities. I had this friend and we went hunting together. By mistake I shot my friend in the foot. I took him to the hospital and Marjan ran back to my house. When my brother saw the dog coming alone, he knew immediately I was in trouble. The dog led my brother to the scene of the accident, blood everywhere. There was a farmer there. My brother asked him what happened and was told the whole story. My friend spent forty-five days in hospital and my dog stayed with him there the whole time. At night he slept under my friend's bed. He never left him. So this is the story of Marjan. That dog was with me for sixteen years. When it got old and sick I left him with another friend who lived some distance from my house, 22 kilometres. Marjan stayed three days with him and on the fourth day he came back to the front door of my house and . . . dropped down and died there. I used to take him to the seaside and he would watch me from the shore and if I pretended to be drowning he would raise the alarm.'

The Father of Skulls wiped away a tear from his eye.

Chapter Sixteen

Three Sultans

A Short History of Pigeons in the Islamic World (5)

There were three sultans once. Brothers, they were bound together by the charms of a woman 'black of obsidian blackness (*ḥālikat al-sawād)*, beautiful of voice and faultless at song', an Abyssinian songstress who was also their father's favourite concubine. Ittifāq, whose name means, appropriately enough, 'concord', has been memorably described by Robert Irwin as 'the Lola Montez of her age'. Al-Nāṣir Muḥammad, the longest-reigning of the Turkish or Baḥri Mamlūks in Egypt, had a penchant for women of mixed blood (*muwalladāt*) and of his many slave-girls 1,200 of them fitted his colour scheme and of these 505 were singers. Al-Nāṣir had a special palace built for them, al-Sab' Qā'āt, which is to say he kept his many other women elsewhere. There was also a special government agency, the Bureau of Songsters, where Ittifāq's name was registered. It says something for her, and her voice, that she was able to rise swiftly to first position in the harem and it says even more that after al-Nāṣir Muḥammad's death in 1341, she became wife to three of his sons in order of their succession. The three brothers seemed to have genuinely adored her. The sexual knot binding them was rather tighter, though, than their grip on the sultanate. After the firm rule of the father, the power of the sons began quickly to wane. And if historically the keeping of pigeons may be said to be emblematic of moral decline, especially with those whose responsibilities lay elsewhere, and if sometimes, though not always, obsession is a form of emasculation, then two of the aforementioned sultans squandered power in favour of what flies up in the air and returns home.

First, though, we should set the scene a little.

The Mamlūk rulers while often dysfunctional in themselves did much to beautify the city which they simultaneously drained for their own pleasures. Similar attention was paid to commerce and agriculture. Ibn Baṭṭūṭa who visited Cairo in 1325 could barely contain his enthusiasm for 'the mother of cities' whose multitude of buildings were peerless in beauty and splendour and whose teeming populace comprised 'the learned and the ignorant, the grave and the gay, the mild and the choleric, the noble and the base, the obscure and the illustrious. Like the waves of the sea she surges with her throngs of folk, yet for all the capacity of her state and her power to sustain can scarce hold their number. [...] Its children are angels, and its doe-eyed girls are houris.'

The angels seem not to have included among their number al-Nāṣir Muḥammad's sons, twelve of whom became sultans. Between them they managed to tear a hole in the fabric of Baḥri Mamlūk rule. Al-Nāṣir was not deluded when on his deathbed he said, 'O amirs, I have fifteen sons. How will one of them maintain his rule?' The first three sultans were shadowy figures whose rapid ascendancy and even more rapid downfall are too complex to relate for the purpose of this brief narrative. The first of them, *not* his father's choice as successor, was the ghastly Abu Bakr who as soon as he took power had his father's chancellor nailed down on a camel's back and paraded through the streets before being forced to watch his own children slaughtered. After a few months, the amirs deposed him. Then came Kulcuk, a child of six. After a reign of six months he was replaced by al-Nāṣir Muḥammad's elder son, Aḥmad who, while adopting his father's name, was too feeble-minded to don his mantle; he occupied the sultanate for a mere two months and twelve days. As far as we know he had no connection with Ittifāq, and indeed the rumourmongers of the time suggested his sexual interests lay elsewhere.

Pigeons were Aḥmad's undoing at an early age. A serious deficiency of character in him was revealed by a eunuch whose pigeon beat his in a race. The eunuch made the mistake of holding a banquet to which he invited all the other palace eunuchs to celebrate, which so irked Aḥmad that he had the victor beaten almost to death. When, in 742/1342, he became sultan, and was already well on the path to insanity, swapping Africa for Asia he absconded to the castle of Kerak in Palestine, taking with him his flock of pigeons and the royal treasure. The amirs wrote to him insisting that he return to Cairo to resume his duties, and when he refused, after another historical tangle best not gone into, the sultanate fell to the fourth of al-Nāṣir Muḥammad's sons, the seventeen-year-old al-Ṣāliḥ Ismā'il who might have been a decent ruler had he not been of such a sickly disposition and otherwise engaged. He is the first of the three sultans who shall concern us here.

A gentle figure, when the severed head of his truant brother Aḥmad was brought to him from Kerak, al-Ṣāliḥ Ismā'il trembled and became deathly pale and entered a spell of insomnia from which he was never to emerge. His one comfort was Ittifāq whom he'd married in secret. She played the oud for him and as best she could calmed his shattered nerves. Alone of all his brothers, al-Ṣāliḥ Ismā'il was a pious figure who nevertheless had extravagant tastes, such that the annual budget deficit stood at 30 million dirhams, which was double the actual revenue. The treasury was plundered in order that he might ply Ittifāq with expensive presents, although it has to be said he also spent lavishly on the rest of his 200 concubines, especially with respect to their clothes. Cairo fashion was set by what they wore. In his invaluable record of Mamlūk rule, *Kitāb al-Sulūk*, al-Maqrīzī writes:

> [Al-Ṣāliḥ Ismā'il] was infatuated with the black slave-girls and he was excessively in love with Ittifâq . . . He fostered all kinds of entertainers, and he discarded his duties as a ruler by his preoccupation with women and singers. The preoccupation reached such a degree, that when he made his seasonal rides to Siryāqus or the Pyramids, his mother, together with another 200 women, would accompany him riding *akādīsh* horses, and wearing coloured satin dresses and *ṭarṭūr* headgear of Bulgarian leather, inlaid with gems and pearls, and accompanied by eunuchs from the Citadel to the promenading area. The Sultan's favourite concubines used to ride Arab horses, racing against each other, playing polo and wearing silk *kāmiliyya* overcoats. In

festivals, feats and other occasions of pleasure rides and entertainments these concubines made things which can not be told.

The telling of them has preoccupied the minds of pornographers ever since. That the concubines often fared better than the wives is, of course, nothing new, but the military aristocracy was less than happy to breathe the atmosphere of effeminacy that began with al-Nāṣir Muḥammad and which the sons turned from a breeze to a gale.

After a reign of three years, al-Ṣāliḥ Ismā'il died in July 1345 and power went to his younger brother, al-Kāmil Sha'bān, aged seventeen. The amirs agreed to this accession of power on condition that Sha'bān relinquish certain pleasures, among them the keeping of pigeons. No sooner did he come to the throne – on which day he married Ittifāq, on account of 'what he had felt for her since his brother's time' – than he broke his many promises, which included the banning of pigeon games. Cairo was rife with them. A youth of extreme cruelty, indolence and debauchery, he was sufficiently self-aware to be able to say of himself, 'My name is Thu'bān [snake] not Sha'bān!' We have a rare picture of him, a contemporary describing him as fair-haired, blue-eyed, large-nosed and with a pockmarked face. Sha'bān accused his younger brother Ḥājjī of conspiracy and had him confined to a room in the Duhaysa Palace. According to the writer, Glubb Pasha, 'these were scarcely more than nursery squabbles, partly due to the fact that the various sons had different mothers.' Sha'bān was generous to Ittifāq who bore him a son, and built for her, during her confinement, a palace whose furnishings alone cost 95,000 dinars. Openly he gave her properties that he had seized from their owners. According al-Maqrīzī, Ittifāq had forty gowns inlaid with jewels, another sixteen with silk hems embroidered with silver and gold, and eighty veils, each worth between 5,000 and 20,000 dirhams. Such extravagance proved too much for the amirs who then released Sha'bān's younger brother Ḥājjī from his prison and within the hour had Sha'bān incarcerated in the same room. Quite literally, the breakfast that had been set for one sultan was eaten by the next. Three days later, Sha'bān was strangled.

On his accession to the sultanate, in 746/1346, Ḥājjī took on the name of al-Muz'affar which means 'victorious', a name not a little ironic in the circumstances. Victory, if it was ever his, came only in feathered shapes. Whatever faults his predecessors had, in him they were greatly magnified. Robert Irwin writes of his ascension to power that 'he was 14 years old and fond of polo, torture and playing with pigeons.' Ittifāq was returned to the citadel, with her many dresses, and there became al-Muz'affar Ḥājjī's wife as well. She seemed able to move along the links of the sultanic chain without the retarding inconvenience of sorrow. According to al-Maqrīzī, 'she took possession of his heart'. While not wishing to underestimate her abilities, it has to be said she was not, as al-Maqrīzī writes, 'his sole occupation'. Pigeons were at the very least equal to her amatory and musical gifts.

At a time when Egypt was suffering from drought, starvation and pestilence, al-Muz'affar Ḥājjī spent his money, or rather the treasury's, on lowlife figures (*awbāsh*) – singers, prostitutes, musicians, jugglers, wrestlers and pigeon fanciers – often literally throwing riches at them. He ordered that pigeon games be allowed in Cairo and Fusṭāṭ and sometimes, to the disgust of the Mamlūks who watched their elite society and the rules that kept it together disintegrate, he went so far as to wear the dress of commoners. This mingling with the lower orders was considered by the Mamlūks to be a disgrace, and the raising of slave-girls and eunuchs to positions of power exceeding their own was yet another symptom of decadence. Once, during Ramadan, al-Muz'affar Ḥājjī scattered 30,000 dinars, 300,000 dirhams and 80,000 dinars' worth of jewellery and fine embroideries. When a group of amirs came to him, complaining of his excesses, as a warning to them al-Muz'affar Ḥājjī took some pigeons and slaughtered them in front of their eyes, saying they could expect the same. Clearly he had not learned from the examples of his disposed brothers. What they should have learned from their father was that the amirs needed to be flattered and rewarded but not to such a degree as to close the distance between sultan and subject. Already during al-Nāṣir Muḥammad's time the Mamlūks were growing out of their breeches. There is a record of them skipping military duties to go boating on the Nile. One day, while in his harem, which is when nobody sane would dare disturb a sultan's peace, fifteen hundred Mamlūks gathered at the palace gates to protest about a delay in their wages. They were, to begin with, an aristocracy of white slaves. Slave rule was fast becoming people rule. Mamlūks were even known to sell their loyalty to the highest bidders. Al-Nāṣir Muḥammad's sons were to suffer the consequences.

What was probably al-Muz'affar Ḥājjī's undoing was the construction, on the pavilion of his Duhaysa Palace, of a magnificent dovecote, estimated by some to be worth the extraordinary figure of 7,000 dirhams. It was said to have been exquisitely carved and decorated with ivory and ebony inlay. The pigeons themselves were adorned with gold necklaces and anklets and a great number of people were employed to look after them. Allāh Himself was relegated to second place. Al-Muz'affar Ḥājjī ordered the muezzins to lower their voices when calling the people to prayer so as not to disturb the birds in their flight. The fact they did so once was enough to arouse his ire. Clearly his passion for pigeons had all but destroyed any moral distance between himself and the populace. Finally, after repeated warnings from a couple of his familiars, brave figures indeed, al-Muz'affar Ḥājjī had the magnificent dovecote destroyed and he bled his pigeons with his own hand. It was too late, however, to escape the wrath of the amirs. Too many times he had gone beyond the pale. Only recently he had confiscated the treasure of one of his amirs and had divided it among his favourites, a rash act that provoked a couple of his own Mamlūks to warn him of the consequences. Enraged by their impudence, he set about to kill the Mamlūks who then escaped and stirred the amirs to rebellion.

There are several versions of al-Muz'affar Ḥājjī's death. The historian al-Ṣafadī relates that an amir caught al-Muz'affar at it again, playing with pigeons, just when it was thought he had freed himself of his addiction to them. The amir seized and slit the throats of two birds and al-Muz'affar was so enraged he threatened to do the same to him. It is here that the chroniclers diverge. Al-Ṣafadī says that the amir, realising what was in store for him, acted first and killed the sultan. Others say that when al-Muz'affar threatened to have the amir executed in public fellow amirs came to the rescue and took the sultan to a mausoleum in the City of the Dead where he was suffocated. It is an interesting case of a man being escorted live to his own grave. Another version has it that a group of amirs, enraged by al-Muz'affar's avian activities, struck the horse which bore him, and then pounced upon him, strangling him to death. Whatever the circumstances, al-Ṣafadī wrote of al-Muz'affar Ḥājjī who had barely made it beyond his twentieth birthday: 'He lost his soul and his kingdom for the pigeons.' He was the last Mamlūk sultan to abandon himself to pigeon games. After his death, the amirs forced the many favourites of the sultan, even his slave-girls, to return the presents he had given them. Ittifāq was thrown out of the palace with only the dress she wore. She left behind her tiara which all three sultans had inlaid with precious stones with a combined value of 100,000 dinars. Quite wisely, after finding that al-Muz'affar had emptied the treasury, the amirs decided that henceforth no sultan would ever again have control of that particular domain. The money they managed to recoup from various sources was enough to restore the public treasury to reasonable health but not before they tortured to death al-Muz'affar's jester, a hunchback called 'Ali al-Kasīḥ, who was slow to surrender the monies given him. Doubtless they also had unhappy memories of his sharp tongue.

A fluttering of wings accompanies the sultans' demises.

All three were teenagers when they came to power and behaved as teenagers often do, with not much of a view to the immediate future. All but one of the twelve sons was removed by the amirs. An early death spared al-Ṣāliḥ Ismā'il.

What happened, though, to Ittifāq? She made her escape, and such was her star, a burning phosphorescent white, that she managed even to avoid the Black Death that followed soon after, from 1348 to 1349, and which claimed almost a million lives. Ibn Baṭṭūṭa had said of Cairo that 'the star of her horoscope does not move from the mansion of fortune.' Compare the scene a few years later: 'It was then that an epidemic of plague exploded such as was never before seen in the Islamic era,' writes al-Maqrīzī, 'which encompassed not just the human species but also the fish in the sea, the birds in the sky, and the animals in the field. Cairo became an empty desert, and there was no one to be seen in the streets.' After the deaths of her sultans one, two and three Ittifāq married a Mamlūk vizier, Hibāt Allāh, and when he died, lucky girl, she cooed her way into the arms of a Moroccan sultan.

Chapter Seventeen

A Turkmen Cloth

Always Yasser has something with which to torment me, some nomadic textile whose purchase would leave me broke, but this last which he pulled from his wooden chest of treasures was most definitely not for sale. Certain things should never be sold in the first place. Commerce defiles them. There's a certain physical routine that one observes in the souqs of the Middle East, which requires of a dealer that he take a carpet or kilim or textile, and, simultaneously bowing a little and shuffling backwards two or three steps, as if in abeyance to the superior qualities of whatever it is he has on offer, then let gravity take care of the rest, so that the piece floats downwards, in a single geometric plane, onto the floor, sometimes hovering in mid air for a split second or two, its brief suspension making for a kind of mystique, and it is in that very instant the potential buyer, whether he realises it or not, is seduced, and, if he is not, which any dealer of experience will be able to register from a bored twitching of the nose or a stifled yawn or an inertness about the eyes, then another piece will land on top of that one and so forth until there is a small plateau of woven treasures. This layering technique has the curious effect of making a buyer feel the seller is being put to considerable effort, which is not really the case because the subsequent folding and putting away of pieces falls to the dealer's assistant who probably learns more about them from this exercise than from any other chore he does. This aftermath also defines exactly the relationship between master and servant and so helps preserve the traditions which Yasser, although he is keen to change them, adheres to nevertheless. It was in one such session, in another shop, I was given one of the very best lessons I've ever had on the subject of carpets. The dealer, who had thrown down an ornate Persian rug, watched me, and then, with something approaching disgust, whipped it away, saying, 'I can see you're not interested.' It was true, although I rather wished, just then, it weren't: I do not like my brain being too easily read. When I asked him how he knew this, he replied, 'It was because you were looking *at* the carpet, when really you ought to have been looking *through* it.' I knew then that my taste ran not towards urban ornate but towards nomadic simple. So does Yasser's, so aesthetically we are of the same weave. Today's exercise had quite a different purpose. Yasser spread out for me, one after another, the textiles that comprise his private collection. It is something he does only occasionally, perhaps more in order to surprise himself than others, but, whatever his reasons, to be party to this is a privilege, as if one has been granted admittance to a secret fraternity with its own hidden language.

Yasser has scant regard for the products of his own country unless they are so obscure as to be almost not of it. Among the exceptions he showed me was a rug whose pattern was a thing of stops and starts, as if some tempest in the mind of its maker had levelled any straight line that stood in its path, a force against which not even the most deeply-rooted tradition stood a chance. It was made by a girl who was simple, that is, she was of a certain mental age. For Yasser who saw in this the holiness of a thing made, which came direct, as it were, from the unfathomable mind of one whom a kindly world would describe as having 'learning difficulties', the rug was endowed with special significance. Would he have felt as tenderly towards it had he not been aware of its history? Probably not, but that's neither here nor there. The point is he knew its provenance, and the intrinsic value of things is set not only by superior knowledge but also by the imaginative sympathies with which one invests them. Otherwise it was pointless showing Yasser local textiles, my recent purchase, for example, of an old Damascene silk shawl whose fleshy pinks shot through with silver threads grabbed whole fistfuls of Syrian sunlight.

'One does not hear the flute playing in one's own garden,' he said.

Any music, for him, required distance.

What he set out for me that day was a symphony of colours and weaves. Adham, Yasser's assistant, when he saw this, shook his head, fearful that his boss was about to make a mistake and sell something from his own private horde. Adham, so serious and so loyal, needn't have worried. This journey we were about to make had nothing to do with commerce. The distance we would cover, some thousands of miles, when translated into fabric covered only a few square feet of floor space. If I journey through people, Yasser journeys through textiles. The avenues we would explore all fed into a main thoroughfare of centuries of tradition, its artefacts planned in the blood almost, and so we made our way, alighting here and there, marvelling at tent-bands, horse-covers, soumaks, Baluch salt-bags (*namakdān*), meal cloths (*soffreh*) saddle-bags (*hōrjīn*) and kilims – no carpets, though, *never, never* – and then we switched routes from the fruits of the loom to the products of a dexterous hand and sharp eye, and ogled Turkmen tobacco pouches, Uzbek *suzanis*, appliqués, Dagestani embroidered mirror and vanity bags, wristbands and puttees, Qur'ān bags (*shanṭa*) and, as proof of a bride's virtue, an embroidered Turkmen square stained with virginal blood, so old the young lovers who lay upon it were already in their graves.

We spoke with respect to the truth of these things or what Yasser describes as their *honesty*, which usually meant that the people who made them did so not for commerce but for themselves, and then, just when it seemed we were fully satiated, we arrived at the item which reduced us both to silence, a sturdily woven textile of approximately six feet in length, tapered, diamond-patterned, and with a curious split of roughly a foot in length down the middle at the narrow end, which served no obvious purpose.

Yasser told me its story, unfolding the details one by one.

'I'd never seen one before and so I had no idea what it was. At first I wondered if it was a piece of tent-band but its tapered shape made no sense. Tent-bands need to be straight, obviously. "Forget the design," our boss used to say, when presenting us with something we'd never seen before. "Where do you *think* this comes from? What does it *feel* like to you?" Once you begin to think along these lines, then you're in business. Only then do you go into the details. As I said, it couldn't possibly be a tent-band and if you look at the wide end the diamond pattern is suddenly interrupted just where you'd expect it to be complete. It has been cut there, whereas

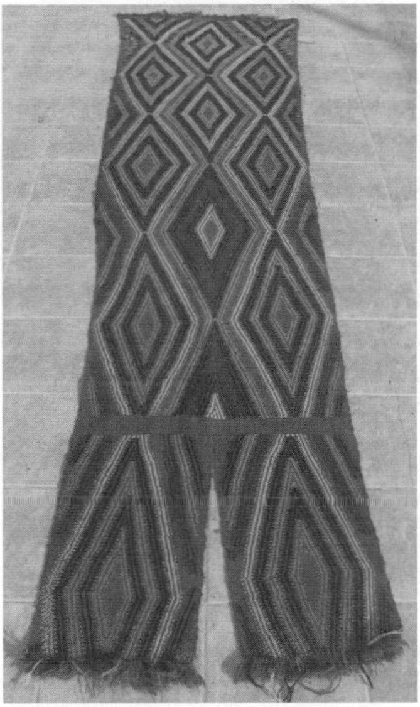

at the narrower end it is properly finished, with a kind of skirt. The weaving technique is called *zili*, one of the more common overlay brocades. The whole surface is covered with these slightly protruding lines which give the *zili* its distinctive look. The soul of the piece is Turkmen. This much is absolutely clear. But what could it have been used for? The man who sold it to me bought it from an old woman in one of the Turkmen villages. I said to him, "Ask the woman from whom you got this what its purpose is." "This will cost me," he replied. "She lives in a remote place." I told him I'd pay for his journey. Six months later, he returned with the answer.'

Yasser introduced a dramatic pause.

'It is a Turkmen coffin cover. Anytime someone died in the village it would be called for and placed over the coffin which was then carried to the cemetery. So this cloth was made for a specific purpose, to be used over and over, and its length is that of an average coffin, the whole of it woven to a coffin's dimensions, which explains the tapered effect. At the fold, where the split at the narrow end begins, those two strands symbolise the legs of the dead person. One could take this metaphysic a step further and say that where the pattern at the head of the cloth is suddenly broken is where life itself stops. One might say the soul is represented by the diamonds, and yes, one could simplify things and stop there, but really it is even more complicated than that. You must consider the combination of the wool, its colour scheme and the historical background. There is, without a doubt, an abstract language in this piece. Something is happening near the head, these small designs like flies, which are not repeated anywhere else. Symbolism? Well, yes and no. Symbolism works unconsciously on us sometimes. And what are we to make of this darker diamond? Why is it not exactly at the centre, but just down a little, where one's sex is? And if this were meant to cover a woman, this is where her womb would be. It seems obvious why the diamond is there, but to say it was positioned intentionally is maybe to push things a little. Also there is something in the abstraction of the pattern, its shifting planes, which makes you feel you are falling to one side or the other. When you stare at it, the perspective shifts this way and that. That makes symbolic sense too. If you fall to the right it is towards heaven and if towards the left then towards hell. Each of us has two angels, one on the right shoulder, Raqīb, and the other on the left, 'Atīd. *Raqīb* notes all the right things we've done in our lives and 'Atīd all the wrong ones. On the Day of Judgement we will be presented with the Book, in which all has been recorded by these angel scribes. If the Book is given with the right hand we will meet our friends and find eternal happiness, but if it is with the left hand then we will go to hell. The history of this piece is what makes it so powerful and what gives it its *baraka,* although *baraka* is also derived from the souls of those whom the cloth covered, and the rituals which attend the preparation of the corpse, the washing of the body, and the reading throughout of Qur'ānic scripture.'

I asked Yasser if he were sure the dark diamond was where he said it should be. It struck me as being maybe just a little far to one end. Without further ado he lay down on the coffin cover, his body enclosed by its trapezoid dimensions, and what he said was mathematically, sexually true. Yasser seemed perfectly comfortable there, a Turkmen in his Turkmen heaven.

There's got to be more, always. A story such as this can never end in just one place. If one does not go deeply into this, one goes nowhere. *Baraka,* Yasser said. The Turkmen cloth had *baraka* in abundance. The strict translation of the word is 'blessing' although the word that best captures it, in English, is 'holiness', so when we say something has *baraka* we say it is invested with holiness. If we speak of a human being having *baraka* what we mean is that somebody is close to sainthood, such that even his saliva is thick with it, and indeed there are stories, none too sweet to contemplate, of holy figures spitting their *baraka* into other people's mouths. The place where a saint lived may be said to be possessed of his *baraka*, and the same will be true of his grave. There is nothing here to puzzle anyone, whatever his religious tradition. The secular world, too, pays fantastic prices for what it imagines are the magical properties contained in a celebrity's discarded clothes. Where is *baraka*, though, in the thing itself or in the imagination of one who beholds it? Can an object that comes with no history of any kind be said to have *baraka*? Maybe one needs to be sufficiently deluded to be able to partake of something true.

What, though, of the metaphysic of which Yasser spoke?

When one reads about textiles, and invariably the books are written by people with a deep love for their subject, only rarely do the words extend beyond matters of technique. It is as if what matters most is form and not what that form is meant to convey. There is in this a hint of decadence even. It may be, of course, that any such discussion inevitably brings one up against the bulwark of the inexpressible. We enter an uncertain zone where junk takes over, and the mind goes all milky with moonshine, and spirituality becomes the most suspect word in the dictionary. Can one speak of Islamic art, however, without reference to the beliefs underlying it? When we speak of the unifying principle that informs the making of a beautiful mosque, we may, if we wish to follow this through to its source, apply that same principle to the pattern in a finely woven cloth. There is homogeneity in Islamic art that perhaps is found nowhere else, which, in its products both great and small, is rooted in a common artistic and spiritual universe. Islam, certainly in its early phases, can be said to have been the custodian of the idea of sacred geometry, which came down through Pythagoras, and prior to him, the Egyptians. Sacred geometry, often referred to as 'the language of God', is the observing in all things the vestiges of the Almighty or what we might prefer to call the primordial truths relating to the construction of the universe. The eleventh-century scholar al-Bīrūnī called geometry *geodesy* and as such it was classified as natural philosophy involving matter and form combined with time and space. A few years later, his friend Ibn Sīnā reclassified it as a mathematical science. That so precise a view of the universe should have been allowed to become, in our society, the preserve of New Age blur ought not to deter us from considering seriously the relationship between belief and the arts but, this said, it is easy to become unstuck, especially when trying to smuggle such notions across the unmarked boundary that lies between ornament and symbolism. Maybe the best solution is to be as simple as possible. It's the only sure way we have of gathering up the world's complexities. Ornament is ornament. A symbol is something which we make, which is tangible, in order to give voice to, or to illustrate, the otherwise inexpressible. A symbol is not so much made as *conjured*. The deeper the culture from whence it comes, the more deeply ingrained it will be, such that even the artisan makes no conscious reference to it. The strongest bridges are made in the psyche. What eludes him, on a conscious level, is that which, on an unconscious one, loads his work with significance. When the things he makes are denuded of significance, all we are looking at in the end is merchandise.

Say that to the weaver, chugalugging over a loom, ash falling from his cigarette.

It could well be the case that on a sunny afternoon, in Damascus, in full swing, temporarily deprived of the oxygen of everyday existence, we were investing the Turkmen cloth with more significance than it could possibly bear. There was, after all, nothing so unusual in the weave – the diamonds were standard Turkmen fare. What overthrew us was the cloth's shape. It may be, too, that the symbolism of which we spoke was that which we chose to feed it, although, here again, it can be argued that interpretation is part of the creative process. It is a perilous form of democracy, though, when we place our own imagination at its centre. We enter intellectual foxholes of our own making that become, the deeper we dig them, all that much harder to escape. The religious interpretation Yasser placed upon the cloth would be necessarily different from my secular one, but there was one thing we shared absolutely – this remarkable object could not help but echo the hum of existence.

My only argument with Yasser, which is no argument at all but rather an extension of our conversation, is that long before the advent of Islam powerful geometric design had been an element of oriental work and surely any unconscious symbolism, while perhaps being fed by, is not absolutely dependant on, the specifics of faith. We are all at least partly prehistoric. Symbolism is deeper and more profound than language can encapsulate. It may be too that it is simpler and more mundane. It not only precedes language but also adores the hidden modalities of existence. A sexual diamond is not necessarily a Freudian one. The weaver does not philosophize, nor does he psychoanalyse, every throw of the shuttle. The task at hand is to keep the warp under tension because as long as form is adhered to there is room for play and where there's play there is always the element of chance whereby a thing may be made anew, what we might otherwise call a *poetic*. Civilisation can be said to hang upon the straight line. A straight line, so rarely found in nature, contains chaos. The ancient Egyptians knew this. Theories abound as to how the pyramids were made, and how it was possible to move even a single one of those stones, but, whether we know it or not, we carry the bulk of the Great Pyramid of Giza within ourselves.

The making of the Turkmen cloth may unravel this prose.

And one has to wonder, too, at what point in the history of this Turkmen village such an object became expendable. What break in its traditions could have allowed for such a sacrifice? After all, this was rather more than a rug whisked from somebody's floor. It had been shared by many people, at a moment of terrible separation in their lives, and because it was used not just once but many times presumably it served as some kind of communal bond between past, present and future. Was it that the new was embarrassed by the old, which, after all, is what happens when modernity swoops down all at once? Suddenly nothing seems more valuable than cheap substitutes. One must consider, reluctantly, the alternative. What were the changes that might have made of the cloth's disposal no kind of sacrifice at all? At what point is *everything* for sale? When everything's for sale, there's no longer any crisis of conscience. Things are merely let go. Yasser says the Turkmen cloth is not for sale, and of course I believe him, and maybe with his demise it will be allowed another airing, which, of course, would be most appropriate. The cloth will then be restored, if only for a short while, to its original purpose. A degraded image has within it the potential for renewal, but it also means we must rediscover what is lost in ourselves. One day, probably, the Turkmen cloth will be for sale and what then? Will it become décor? Will it become, as if the very words themselves confer holiness, a *museum piece*? Will somebody else's exquisite taste apply a deathblow to significance? And once significance is gone, where goes symbolic value? Who is responsible, though, for their ultimate demise? The collector who is willing to pay vast amounts of money for a rarity or the person who, maybe penurious, is willing to sell? Suppose I had been offered such a piece, at a bargain price, would I exercise high moral principle, or, as would be more likely the case, would I rescue it from ending up in my neighbour's house?

§

'Tell me, Yasser, are Muslims half in love with death?'

'I see a great deal of beauty in death. If you want to feel it, just consider the death of a friend. I have lost two friends my own age, one of whom was very close to me. I remember vividly walking after his coffin to the grave. When you are close to someone you have agreements, disagreements, disappointments, and then, all of a sudden, everything is brought to nil. This stage doesn't last for a long time. Death is not permanent. If it were, I would retain the same feeling about this person for the rest of my life. When I looked at my friend's coffin, I felt this peace – all his ambitions, all my ambitions built on his, our quarrels – and here we were, at *zero*. This is something beautiful, which you experience maybe only once in your life. So many people say to me, "I dream of coming to the point of nothingness, when I have no debts and I do not expect anything from anyone and I do not have to worry about anything." You experience this only with death. I am not talking about one's own death, of course, because nobody can talk about it, but about the deaths of others. When our President died, I regretted not being here. I heard the news at a petrol station in eastern Turkey. I was working voluntarily with the Red Crescent in the middle of nowhere. "Where are you from?" the attendant asked me. "Oh," he said, "Hafez al-Asad died today!" And for just for a couple of minutes or so, I felt I had nothing more to say against him. When someone you think you know dies, this is a great moment. And the ultimate beauty of this moment is in one's relation with the other. And with a woman one loves? I always expect her to say or do something, but if I were to die she would expect nothing of me anymore. At that moment she would really love me. Do you remember the first moment you saw your newborn child? I cried. I felt like I had been injected by a soul and this was pleasure. The opposite form of pleasure is having a soul taken out of you. A soul removed has a beauty one cannot describe. What was that line by Milton? "And day brought back my night." Incidentally, the best description of a woman's eyes in Arabic poetry was written by a blind poet. "When she looks at you, she almost makes you drunk." Actually it is impossible to translate. Bashshār ibn Burd was blind from birth and had an ugly pockmarked face. What he wrote is what you feel when you look into the eyes of a woman you love. You lose your balance.'

Whenever Bashshār ibn Burd began to recite verses it is said he spat first to the left and then to the right. Once he got going, though, his mainly young audience was enthralled and most enthralled of all were the females.

We took the path any poet might choose, from death to love.

§

That same evening, on 3 April 2006, we were at a small gathering when a friend of Yasser's, a journalist, arrived with the news that the poet Muḥammad al-Māghūṭ had died earlier that day. He was 72, which, although not a great age, was ripe enough given his predilection for alcohol and cigarettes. We barely spoke about it until the following day by which point the immensity of that loss had begun to sink in, not just with Yasser but with Syrians everywhere. Syria had two great poets in its recent history, Muḥammad al-Māghūṭ and Nizār Qabbānī, and it was strange that I should have been in Damascus for the deaths of both of them. Qabbānī died in England but it was here where his dying *really* took place. I went to his funeral, which was attended not only by the adoring masses but also by the secret police easily identifiable by their American Levis and imitation Gucci sunglasses. The doors of the mosque where the final rites were conducted were slammed shut to the public. Only about a hundred or so people got inside. One man in a hysterical rage hammered at the door with his fist, demanding to be let inside, but after a while he gave up and was swallowed back into the human throng. Squeezed this way and that between the press of bodies, somehow I found myself at the same door. I tapped lightly and suddenly it opened and a uniformed arm pulled me inside. The door was quickly closed again, and I was allowed to observe the funeral rites. What I have just described may serve to demonstrate that if someone wishes to be heard in this country he should knock lightly. While Qabbānī's death was only weakly registered in the Syrian media, the popular outcry was immense. With al-Māghūṭ's death things were strikingly different. The media, which by implication means the government as well, was absolutely awash with tributes and articles. Al-Māghūṭ was accorded something like a state funeral in his hometown of Salamīya. Among the mourners, representing the government was the Minister of Information, Muḥsen Bilāl, whom I'd met a couple of weeks before, in his chandeliered office.

The shy, slightly bovine, face of the man I'd met in 1999 was now plastered everywhere. Doubtless he would have relished the irony that on his death he was saluted by the very regime that had been the target of his many satires written in collaboration with the comedian Ghawwar. There is probably no writer in Syria who has got away with more, which is not to say he did not get himself into serious trouble at times. An earlier century might have seen him strangled with a silk scarf or else fed to the wolves. The story is told of how at the opening night of one of his plays most critical of the regime he took his curtain call only to discover the late President Asad seated in the front row. Addressing him from the stage, al-Māghūṭ asked whether he might be permitted to go home or whether he should go directly to his aunt's house. Asad laughed, saying he could go home in peace. In Syria, one's 'aunt's house' is slang for prison.

I was lucky to have met him. It would be some time before I realised just how rarely he ventured into public, and from what I heard of him thereafter it seemed that he'd slipped into worse and worse health. What I'd heard too was that he was writing ferociously against the dying light of day, and that his recent poems had gone further than anything he'd ever done before, that they were the words of a man who no longer had anything to lose. There had been stories too of a terrible falling-out with another Arab writer living in London, a rivalry that ended in a betrayal so deep that, in his final year, al-Māghūṭ was reduced to poetic silence. One should wait for more evidence before naming names, but I need hardly say in whose direction the greater number of accusations has been made. The crime was seen as nothing less than *poeticide*.

Providence must have brought Bashshār ibn Burd to Yasser's mind earlier that day because it could be argued that Muḥammad al-Māghūṭ was the other's drunken spiritual twin. They might have fed from the same bottle. The career of Bashshār ibn Burd (c.97-167/714-84) spanned a period of historical change, the transition from the Umayyad to the Abbasid age, which marked a shifting away from the desert and its lore towards the city and its laws. The austere was traded in for arabesque. Bashshār, who claimed to be of noble descent, was in fact the son of a bricklayer, a freed slave. He was blind since birth, his eyes, according to the biographer Ibn Khallikān, bulging and overlaid with red flesh. Blindness, though, was no obstacle. 'You say that I am led by one whom I never saw,' he wrote. 'Know that the ear, as well as the eye, can inform the mind of facts.' Also: 'Sometimes the ear falls madly in love before the eye.' And he could turn his own infirmity into a joke. According to Abū l-Faraj al-Iṣfahānī's *Kitāb al-aghānī* (*The Book of Songs*), the great tenth-century collection of poets' biographies, Bashshār was among a group of people when he let a loud fart. Dismissing it with a wave of the hand, he said, 'It's only a noise! Do not believe anything until you can see it!' Ugliness was no obstacle either. Although he had a bulky frame and his face was hideously scarred from smallpox – and remember those pockets of ruddiness that were meant to be his eyes – there was no shortage of women in his life. Women inspired his very best verses, especially his muse 'Abda, the wife of a Basra notable. Those were *her* eyes which pickled Bashshār with wine. As for his religious beliefs, he was too much of a freethinker for his own good and was charged several times with heresy (*zandaqa*). This may have been a consequence of his justifying Satan's refusing to fall prostrate before Adam, and also, given his Persian background, a whiff of Zoroastrianism was another possible cause. Scratch a Persian deeply enough, though, you'll often find a Zoroastrian. The writing of panegyrics, which kept him in funds, was nullified by his lampooning the very same people he praised earlier. One satire too far, this time against the vizier, although the suggestion was that the vizier worked while the caliph played, resulted in the latter sentencing him to seventy lashes, which, coincidentally, was Bashshār's age, after which, close to the point of death, he was sewn into a sack and deposited in a swampy part of the Tigris. A poet of even the most considerable talent could still be thought an annoyance.

As with al-Māghūṭ, the anecdotal life threatens to overwhelm the poetical. Both poets were progenitors of a new style, although in Bashshār's case it was a move away from Bedouin poetry, which was stark in tone, outward-looking and objective, towards the rhetorical flourishes that were to be the hallmark of a new Arabic poetry which was both subjective and introspective. Al-Māghūṭ's poetry is also brimming with outlandish images and wild flourishes. It is derisive in tone, negative in the extreme, and ironic, while at the same time full of anguish, with the poet in a state of both terror and rage and whose task it is to let loose his arrows at all forms of oppression. With Bashshār sensuous images were no longer enough – the new poetry called into play the intellect, the highly allusive, and an intensity of feeling quite out of keeping with Bedouin sensibilities. Bashshār's poetry wore fancy clothes while al-Māghūṭ's never stepped out of its dungarees, and yet both writers chose a simple diction, close to spoken language, while introducing daring licences of language. They were both wild cards, al-Māghūṭ with his rapacious persona and Bashshār with his willingness to forgo a life of virtue for the sake of a woman's charms. They shared a natural irreverence which, in a poet, is the next best thing to reverence. Bashshār's poetry was condemned for its licentiousness; al-Māghūṭ's poetry was condemned for its excesses. The Caliph al-Mahdī, with whom Bashshār had a tempestuous relationship, forbade the writing of further amatory verses, which only fuelled Bashshār's desire to write even more. The two poets were unstoppable.

When I asked Yasser a few years back whether he believed al-Māghūṭ was an outsider, his response was: 'I would say of al-Māghūṭ that he is a real insider. If you were to speak of this in biological terms there are certain kinds of viruses that build a protective layer, which enable them to survive in the body. I find this close to the character of al-Māghūṭ's work. He is the germ inside all of us, and it is as such that he feels and understands our real problems.'

al-Māghūṭ

Interestingly I would get a similar response from Kosay Mustafa.

'One thing about al-Māghūṭ,' I said to him, 'is that he is seen here as a man of the street who was fearless in his criticism of the regime. How would you evaluate him from the other side of the coin, as it were?'

'I do not exaggerate when I say he was very popular with both the people and the authorities. Even those who are in power appreciate these ironic jokes. Al-Māghūṭ could describe any situation ironically. We liked this, so he was allowed to produce these plays with Ghawwar. The language he used was very special. There was always some element of exaggeration in his writing, but if you were to mention this to him his response would be, "What are we witnessing in Syria, do you call that normal? The situation is already exaggerated, way beyond anything our imagination can produce. If there is anything unusual in what I write, it's because what is going on all around us is unusual." Yesterday I was watching TV when his death was announced, and, believe me, every Syrian had the feeling he'd lost a personal friend. I really felt that one of the people I am most familiar with had died.'

'Yes, but he got into trouble with the regime, didn't he? He was arrested a couple of times.'

'Sometimes when you overstep the mark you are not accepted here, but in Syria, and I am not speaking as a spokesman of the regime, there is some kind of marriage between intellectuals like al-Māghūṭ and the authorities. Actually he had the freedom to express whatever he liked. Sometimes we approved of what he said and sometimes we didn't, but it did not affect, even in government circles, the image of him as a national figure, that is, a man who wrote about national and pan-Arabic issues, somebody who could be considered a spokesman of the people.'

'Would you go even further and say the *conscience* of the people?'

'No, I'd think twice before saying this. Nobody can lay claim to this honour, but people liked him. Ironically, the day before he died, I started to read one of his collections of articles, *I Will Betray my Homeland*. The man who wrote the Preface was someone who would later betray him. He wrote, "Do not be shocked by this title. Al-Māghūṭ says he will betray his homeland, but you have to differentiate between the homeland we live in and the homeland that those who are controlling us think is theirs. Al-Māghūṭ will betray *their* homeland." Sometimes such people do not differentiate between the homeland and the government. This is a mistake. Culture is not the government. It is not owned by the government any more than it owns your history.'

'Yes, but isn't the poet always, in a sense, bigger than the regime?'

'Nobody is bigger than the homeland, which is our father and mother, the great mother that contains everyone. The government is something temporary in the life of the homeland. I'm not saying the government is good or bad. I am simply stating a fact. I think everyone must share in making his homeland greater. This applies even to this office boy who is easing our lives a little by bringing us coffee. Al-Māghūṭ gave us spiritual coffee. Anyway I started reading the book at nine o'clock and stopped at three in the morning. This is his magic. You live these stories, but the language he uses is different. That's his greatness. He will catch your ear and force you to follow him. He was so moody. Ask him about what he wrote twenty years ago and he'd say it was rubbish. If you asked him the same question the next day you would get a different answer. This was his character. He didn't believe anything in life was fixed.'

Finally I asked Kosay the question I asked of most Syrians: 'Which of the two poets do you prefer, Nizār Qabbānī or Muḥammad al-Māghūṭ?' The majority of people usually chose Qabbānī, saying that if one were to find a single line of his on a scrap of paper on the street it would be recognisably his. This is the aspect of Qabbānī which is least translatable, which is invariably flattened in English, whereas with al-Māghūṭ something of the content always shines through.

'It's like making a choice between tea or coffee, an apple or an orange. Each has it own taste and each has it own environment and each is good at a specific time, but in terms of what it is to be human I wouldn't hesitate to say I feel greater sympathy with al-Māghūṭ. You have to know first of all the environment of both poets. Al-Māghūṭ was from a very poor background whereas Qabbānī belonged to the high society of Damascus. They both addressed national concerns, but Qabbānī never actually wrote about the suffering of the people. We called him a "pasha" or "court" poet despite the fact he never embraced Arab leaders, except, ironically, Saddam Hussein, who gave him money. Al-Māghūṭ, on the other hand, was a tough character from peasant stock. He suffered a great deal, often ended up sleeping in the streets, and this suffering can be interpreted into all languages. So there is considerable difference between the two poets as human beings. Qabbānī was very proud that he cut short his Swiss holiday when the Intifāda broke out. Can you imagine? He thought he was doing something of national importance by saying, "I can't spend my holiday in Switzerland, not while children are being killed in Palestine." What is the point of cutting your holiday? What do you *mean* by *holiday*? We would never go to Switzerland to begin with, it being something beyond our imagination. 95% of people in Syria have never been anywhere. So to say that you have cut your holiday in order to come back to Beirut or wherever, this is rubbish! People here criticised him for this. Al-Māghūṭ, on the other hand, was one of *us*.'

'And he addresses the pain of people here?'

'He describes the pain in a very simple, complicated, clear, complex language. When you read his poetry you think it is simple, but you'd never be able to achieve what he does.'

Al-Māghūṭ's life is a biographer's paradise.

There are numerous anecdotes concerning him, many of them too ridiculous not to be true. Among the many articles that appeared after his death was Ghassān Rifā'ī's, in the *Tishreen* newspaper, a piece called "Al-Māghūṭ, *Tishreen* and the Cock's Beak". The story he relates describes perfectly al-Māghūṭ's appetite for the perverse. There were plans afoot for the opening of the new Meridian Hotel in Damascus and its head manager wanted to turn this into a major event, which would include even literature. So he invited the then editor of *Tishreen* to invite some literary people. Al-Māghūṭ was invited. The evening came and he didn't show. Where was al-Māghūṭ? After telling friends he didn't go to such places, he disappeared. The editor sent his newspaper army to look for him in the seediest bars and cafés. Finally he went on his own and found him in this rundown place, the *Hanī*. 'What in the hell are you doing here? The opening is in an hour's time and your name has already been mentioned.' Al-Māghūṭ replied 'My shoes don't have laces. I don't have a tie. I'm not handsome. What do you want with somebody like me there?' So the editor sent one of his staff to buy shoelaces, a new tie, and then he took Al-Māghūṭ to the opening. Al-Māghūṭ watched everything. The following morning he wrote an article in which he describes how the tables had been laid out with luxurious foods cooked by chefs from all over the world, and in particular he dwelled upon a cock that was cooked and decorated with nuts, etc, saying he was too scared to even touch it. He concluded his article with a call to all the hungry people of the world to unite. The Minister of Tourism at that time sent a letter to the editor, 'You must fire this man. He has insulted us.

We want investors to come and he goes and ruins everything. He must be forbidden from writing.' The editor replied, 'You want to fire him? This man is making our paper readable!' So they sent the same article to the head of the French Meridian in Dubai and this man went crazy, saying this was the best advertisement ever, indeed the best thing in the history of the Meridian. He sent al-Māghūṭ a present of $1,500.

My favourite story was related to me by a journalist friend of his. It dates from the late 1950s when al-Māghūṭ was living in Beirut, which was then the centre of a poetic revolution. There, during the heady days of the avant-garde *Shīr* magazine, one might give voice to matters which were not allowable in other Arab countries. Al-Māghūṭ was extremely poor, and had come straight from the farm, manure still on his shoes. He stayed at the house of the Lebanese poet, Yūsuf al-Khāl, who was also poor but not quite as poor as he. One day al-Māghūṭ was approached by the organiser of a series of weekly lectures who offered him 1000 lira, which was not an inconsiderable figure in those days, if he would deliver a speech demolishing his friend's poetry. Al-Māghūṭ agreed to do so and returned to al-Khāl's house and began to write furiously. When al-Khāl asked what he was up to, al-Māghūṭ answered that he was preparing a lecture on his work. Al-Khāl was greatly pleased by the prospect of praise coming from someone already considered by many to be his equal in poetic stature. When the night of the lecture came, al-Khāl sat in the front row while, onstage, al-Māghūṭ began to criticise him in the most brutal vein. By the end of the harangue, al-Khāl had slipped to the back of the auditorium. Afterwards, he visited all the bars in Beirut looking for his treacherous friend. After failing to find him, al-Khāl stormed home. There he found al-Māghūṭ on the floor with a massive kebab and a bottle of wine. Al-Khāl advanced, ready to thrash him. Al-Māghūṭ cried out, 'Stop! Wait! Look, 500 lira for you, 500 for me.'

Al-Māghūṭ was, in many respects, a baffling figure. Some people were disconcerted by the fact that shortly before he died he accepted a medal, the highest in Syrian letters, from the younger President Asad. Others spoke of even having felt personally betrayed by him and that the prize was something he ought to have refused, especially after having been, for so many years, critical of the regime. And then still more people saw this as a sign that the authorities were more tolerant than they used to be. What is to be said, though, of a poet who had recently penned lines in praise of Stalin? Or was al-Māghūṭ being ever the supreme ironist? Certainly he was a joker. Once he obtained a jar of rotten olives, which he reserved for public occasions in order to throw at people he didn't like. While the al-Māghūṭ who resisted authority in all its forms was crystal clear in his principles, the political al-Māghūṭ was a curious muddle. Prior to his escape to Beirut, in 1956, he had been accused of belonging to the rightwing Syrian National Socialist Party when it was in its most ideological phase and indeed he was imprisoned for his political activities. Years later, when reminded of this, his response was, 'Yes, I used to go and attend all the meetings and sometimes I'd even sleep in the party headquarters but it was not because of the ideology. At that time I was living in a cold room and in the party headquarters there was a huge stove. I used to sit next to it in order to keep warm.' One suspects here a curious blend of the disingenuous and the sincere. After being imprisoned in Lebanon on some charge, he fled back to Syria in 1961 where later he got into other kinds of trouble. Al-Māghūṭ seemed to have been caught in an eternal political shuttle.

'Strange,' said Yasser, 'only yesterday afternoon we were discussing the Turkmen cloth and it was as if we were preparing ourselves for the news of his death.'

That very morning he'd gone to see al-Māghūt's coffin which was taken from the hospital and loaded into the vehicle that would take it for burial in the poet's childhood village of Salamiyya. Yasser then read out another newspaper article by Walīd al-Mārī, a Communist writer, which relates how just before al-Māghūṭ died he took him quietly aside as if he were about to reveal the great secret of his life. Al-Māghūṭ showed al-Māri his writing table and made him swear never to repeat what he was about to be told. 'I have never written anything on this table,' he said. 'Every poem and article I have ever written has been done on my right thigh.' There al-Māri concludes his article, reminding his audience of al-Māghūṭ's nickname, or, rather, the epithet by which he was commonly known *al-h'amām allatī taṭīru khārija al-sirb*, which translates as 'the pigeon that flies outside the flock'.

Chapter Eighteen

The University of Pain

Abed told me, years ago, that both he and Sulaymān are graduates of the University of Pain. Yasser, when he got wind of this, decided he, too, is a graduate. Muḥammad al Māghūṭ, author of *Joy is not my Profession*, was surely another. All Syrians are. There are no maybes in the Slough of Despond or maybe there are *only* maybes. All I had to do was mention the University of Pain and people were either clambering to get in there or clambering to get out of there, always with a twinge at the centres of their stories of things lost, things gained they never wanted in the first place, platonic loves, horny loves and spiritual loves, or else loves that never materialised. The University of Pain wasn't a place one could *not* pass through – it was an obligatory, crowded thoroughfare. This is not to bemoan absence of humour; on the contrary, Syria has provided me with moments of hilarity such as I have not experienced since. There was Fatina's blue door for one, Abed's problem with oxygen intake for another. And there's a story which I've yet to tell, which concerns the music of a German composer and the Bedouin who loved it, only it seems not to want to fit anywhere. There's still time. The only way one gets admission into the University of Pain is with a joke. The only way out of it is with a joke. Laughter, though, is misfortune's bastard child, and where it comes from, there the teardrops fall at record levels. You could easily mistake them for climate change.

Orhan Pamuk beat me there.

I had been intending to write on the subject of collective melancholy, a feeling so elusive as to be indecipherable, when I read *Istanbul, Memories of a City* and there discovered Pamuk had already cracked the code of his tribe. At roughly the same time, in Damascus, Yasser read it, in the same lucid English translation. A few months later, a stalker of the intellect's abstract beauties, he walked up and down the street where Pamuk lives. The city as autobiography, I wager there is nothing quite like it in all of world literature. There I located the word I hadn't realised I'd been looking for. What was the English for this sweet and terrible virus that resides in one? I'd ransacked Roget's *Thesaurus* and came away empty-handed, concluded that if certain terms do not exist it's because there is no call for them, and, in any case, the words that most closely define the soul of a people are the ones that are least translatable.

The Turkish *hüzün* is the Arabic *ḥuzn*.

Pamuk's essay on the subject is unsurpassable. This melancholy which he so lovingly describes is more properly an essence. It is the stuff with which one dabs one's soul in times of trouble. Pamuk says *hüzün* cannot be observed from the outside and goes on to say that it is 'a way of looking at life that implicates us all, not only a spiritual state, but a state of mind that is ultimately as life affirming as it is negating.' One needs to be schooled in it from birth or maybe even earlier. If Pamuk is correct and *hüzün* can only be seen and felt by those on the inside, by what rights, then, am I allowed to stake a claim to understanding it? The answer's simple: I'm a deadly carrier, well, at least that part of me which is a Pole. I grew up so deeply in the thick of it I didn't know it existed until I acquired sufficient distance. The Polish equivalent of *hüzün* is *żal,* and if there is nothing in English to duplicate its meaning the Turkish and Arabic most certainly do. Could it be a complete fluke that the softer-sounding Arabic *zal* also denotes a form of sadness although not as powerfully expressive as *ḥuzn*? If by some weird serendipity the Arabic word did squeeze its way into Polish coinage, and probably I'm pushing things a little, the Poles invested it with a life, or death, of its own. In Paris, when Chopin was asked about the wellsprings of the emotional depth in his music, he replied, 'C'est *żal. Żal* est une émotion uniquement polonaise.' There comes with *żal* a dash of mysticism that is Oriental in character, notably in its fatalism, and which is savoured as one might savour a fine wine. *żal, hüzün, ḥuzn* – this pain which is something one nurtures almost, which is as positive as it is negative, is found in very few cultures. 'Bittersweet' is too weak a word to describe it; 'regret' is only a partial interpretation and 'loss' only barely touches the surface.

A couple of yellowing leaves fell from the potted tree beneath which Yasser and I began to tackle the elusive. He had just come from punching a bag in the gym and there was a frog in his voice. Apparently, the night before, he had been screaming at the Fates. The good news was that he had any voice at all.

'Actually *ḥuzn* is a much more profound word than simple melancholy,' he whispered. 'It describes that which cuts into your heart. The word *ḥuzn* has pain in it, is something that engulfs you. It can kill you or it can make you tired.'

Yasser, too, was at a loss to say exactly what it is.

'Can one speak of a distinctly Syrian *ḥuzn*?'

'If the Syrians don't have it, who does? If Damascus has no *ḥuzn* about losing its river and its greatness, where else would have it? Pamuk speaks of the loss of the Ottoman Empire and how profoundly felt that was. So it is with Damascus, which, after all, was the Umayyad capital once upon a time.'

'But are there ways in which it is distinct from the Turkish?'

'What makes our *ḥuzn* more profound is that we have not even begun to raise ourselves from the hole we've sunk into. We are *down* there. Istanbul has regained some of its dignity by re-establishing itself as a centre for trade and commerce, whereas Damascus is still at the bottom. Add to this our feeling of *ḥuzn*, which I feel more deeply than many people, not because I am more paranoid than them but because it's always the artist or poet who feels it more. Damascenes have this sense of a conspiracy against them and unfortunately it is beginning to prove true. Even the whole *zamān* [the time we are living in] conspires against us. Talk to any Syrian who finds himself in a moment of anger. He swears at the *zamān*, crying, "Everything is against me!" Which are the cities that most influenced Arabic civilization? Medina, Cairo, Baghdad . . . yes, but *first* came Damascus. The Umayyad rulers shifted the capital of the caliphs from Medina to Damascus. The first was Mohayila who fought with 'Alī; he brought everything to Damascus. The Umayyad was the greatest age, which coincided with the spread of Islamic civilisation all over the world, and then came the

Abbasid, which shifted the centre of power from Damascus to Baghdad. Damascus had the pride of being the capital of the greatest civilisation for a while. If you compare Damascus at that time to what it has become, you will see it ranks close to the bottom even among Arab cities – even Dubai is twenty times more important than Damascus; Beirut is more important than Damascus. *Any* city is. What, then, do you suppose goes on in the backs of the minds of Damascenes? This is why this feeling of *ḥuzn* is more profound here than anywhere else. When in its history was Damascus as down as it is now?'

I asked Yasser whether the terrible weight he carries comes of his continually striving for the unattainable.

'I wouldn't call this a weight or a sorrow. On the contrary I would call it something that lifts me from all the trouble in my life. With this thing you mention, the University of Pain, when inside it we look for pain in even the most pleasurable things. Sometimes the holiest thing in my life is seen by someone else as the most sinful. What you get then is catastrophe.'

'Anyone with a poetic nature is half in love with catastrophe,' I argued. 'We speak of it as if it's always just around the corner and then we discover, to our embarrassment, that it has been postponed for another day. What about more recent, more localised catastrophes? Someone told me the oldest Qur'ānic school in Syria stood in front of the Umayyad mosque, in what is now the square. What could have possessed them to tear down that place? And why this hideous construction off Martyr's Square, where there was already a famous and beautiful mosque which they tore down to make way for this one? What is in the mindset of a people who can allow the destruction of things so central to its history?'

'Maybe this is where our *ḥuzn* stems from, the inability to take action. If you want to go down that road what always haunts me is that you can spend forty years building something and then destroy it in an hour. So how long will it take to rebuild what has been destroyed over fifty years? When you go down this road, your *ḥuzn* becomes a hundredfold more. A more optimistic approach is that a pendulum always swings back. All which is going in a bad direction will one day swing back, but how or when we don't know.'

'Surely, though, the result would be a technocratic society without the graceful Arabic line. Damascus would be all shiny skyscrapers.'

'I don't see this. This is the greatness that I still see in this city. It refuses to be anything like Jeddah or Beirut or Dubai unless, of course, the world goes crazy and drops an atomic bomb on it. The other thing, when considering where one lives, has to do with the genes. This is a very Islamic notion. The Prophet says, and this is a strong hadith, that when you want to marry first choose the aunts and uncles of your children before they are born. The bloodlines will show up somewhere. There are some stupid people here who are proud of being Damascene just because they are of such and such a family, but it's not this that's important. Being proud of Damascus is to be proud of a city that has always cared about its connections. I come from a Damascene family that is *rooted*, which means you *know* where you are. I am not speaking of pure race. This is a kind of nonsense that gets blown up into racism, but the opposite of racism is *not* destroying everything that has to do with your blood. This is what modernity is trying to do. We are fed stories about thieves and prostitutes who are more honourable than those who only yesterday were thought respectable in society's eyes. I am talking about Arabic literature, especially in the 1940s, when writers here began to be fascinated by the West. All these stories do not prove the opposite. Their message is that there is no black and white, which may be true, but what they actually achieve *is* black and white – the Axis of Evil and the Axis of Good. There is nothing in between. It is good to know who you are. Without roots, you cannot survive.'

'What are the forces that would cause such a collapse? What do you see as threatening the Damascene way of life?'

'The biggest threat for us, and I feel this more than other people because I have been exposed to a good many things, is of having been in a conflict that resulted in our loss of self-confidence. I am not exaggerating when I say that 90% of Muslims have lost their self-confidence.'

'You are speaking of an internal conflict?'

'Exactly! We have reached a point – let's not deny it, let's be objective – where there is globalisation or if not exactly globalisation then the most powerful seeking to make the world in an image they choose. The Coca Cola world. And from where we are, looking always at the other, we think, "They do things better than us." We are, in a sense, attacked not by people, but by ideas, and in the process we have lost our self-confidence. We have this inferiority complex. Try this experiment: take the very best Syrian product and the very worst European one; go to any ten people here and say, "Choose between this European shirt and this Syrian one, which is one-tenth the price." Most of them would go for the European one. We have this complex and there are reasons why we got to this point, starting from the top of the pyramid, with our leaders who do not have the slightest respect for us, who are willing to do anything to stay there. And if they are losing now it is because they realise that you can never build an army strong enough to protect you when you no longer have the respect of the people. You see what happened in Iraq. We have reasons for this loss of self-respect. Our legal system is not working, our leaders do not respect us, and even our own families don't give us a chance. Our history books are full of stories of Usāma bin Zayd who, when he was just seventeen, led an army, and here I am, aged 36, and I cannot even face my own family when I do something they don't like. What *is* this? We are filled with these big stories. We have the example of Haldi ibn Walīd, a great army leader in Homs, one of the symbols of manhood. His sword alone was something great in Islam. With every city he conquered he'd marry a beautiful woman from there and this was why we were all somehow related to this great leader. "Why aren't you more like him?" we are asked. Our history which, after all, is the only thing left to us, is presented to us in such a way as to make us feel even smaller. Our religion is built on the idea of being yourself and that if you believe in Allāh you can do anything. We are nothing. Anyone who comes from abroad is better. This idea is so humiliating. If you apply for a job in Damascus, and you are a graduate of some minor university in the USA and the other applicant is a graduate of Damascus University, with a degree in Arabic literature, they will hire the other. This is what endangers us. We have lost it all, which is not to say that we at the bottom are always good.'

'One sees a new conservatism in Syrian life. Take, for example, the fact women are covered up as they weren't even a year ago. Would you say this is a false way of trying to restore Arabic pride? Isn't there some other way?'

'I think that in every crisis that faces the Arabic world, Muslims automatically divide into two camps. We have always had this problem. Hopefully, we will learn from it one day. Once we are hit by something like the war in Iraq and we see women there raped, people tortured, what affects us most is the humiliation. An old man with a beard and his face on the ground, an American soldier standing with his boot on his head, this is humiliating, and when our media show you this all the time, it humiliates us even more. What more do they want of us? As if we need *more* self-erasure! So Arabs divide. One side loses all confidence in anything that is Arabic and the other side goes back to the roots, or, rather, to the way by which they perceive those roots, which, unfortunately, is hardly ever the right one. We are having a crisis and it is a big one. This is Baghdad, for God's sake. It's not Algiers or Amman but one of the centres of civilisation – Baghdad, Damascus, Cairo. People are pulled in two directions. If this is what you see, women covering themselves, what I see are friends of mine who can't pray anymore. When Baghdad fell one of them phoned me in tears, saying, "Whatever you call me from now on, let it be anything, but do not call me by my real name anymore." This man no longer prays and if you try to talk to him about any Arabic or Islamic matter he replies, "*Khalaṣnā!*" – "Let's leave it be!" And then we have the others, who say we must grow our beards and show everyone we are Muslims, as if what truly matters is to present ourselves with these surfaces. Unfortunately those who try to follow a middle road are not given a chance. They are very few. I wouldn't even consider myself one of them because, in truth, I keep swinging from one side to the other. Let's learn from this. It did not work one way, and in fact created more problems, and it's not going to work if we go the other way either. We are losing our culture, our music, our literature, our architecture. You are hit by something big, so why not use it instead of just being black and white all the time? If you are not this, then you are that. This is not our culture, which basically is an Islamic one. We have the most flexible religion. If you read enough and know enough about Islam, you'll see it is the most flexible. I will give you an example: you are faced by something and although you don't know what the solution is you do whatever you think is best. If you do it right you are rewarded twice, if you do it wrong you are rewarded once. You are rewarded because you have *thought* about it. This, for me, is the peak of flexibility. Meanwhile, they stick to hadiths like, "If you do not pray, you are blasphemous." This is no kind of solution in times of crisis. We will continue to fall and there will always be something else to hit. If they think Iraq is the end, there is worse to come.'

'We have spoken about what happens to people on the inside, but what about what's on the outside? What of Damascus itself? Do you fear an apocalypse here?'

'No, not literally, not in the sense of more cities falling, but there'll be even more humiliation. There are so many things in daily life more humiliating than the fall of Baghdad.'

'When one speaks to people the fear they express is always of destruction from outside, but I wonder if the greater destruction is not from inside.'

'With all the shortcomings and misdeeds of the inside, which include serious violations, the city has stayed put over the past forty years. The destruction, such as it is, came mostly of ignorance rather than intention. But when you turn on the TV and look at the news and you see a bomb that weighs half a ton being dropped on a city from God knows how high and it explodes and destroys who knows how many layers underneath, then your fear comes from the outside. If you want to take it to the lowest level no one today, certainly the majority of people who live in the old city, would allow me to knock down this building, even if the law gave me permission to. And if they are stupid enough to allow it to happen there would be other people sufficiently aware of the value of these places, who would come and say, "Okay, how much do you want?" and offer money for their rescue. There is sufficient awareness. I am optimistic enough to say this, but you can't control what comes from the outside. I don't think someone sitting in an office somewhere says, "Go, destroy our history." No one would do this, but if someone issues an order to drop a bomb on Nagasaki then he is issuing an order to destroy.'

'We are going back into the University of Pain here, the only place we feel comfortable.'

Yasser's earliest memory is of standing on a balcony with his sister who was a year older than him and looking down into a building site of what was later to become the Abbasid Sports Stadium. There was a cart there, one of its wheels stuck in the mud, and a donkey trying to pull it free. A man was beating the donkey which, poor thing, couldn't move.

§

Kosay Mustafa was born with a tulip smile, which is really not a smile at all but an endowment of nature. The shifting moods of its bearer are difficult to gauge at times. A smile such as this, which stays put, is a form of espionage. You can look at the world from behind that smile, invisible. Kosay would appear to be in love not so much with power as with its intricacies, and any mastery of them is akin to mastering the steps in a Fred Astaire dance routine. The way things are put together fascinates him, whether it be government policy or a television programme. The recent move from diplomacy to media is not such an unlikely change of career, although for Kosay it is a return to something he loves. I would say he is brilliant at manoeuvres. If, as he says, the government is something temporary in the life of the homeland, what if suddenly the object of his loyalty were removed? What would he be, *where* would he be? I'll hazard a guess: things for him would be roughly the same. Charm, which is to say charm in its original sense, charm as *spell*, would get him through even a band of meteorites. There he'd be, still tinkering with the controls, crying *action!*, maybe just a little nostalgic for the days when one made splices in film.

I should imagine, when crossed, he can be extremely fierce. There are elements of both panther and teddy bear in him. Maybe because of what they have seen, his eyes are never quite in the same place as his smile. And equally fierce is his laughter that never comes by halves. His whole body joins in the execution of any single laugh and it is, all in all, quite an explosion. It makes him fun to be with at table. When he talks of serious matters his voice goes as low as it can possibly go while remaining perfectly audible, and the words, at least in English, seep out one by one, as if to emphasise a point that might be easily lost otherwise. Squarish not so much in physique as in attitude, as those who are in power tend to be, when touched by something, a government minister's poem or a child's cries, Kosay dissolves into curves. A man who loves his children will shield them to the best of his abilities. A man who loves his country will want it to be a fit place for his children. These are standard truths from which he does not deviate. What is troublesome is his politics, although they have never been cause for strife between us. We beg to differ and we beg to agree. We are perfectly happy to leave our bunkers and step into the sunlight. There is little doubt that he, too, is a graduate of the University of Pain.

Kosay and I sat on a park bench while his children played. An old man stood by one of the gates, selling flowers, while, at another gate, a younger man sold spicy chick peas, a bag of which Kosay shared with me. The air was alive with the cries of children at play, the sky was a snappy blue, and, just then, for a couple of minutes, the world really did seem at peace. A couple of pigeons looked askance at the chick peas, which they wouldn't have liked in any case, not with red chilli pepper, thank you, and Kosay scooted them away. I was rather fed up with them too. They weren't giving me what I asked of them. They'd just waddle about here and there. I spoke to Kosay of my various frustrations in speaking to pigeon fanciers, pointing out that they were all afraid of the police, and that they were reluctant to speak of other people's crimes as if to reveal those would be to confess to crimes they themselves might contemplate. Admittedly I was at a low ebb because whenever it seemed I'd come close to making an analogy that would stick it would just as quickly dissolve, either that or I was perpetually in pursuit of certainties which required, as backing, still more certainties and behind those still more.

'I do not have a scientific approach to this, but those people are *so* naïve.' Kosay drew deeply on his cigarette. 'On the other hand, we are careful about preserving Syria's image. You will not find this with the Egyptians, the Jordanians or the Lebanese. This is an absolutely Syrian trait, it's in our blood. We think of those who criticise our country as traitors. This may be a form of exaggeration but we get very sensitive when we hear our country being criticised. Maybe it's because we are a conservative people, conservative in our government, in our families, and as employees. You don't have to read the word "conservative" in the fullest sense because we are also an open people. We like foreigners. We like to talk and to hear other opinions. I am not saying we are perfect and don't like to be criticised, but we do take really harsh criticism badly.'

'Some of those people I speak to are illiterate. The smarter ones think I am looking for political parallels. I'm aiming for something more subtle.'

'It is the mistrust between West and East, so it's back to the clash of civilisations and back to the Crusades. If you asked your questions ten years ago, people would have been more open with you. The government has nothing to do with this. It has to do with the people themselves, mainly because they are watching what is going on. Yesterday I was talking to a cameraman in the TV studio. He is so worried about his children. He kept saying, "I don't know what will happen to my children. If they want to fight against America and Israel there'll be nothing I can do to stop them, but at the same time I want them to grow up and become doctors and engineers. We don't have masses of children like the old families used to have. I have only three boys. I do not want them to fight but look at what has happened in Iraq and Palestine." My own daughter, she is ten years old. She watches TV. Once, during 'Īd, she said to me, "I do not want to celebrate because yesterday I saw children my own age being killed by the Israelis. How can I celebrate 'Īd and be happy while my brothers and sisters in Palestine are being buried." You know burying children in this part of the world is unlike burying children anywhere else. It's not like anything you'd find in China or any other country in Asia. I am not saying people elsewhere do not consider their children as dear to them, this is the basic fact of life, but melancholy in this part of the world is something different. One of my relatives died last year. Her son died in 1973, in the October War, and she cried every single day until her death. I don't know if you can understand what it is to cry every single day. She never wore anything except black. She never went to weddings or birthday parties. She remained like this until the day she died. President Hafez Asad, when his son Basil died in 1994, he died too. When the son died, everyone in Syria knew the father would follow soon after. We cannot accept easily the fact of death. Of course Muslims accept death as a principle, but if you attend a funeral in my own city of Latakia, especially if the deceased is a young man, just watch how people react to his death and you will have the impression that everyone there is a complete *majnūn*. The women who are so very conservative will tear their clothes and show their breasts to everyone, which is considered a shameful thing to do. People here are obsessed by sadness. When my mother comes to Damascus and meets with my aunt, after five minutes or so they will start crying because they love to remember those who died 45 years ago. They keep on crying throughout the whole visit and then the younger people look at them and think they are crazy and actually *enjoy* sadness. Sadness is a profession here.'

'That explains the title of al-Māghūt's book! *Joy is not my Profession*.'

'It has to do with history too. We live in an unstable area. Syria was occupied countless times. Those invaders were not angels coming from the sky. They were brutal and savage. We witnessed all this violence and when you see human blood and get used to it then this is really something terrible. People here like to worry and they get worried if there is nothing to worry about. If I am driving from Damascus to Latakia my mother and wife will each phone four or five times to see if I'm okay. We were talking about death, especially with regard to those who die young. It's tragic everywhere, but here it is even more tragic. The news of a death spreads quickly here. I think your next book on Syria should be about melancholy.'

Surely Kosay might have guessed it already was.

'Arabs seem to feel everyone is against them,' I said, 'which is as much a misconception as saying all Arabs hate us.'

'Yes, of course those who think this way should see a psychiatrist. Nobody in his right mind thinks all Americans are against us. We know this is not the situation. When those explosions took place in London everybody here said this was something crazy.

Why London? When two million people there protested against the war in Iraq? Are we rewarding those who were against it by killing them? September 11th, despite the fact people here knew the victims were innocent, and we really don't like the killing of innocent people, there was gloating of a kind but it was not directed against the American people but towards the American government because those bloody officials over there are trying to convince the whole world they can do whatever they like. "We know the colour of your underwear!" So this failure of security and intelligence was a source of happiness for people in the Arab world and also because they bury their beloved ones every single day, in Iraq and Palestine, they think, "Thank God, this time I don't have to bury mine. Let them drink from the same glass. Let them understand what it means." If you count the number of Arabs who have been killed by American weapons and compare this to the number who were killed on September 11th, you'll see it's many, many more. Of course, we know it is not something between "them" and "us" – this is not the situation. We are all human beings. Sometimes you don't get on with your own brother or child. When I was living in America I found people similar to myself, but unfortunately the current administration there is creating these great distances between people. Those people really are fools. Why are they inventing enmity between Muslims and the rest of the world? Who cares about Islam? You see those veiled women. Give me half an hour and they will be in bed with me. These *ḥijābs*, they are wearing them as a reaction to the American policies in the Middle East. If you do not want me to exaggerate, okay, then 75% of those veiled women are wearing them as a consequence of American policies. Everyone feels he is targeted because he is Muslim. If that's the case, why not at least *pretend* to be a good Muslim? So now Islam is becoming an identity. It wasn't like that twenty years ago. If you went to the swimming pools in Latakia the women wore bikinis. If you go there now you won't even find any women swimming. So what is going on? I'll tell you what's going on: people are retreating instead of moving forward. I started working in television in 1987. We had fifty-three women working in that place, most of them unveiled, but when I left, in 1995, there were only seven unveiled women. Do you understand my point? This is a reaction. There are different reasons for the rapid spread of the *ḥijāb*, but American policy is playing an important role in this respect. I mean, of course, Islamic extremism. I never go to the mosque, but now I feel I am a real Muslim. I might be killed for this, so why should I ignore it? That's what everyone is feeling here. This administration and the previous one were not angels, but what I can say is that something has got to be done. I don't know what. All this so-called dialogue between West and East, East and West is rubbish. There must be some credibility – honesty is the best policy. Why should I talk to you if mistrust is there all the while? I think the Americans should try to find a fair solution for the Palestinian question. They should stop interfering in the Arab world and also I think Europe has a role to play. Instead of blindly following the USA they should have their own policy and reactions, otherwise this world really is becoming, day by day, more unsafe and insecure. If you watch the news, you feel there is something wrong. If you live in Britain you cannot observe and monitor the world's events so accurately anymore. Believe me, this man over there selling flowers, if you were to ask him about current events, he would be able to talk for hours. Here we listen carefully because it is important that we do so for the sakes of the lives of those children who are playing now and who'd love to see their sons in the future playing as they are playing. We are the weak ones in this game and they are the strong and if you are the strong you can do good things or horrible things. If you are strong it might be you don't care about others simply because they are weak. Do you think anyone in the Arab or Muslim world would believe this fucking stupid man, this primitive, Osama bin Laden, is really a threat to international peace and security? Nobody in the American media mentions his name anymore. It is not the right moment to exploit him. What do they mean by Islamic extremists? *I'll* tell you what they are. Those people look at me in a horrible way. They think I should be killed even *before* George Bush is because my wife doesn't wear a veil! Those people were nothing in our society but now they are becoming an issue. Anyone who fights America is a hero according to Osama bin Laden. Can you imagine someone like him controlling this country? I would prefer to kill my children one by one rather than see him leader of Syria or the Arab world. They are over-exaggerating

Osama bin Laden and al-Qaeda in order to achieve their own political aims. We are fighting al-Qaeda in Syria. We do not want to announce this. I am telling you this, and I am a Syrian official, firstly because we do not want to frighten people, secondly because we do not want to go openly with this war because al-Qaeda is very popular. If you fight them, you become unpopular. I am not supposed to tell you this because you are a foreigner and might be a spy, but we are fighting them on a daily basis. Those people are really crazy. If you work as a driver for a secondary school in Syria they will consider you a traitor and deserving of death just because you are working with this unIslamic government. Can you imagine! Their ideology is horrible. If there was a government official in this park and they had to kill him and the result would be the killing of everybody else here they wouldn't mind. According to *their* idea of Islam, this would not be considered *ḥarām*. Any innocents killed would go to heaven. Can you imagine my son dying here because of those people? It's horrible! I think American policy in the Middle East, American interests and the way they are defending them are all absolutely horrible. Every Arab citizen knows they are stealing our oil and we remain silent. We know they are occupying our lands, whether in Saudi Arabia or Kuwait, and we know those are not military bases – they are occupation forces. We know this and we are keeping silent. They are taking everything they want. If you want to talk about international relations, they are supposed to be based on interests. According to this line of thought, American interests should be with the Arab world and not with Israel. They are taking our oil, all the natural resources. What is happening? They are not dealing with us according to any principle. They support Israel which occupies our lands and which brings people from all over the world to their homeland. Why? They want to humiliate all of us.'

'There is one issue which I come across endlessly. You will probably argue with me. There is this notion shared by almost all Arabs that the Press everywhere is run by Jews. This, surely, is one of the great Arab delusions. One could look at the other side of the coin. In America, the fiercest critics of Israel are invariably Jews, Noam Chomsky, for example. Who exposed the atrocities at Abu Ghraib? Seymour Hersh, another Jew. There are some terribly wrong ideas floating about in the Middle East. I have yet to see any evidence of this supposed control of the Press. Where in England do Jews run the Press? When you look at America and the editors of newspapers and magazines, how many of them are Jews? We are talking Arab madness here.'

'I do not think they are mad. I do not think they over-exaggerate. What do you make of the fact that you can criticise Israeli government practices within the Knesset but you can't do so within the American congress? Isn't it ironic? You are speaking about individual Jews. We appreciate those people. They are precious. We love them very much. If you go to any Muslim shaykh they will tell you what their grandfathers used to tell them about the Jews. We never had any problem with them. We were cast out of Spain at the same time. We have been living side by side because our traditions are similar. Jews love money, Arabs love money. Arabs are good businessmen, Jews are good businessmen. We used to compete with each other. I still remember my Syrian Jewish friends who regretted leaving this country. They never had a fight with anyone. The government here used them as bargaining chips, otherwise they were doing very well here. I don't think Arabs have anything against Jews, but now the word "Jew" is so deeply connected with Israel that when people say "Jew" it has come to mean *Israeli*.'

We were getting to the heart of the matter when a friend of Kosay's strolled by. When Kosay told him of my mission, the friend began to tell me of a recent murder case. A couple of fanciers posing as policemen came to confiscate this man's pigeons, but when the man twigged and realised they were out to steal his flock he shot dead both of them.

Suddenly Kosay's friend stopped in the middle of his story.

'Is that thing on?' he asked, pointing to my microphone.

I explained it wasn't that I'd switched it on but that I hadn't switched it off. The man sped up his story more and more until it became a meaningless jumble, made his excuses, and fled through the gate where the spicy chick pea seller stared into the chemical-enhanced azure.

Kosay gave me an ironic smile. Or was it a smile?

§

I'd better tell a certain story now because there's nowhere else it will go, and besides, after almost a decade of floating in space, it seems to find a natural landing place here, where it is cushioned by a zone of tears, where *ḥuzn* is the very stuff one breathes. The story wouldn't be so comical otherwise. The people who lived in this zone are no longer there. Those who yet survive visit it sometimes, and they carry with them megaphones through which they address family and comrades caught on the other side of this zone. Otherwise all you'll find are ruins, and as such they stand as testimony to man's callousness. It is where St Paul is said to have stopped on his way from Damascus to Jerusalem and it was there, too, that Pope John Paul prayed for peace.

I had gone to the Golan Heights to visit the ruins of Quneitra, once home to 37,000 people. Israel occupied Quneitra during the Six-Day War in 1967 and forced the population to flee, leaving it as a ghost town for several years. During the Yom Kippur war of October 1973 the town suffered much damage. The UN-brokered disengagement agreement of the following year stipulated that Israel return Quneitra to Syria. Before withdrawing, however, Israeli troops called in building contractors to remove anything of value, even window frames and light fixtures, and then with bulldozers they systematically destroyed every single building remaining in the place. If they were going to hand anything back to their old enemy it would be a pile of ruins. It is close to unfathomable this penchant for destroying other people's houses. What they really gave Syria, of course, was a propaganda exercise, because if one obtains a certificate from the Syrian Ministry of the Interior one may go to see just how iniquitous those Israelis were. The Israelis, from their side, say the town was already blown to smithereens, massive Syrian shelling the cause.

What nobody will admit to is the disinterment, in the Greek Orthodox cemetery, of a number of corpses. This I did not see with my own eyes, but an acquaintance of mine, escaping, a little too easily perhaps, the clutches of the secret police, showed me photographs he took of the bodies. A desiccated corpse, recognisably a woman's, had been beheaded. There was still no clear answer as to who could have desecrated these graves nor was there any clear idea as to why the bodies weren't reburied although maybe I have just answered my own question. Whoever one chooses to blame, Israeli or Syrian, neither answer seems plausible, and in recent times, maybe because of brewing prejudices, mutterings have been made in the direction of the Druzes, but after meeting Druzes this, too, strikes me as implausible. Surely, though, the Day of Judgement has not yet come, when, quite of their own accord, the dead, even the headless ones, arise from their own graves.

After going through a couple of checkpoints I was taken by minibus, for a price, through the ruins, accompanied by a grinning *mukhābarāt*, a holsterless gun shoved in his trousers, who kept feeding me bits of chocolate. I was his only custom that day. The buildings resembled collapsed pastries. I did not see any other materials other than twisted bits of metal sticking out of the concrete. It was as hopeless a scene of destruction as one could imagine – a destroyed mosque here, the surviving towers of a church there, a nearby hospital wall pockmarked with bullet holes. The rocky crest of Mount Hermon was just a few hundred yards away and along its ridge was a row of Israeli radar defences. I could make out the Star of David on the flags. Occasionally, I saw in the distance the blue flash of a UN soldier's helmet. This remains a UN-monitored zone. The *mukhābarāt* gave me another piece of chocolate. I did not ask to see any corpses. After finishing my 'tour' he escorted me back to the military checkpoint where a somewhat grizzled, uniformed officer with a comedian's face, probably in his late fifties, a Bedouin as it turned out, summoned me over.

'Tell me,' he said, 'What do you think of Israeli Netanyahu?'

(Benjamin Netanyahu was Prime Minister at the time.)

The officer walked full circle around me.

'Well, in truth,' I said, 'I do not much like him.'

The officer poked me in the chest.

'Very good!' he cried. 'Now, tell me, what do you think of chief?'

'Who?'

'Chief! Our President!'

'Well,' I said, truthfully, 'I think he is a very clever man.'

'Very good,' he cried, again completing a full-circle before poking me in the chest. 'Now tell me, what do you think of Beethoven?'

I really didn't know which way to go with this one.

'Beethoven?' I asked, thinking I must have misheard him.

'Yes, Beethoven, *dah-dah-dah-dum*!' He sang the opening bar of the Fifth.

The officer looked pleadingly at me.

'Yes I – I like him.'

'You like Beethoven!' he screamed. 'Go, go into the building over there.'

'I must get back to Damascus,' I pleaded, but already he and the grinning *mukhābarāt* were leading me to what was certain imprisonment. I was pushed inside a building, which was more of a shack really, when the officer suddenly turned on the *mukhābarāt*, cuffing him across the head. 'You think *you* are police? *I* am police. You are *nothing*.' The other fell back under his blows and whimpering he put on a kettle. I realised this was part of some ritual play whose author was boredom. What else was there to do on the edge of a ghost town? I was kept in detention while the officer bellowed, 'Beethoven Symphony One, Two, Three, Four, Five, Six, Seven, Eight, Nine. Which one do you *like*? Beethoven *best*, greatest. Very good, *yes*, Beethoven make good sleep, make happy dreams too!'

'What about Mozart?'

'Very good, yes, but Beethoven is number one *and* number two for me. I love Beethoven more than Arabic music.' And so he continued, determined that the subject of a certain German composer be approached from every conceivable Bedouin angle. We had exhausted all possibilities within a few minutes, but it was another hour before I was allowed to leave. We sucked thick mint tea through thin metal pipes. I kept jamming mine.

§

'*Ḥuzn* is a very special Syrian condition, is it not?'

My first graduates, Abed and Sulaymān, blinked at me as if somehow, during the course of the past decade, I had ignored the sad hub of their existence, either that or I had forgotten what they already knew in the cradle.

'Of course! It is our education. Melancholy is our culture.'

A rather odd contraption dangled from Sulaymān's right earlobe.

'What's *that*?' I asked him.

A small light on it flashed blue.

Chapter Nineteen

The Caliph an-Nāṣir's Ardour

A Short History of Pigeons in the Islamic World (6)

The Spanish traveller, Ibn Jubayr, when he visited Baghdad in 580/1184 found the city 'a remain washed out, or the statue of a ghost', although soon enough he was to discover, and appreciate, its teeming religious life. According to his *Travels* the five days in Baghdad were spent mostly listening to sermons. Although the city 'has no beauty that attracts the eye, or calls him who is restless to depart to neglect his business and to gaze', Ibn Jubayr was impressed with the suburbs and its gardens and meadows. And there, three times, he caught sight of the Abbasid Caliph an-Nāṣir li-din Allāh – once in the courtyard of his palace, another time on a pleasure barge on the Tigris, and finally on the palace belvedere where he stood, dressed in Turkish mode, gazing out across the metropolis that had been so great once, and which in the years immediately following his reign would be reduced from shabbiness to rubble.

> We saw this Caliph in the western part in front of his belvedere there. He had come down from it and went up the river in a boat to his palace high on the east bank. He is a youth in years, with a fair beard that is short but full of handsome shape and good to look on, of fair skin, medium stature, and comely aspect. He is about five and twenty years of age. He wore a white dress like a full-sleeved gown, embroidered with gold, and on his head was a gilded cap encircled with black fur of the costly and precious kind used for royal clothes.

What is it about this brief word portrait that puts one in mind of certain Persian miniatures, which bespeaks a certain delicacy or vulnerability even?

The facts demonstrate otherwise. At the centre of all activity, great and small, was the omnipresent figure of the caliph. If there was little that escaped his notice, it was not without an intricate system of spies. When Ibn Jubayr saw him, just four years into his reign of almost forty-seven years, the longest in the Abbasid caliphate, an-Nāṣir had already proven himself a tyrannical figure. One of his first acts as caliph was to murder his vizier, having him dragged through the city by his genitals. Suspicious of all who served him, he regularly dismissed officials; given the court intrigue of the times perhaps he was right to do so. Historians seem agreed that he was intelligent and, despite his failing to assist Saladin in his defence against the Crusades, courageous, and also that he understood perfectly the intricate machinery of government although his inability to delegate would ultimately weaken the caliphate. An atmosphere of terror descended over the city. This said, an-Nāṣir's reign, despite the perennial feud between Sunni and Shī'ite, was a comparatively calm one. Any question as to whether this was due to the caliph's strength or weakness is perhaps best answered by his failure to anticipate more fully the threat from Genghis Khan's hordes.

A pigeon called Balqā' will be called upon as key witness.

The people close to an-Nāṣir were few – his Turkish mother called Zamarand; one of his wives; a son whose death would greatly affect him; a few *'ulamā*; and a servant, a black called Najah, who as a boy used to play together with the future caliph. In 570/1174, when the young prince fell from the roof, Najah leapt after him: 'I did not wish to remain behind my master,' is how he explained his action. The caliph remembered this when he repaid his loyalty by retaining him as manservant and cupbearer. We may hazard a guess as what led to the boy falling from the roof; he was chasing pigeons.

There had been royal pigeon fanciers before, most notably Hārūn ar-Rashīd who, according to al-Maṣūdī's *The Meadows of Gold*, once asked Ibn al-Sammāk to make a poem from the dove he was watching pecking at some grain. The poet responded thus: 'It seems as if she looks through two rubies and pecks at the grain with two pearls and walks on two cornelians.' The caliph, an avid fancier, realising the extent of his folly, later had his birds slaughtered.

Under an-Nāṣir old passions, which had been suppressed for religious and social reasons, were rekindled. Despite attempts by the religious authorities to ban pigeon-racing the sport was legalised on the grounds that pigeons could also be employed as a means of communication, especially in time of war. Avian business boomed. At the *souq al-ṭayr* a young pigeon would sell for 20 dinars and an egg for five; large amounts of money, sometimes as much as 500 dinars, were paid for birds with recorded pedigrees (*dafātīr al-ansāb*) and under an-Nāṣir the pigeon range was reorganised; various books of pedigrees were compiled, including one especially written for the caliph by al-Qawwāṣ al-Baghdadī; the pigeon-shoot competitions intensified, and much distinctly unIslamic betting took place. According to a fragment of an otherwise lost source, the *Ta'rīh* of Qādisī, the carrier pigeon system was restored. An-Nāṣir invited several of his subjects to construct dovecotes and anyone seeking to enter his presence was obliged to receive a pigeon from his hand, a gesture that symbolised a bond between subject and ruler. A pigeon was a guarantor against lies. For the first and only time, pigeon fanciers were unburdened of the stigma of their passions and men of vice suddenly became men of virtue.

In 590/1194 an-Nāṣir, who saw himself as the focal point for all activities, ordered all the fully-grown carrier pigeons to be slaughtered and the younger birds to be retrained according to his own system. This seemingly gratuitous carnage actually had a motive behind it, which was the caliph's monopoly over the entire postal system, which in turn was linked to the official spy system. Most bizarrely an-Nāṣir's ardour developed along quasi-religious lines. What he did, in effect, was to legitimise an activity that had previously met with disapproval by involving the *qāḍī* or civil judges, entrusting to them the raising of young birds, and even providing them with flight directions. The pigeons were divided into twelve groups thereby mirroring the twelve imams. Some of the groups took their names from them and even members of the

Prophet's family were evoked. These twelve categories were taken to sanctuaries that were already centres of religious pilgrimage – the 'Alawiyyāt were taken to the grave of 'Alī near Kūfa; the Mahdiyyāt to a dark cave at Samarra where Shī'ites say the last imam disappeared; the Hāsimiyyāt to the grave of Hāsim b. 'Abd Manāf in Gaza; the Ḥasaniyātt to the sanctuary of his son; the Bāqiriyyāt to the sanctuary of the fifth imam, Muḥammad Bāqir; and the Ṣādiqiyyāt to the sanctuary of the sixth imam, his son, Ga'far Ṣādiq. As for the others their destinations remain a mystery.

These sanctuaries had no practical use. Soon after, maybe a year later, an-Nāṣir established dovecotes in various towns, thereby covering the territory which formed his empire. Baghdad was now able to exchange communications with faraway regions such as the town of Irbil in High Mesopotamia and the province of Hūzitān which the caliph had recently made part of his empire. The caliph instead of concentrating on his northern frontiers extended his empire southwards. Predictably the most imposing dovecotes were those in the heart of the caliph's palace. The pigeons there were mostly for pleasure.

A passion for pigeons blinded an-Nāṣir to the point where it made him forget his duties and the conduct of his affairs. Also he was going literally blind. A young slave girl mastered his hand and produced documents. An-Nāṣir isolated himself more than ever, even from his doctors, which may have been sensible, given that the doctors might be persuaded to poison him. There were periods during which he was unable to discharge his duties, and the city fell into confusion, subject to the idiosyncrasies of a half-blind man. We are afforded one final glimpse of him squinting towards the skies. His vizier came to him with news that Transoxiana had just been taken by the Mongols who were sweeping over the northern empire. An-Nāṣir did not wish to be interrupted with such trivial matters, not when it had been three days since he had seen one of his favourite pigeons, Balqā', so named because of its black and white plumage.

A passion for pigeons passed from father to son. Ẓāhir whose caliphate lasted but a year (622/1225-623/1226), associated with the very dregs of society. The games continued under Mustanṣir who recruited from the lower echelons a scoundrel called 'Abd al-Ganī b. Darnūs and attached him to one of the dovecotes. After Mustanṣir's death in 640/1242, his successor Muṣta'sim inherited this man and promoted him to the grade of chief of guardians as well as giving him the title of *Nagm al Dīn al-Hāṣṣ* 'the confidante'. Darnūs attained a pinnacle of grandeur quite out of keeping with his station and was able to accumulate a large fortune. Such was the liberality of the caliphs towards the end of the Abbasid empire that only the unworthy could expect advancement. Even the vizier was obsequious towards Darnūs in order that the latter might put in a good word for him with the caliph.

As for Musta'ṣim, dubbed, without any trace of irony, *mālik al-dunyā* ('master of the world'), he truly was the appropriate figure upon whom to conclude the Abbasid caliphate. A man of seemingly no will whatsoever, he amused himself with his coterie of clowns and musicians and continued to play his pigeon games. According to one tradition, he removed himself from the populace, and had a cloak of black silk hung outside the palace gate so that a person wishing to pay his respects might kiss it. In 643/1245, very much in the manner of an-Nāṣir, he gathered carrier pigeons from four towns in order to create from them four new breeds. Of the resulting breeds one was sent north to Samarra, to the mausoleum of the eleventh imam, 'Askarī; the other three went south, the first to the sanctuary of Ḥudayfa b. Yamān at Madā'in, the second to the sanctuary of a now unknown saint, Gani, in Kūfa and the last to Qādisiyya. A mandatary and two witnesses accompanied each of the four groups, their official task being to authenticate the new breeds, this being concluded in the presence of a *qāḍī*. Their four releases, probably their first and last voyages, were celebrated by servile verses of courtesans eager to stroke the vanity of the caliph.

The year 1256 was marked by one of the worst floods in the city's history. Water overflowed both banks of the Tigris, and most of Baghdad was submerged for the next fifty days, with such houses as could be reached becoming, in the absence of their owners, the targets of looters. Chaos now ruled in a people whom Ibn Jubayr had censured as being vain and proud, 'as if they are persuaded that God has no lands or people save theirs.' Almost symbolically the waters reached, and rose, about the caliph's palace. In 1257, despite rumours of the approach of the Mongol army, now commanded by Hūlāgū, and despite the repeated warnings of his vizier, who meanwhile was stirring up trouble between the Sunnīs and Shī'ites, and despite even a message from Hūlāgū himself, demanding his surrender, nothing could shake the caliph Musta'ṣim out of his lethargy. A message was sent back to Hūlāgū, which might have been bold had there been actual strength behind the words. 'Young man,' the foolish caliph wrote, 'misled by the day of good fortune, you have become in your own eyes the Lord of the Universe, and think that your commands are the decisions of fate. You ask what will never be given.' Hūlāgū, when he received this, remarked, 'The caliph is as tortuous in his policy as a bow, but I will chastise him until he becomes as straight as an arrow.' In fact if Musta'ṣim had read the signs he would have had time enough to muster forces from all over the Arab world but instead he followed the advice of his vizier Ibn al-Alkami who, while saying to the caliph the walls were unbreachable, secretly sent messages to the approaching Hūlāgū, saying it was time for him to strike. Al-Alkami was probably motivated by persecutions against his fellow Shī'a.

On January 11th 1258, a cloud of dust appeared to the east of the city, and soon covered it. The inhabitants climbed to their roofs and to the tops of the minarets and from there they could see the surrounding Mongol horde. A horrendous bombardment followed. On February 5th, the Mongols breached the walls, and, in the words of the Persian historian, 'Abdullāh Wassaf, 'they swept through the city like hungry falcons attacking a flight of doves.' A few days and 800,000 deaths later, including some 700 women and eunuchs from the caliph's harem, Musta'ṣim, when summoned by Hūlāgū, asked al-Alkami whether there was any hope, to which he replied, 'My beard is long.' This cruel response referred to the Arabic proverb, 'Long beard, short wit.' Together with his harem and children, Musta'ṣim surrendered to Hūlāgū who mocked him for his nonchalance. Hūlāgū, after keeping him without food, offered him an ingot of gold. 'Eat this!' The caliph answered, 'But no one can eat gold.' 'If you knew that,' retorted Hūlāgū, 'why did you not send it to me? Had you done so, you would have been eating and drinking peacefully, and without a care, in your palace.'

The Mongols were superstitious about shedding royal blood, and so, in order to avoid any divine retribution such an act might bring upon themselves, Hūlāgū had Musta'ṣim and his family sewn up inside carpets and trampled to death beneath the hooves of horses. Meanwhile, the stench from the rotting corpses of the populace was so powerful the Mongols had to evacuate their campsites. Thus ended 500 years of Abbasid rule, and so too the fortunes of the city, which its founder, the first caliph, Jaffar al-Manṣūr, called Madinet as-Salaam or 'the city of peace'.

The Great Library of Baghdad or 'The House of Wisdom' (*Bayt al-Hikma*) was destroyed, and the Tigris was said to have run black from the ink of the many thousands of books that were thrown into it. So thick was the pile of volumes at one point a horse could step across the river on them. The waters were also reddened with blood, which gives added poignancy to the Prophet Muḥammad's words that 'the scholar's ink is more sacred than the blood of martyrs.' The city from which the word 'algebra' came, which was the centre of the intellectual universe, lay in ruins for many decades to come. The Mongols, never a people for frivolities, set fire to the dovecotes, with scant regard for their wildly thrashing occupants.

Chapter Twenty

A Reunion of Parts Broken

We had come full circle – the same rickety table at the Hejaz Café, a pretty ghastly painting of Arab horses on the wall above, the familiar smell of the *nargileh*, which sometimes, where there is none, I pick up in London in the most unlikely of places, even on the tube once, as if I had been breathing in memory spores. And there was the small arms fusillade – *clack, clack, clack* – issuing from the backgammon boards followed by even bigger explosions of voices. It would seem nothing had changed, not for a decade or more, except that now, dangling from the right earlobe of the man who when I first knew him still wore Bedouin robes was a Jabra SP500 Bluetooth Speakerphone.

'What has become of our holy fool?'

An eavesdropper with crooked teeth laughed noiselessly from a neighbouring table. Sulaymān made some adjustment to his new electronic device, a clunky piece of jewellery from some Bauhaus of the future.

Soberly I pressed my case.

'When I first met you ten years ago you were picking at your teeth with a carved stick, just like your fellow Bedouin do, and now look at you. There is a blue light flashing at your ear. What will you be like next time I see you?'

'Should I go back to the manufacturer and tell him he was wrong?'

Sulaymān was a shade exasperated with me, just as he had been a few years earlier when I expressed doubt in his alchemical abilities. What he did then was to give me the product of his several recent attempts, a pill-shaped chunk of metal of roughly four inches in circumference, which I still have, which I hope I'm not mistaken in thinking has *baraka*, and while it's certainly not gold it is quite unlike any metal I've ever seen. Surely, then, this increases its value. Gold is commonplace. People tell me to get it chemically analysed, and I say I'd rather not. There's no gold in it – of this I'm sure. And besides, it is impolite to analyse gifts. When Sulaymān gave it to me, with something like sorrow, he told me to tell people in London a crazy person had made it. Maybe I'd be able to buy a loaf of bread with it, he said. It wasn't just something that came from a moment's generosity. It came from somewhere much deeper, where some alchemy in the soul took place. Who am I to prove it is not what Sulaymān so badly wished it to be? And I don't really believe he thought it was gold either. My fear had been that he would bring financial ruin upon himself because in order to cover the costs of his alchemical activities he had already borrowed money from people, Abed's mother included, and failure to produce the real thing would sooner or later bring their wrath upon him. As Sulaymān himself told me, 'There is either success or failure', and then he quoted a line from one of Nizār Qabbānī's poems, 'There is no compromise between heaven and hell', which was to say there couldn't be any between gold and base materials either. The alchemy session I attended eight years ago occasioned one of Abed's best lines, 'I will now cut the watermelon and live normally.' That watermelon was not a metaphorical one, but a green monster beside which lay a much too short knife. This year Sulaymān seemed finally to have come to his senses. All such activities, he recently told me, were now firmly behind him.

'When you first met me, I romanticised everything – even Allāh. A child will stretch his hand to the stove and get burned and learning it is dangerous he won't do it again. I thought what mattered in this world was prayer alone, but then I realised there are other things – experience and knowledge, for example – and that there are people of whom one should ask certain things before they die. I mingled with clergymen once, but they presented only a single horizon to me. They haven't broadened any horizons for us as a people. We pray five times a day and we claim to be followers of the Prophet, so why can't we be constructive? I pray that Allāh might construct our hearts. It is easy enough to build a house but to construct a heart – this is something that lies beyond reason. Also one needs people from outside one's own experience. I was immature and childish. Things have changed. You spoke to me through this earlier. It is harmless. If I were unable to meet you in person, then it would be of no use. Sitting and talking with you, *this* is civilisation. This object merely brings us closer. Wherever I am, you'll be able to find me. Astronauts went up in the sky and made space stations there and they came up with this. Those men up there were *mujāhidīn* risking their lives for the sake of bringing something new into the world. So why do you criticise me?'

'It's just that technology, especially here, creates distances between people. What will it do to your desert spaces? It will eliminate all sense of space and time, and *then* where will you be?'

I was appealing to Sulaymān's Bedouin sensibilities. And Sulaymān, having none of it, pointed to my small blue Sony Walkman MZ-N707 Type-R recorder.

'So it is *ḥalāl* for you and *ḥarām* for me?'

Sulaymān was ever the adventurer, journeying in opposite directions at the same time, casting ancient spells while fidgeting with the controls to the future. Whatever was going on down here, whatever the latest technological advance, he kept one eye on the Pleiades.

Sulaymān, ever perceptive, noted some disturbance in me.

'What are you trying to reach? I will help you.'

Yet again, and with my researches now at an end, I had become weary of all the contradictions, all the denials, and, worse still, all the empty promises. There were too many for me to enumerate. My prose would go all soggy with them. I remembered how fired up I was three years before, when Waseem told me that if I wanted to understand the Middle East all I needed do is look at his birds. A whole book was meant to have sprung from a single utterance. With Waseem behind bars, I was selfishly prowling about on the outside, wanting him for what he could tell me. It wasn't enough that I'd gathered all these voices, which, when transcribed, would fill maybe three hundred pages: I wanted more. I needed one final proof and because I am wary of facts alone it had to come from somewhere other than the obvious sources.

'These connections I've been trying to make, no sooner do I make them than they begin to disintegrate. I've had more failures than successes. A few hours from now, I will be getting on a plane. So yes, if you can help me . . .'

It had always been like this. Each time I left Damascus my last hours would be spent with Abed and Sulaymān, which were a summing-up, a verbal reprise of various themes. And it was at such times that Sulaymān seemed to come up with the goods as if purposely having kept them on reserve. Almost always he hatched a surprise.

'You have known me for ten years. Anyone asks me who you are and I tell him you are my friend even though I don't know how to communicate with you in English. Can you explain this to me? This is a miracle. The nature of our friendship is more reckless than alchemy itself. This is the first thing. The second thing is that I will demonstrate how the pigeon man is an integral part of Damascene life, even if people here appear to reject him. They would never let him be otherwise. The pigeon wars and Damascene society are one. And you're afraid they are separate! You are not meeting pigeon men in Egypt or Jordan – you are meeting them *here* in Damascus. There are bakers and there are pigeon men too – every profession has its secrets. If I take you to my friend who is a moulder, you will find his shop is closed except to those whom he trusts. The pigeon men are like him. As a matter of fact we are *all* pigeon men. The pigeon man worries over his pigeons and I worry about my son and wife. The pigeon man is afraid for his belongings. I, too, am afraid of thieves. There are things tangible and intangible, and both the physical and spiritual worlds are in a bad state. We each have our own way and want to survive. You can't let go of your secrets unless you love and trust the others. They often come to me, asking for the secrets of my trade. I put on the mask of an imbecile. When I go to those jewellers I don't tell them what I am really up to. I just say I'm buying and selling. If they knew, they wouldn't speak to me. So you see: I am the biggest pigeon man in Syria! This is why I took you to a pigeon fancier of forty years' experience. Likewise, I deal only with professionals in metal and quite frankly I'd refuse to work for them as an apprentice. They say to me, "Take so much a month, but work for us." I refuse because once I start to work for them they will catch my inner pigeon – they will imprison me. I won't let them catch me. If they capture me, I'll suffocate. Once they know my secrets they'll try to imitate me and I won't benefit anymore. The pigeon man has his own world. The one we went to has been in this game for forty years. Did you notice he said he knows exactly where his pigeon lands? And who has caught it? So there you have *knowledge*. All professions are like this. What is it that you find so strange? What hasn't been solved for you?'

Sulaymān gave me one of his steely looks and I waited for him to continue.

'I will make another analogy. Imams have become pigeon men too. Once upon a time, when a follower left his guru or his Sufi way, whether it was Rifā'ī or Naqṣhbandī or whatever, and went to another order the new imam would reject him, and send him back to the previous one. "Don't come to me," he'd say. "Return to your original guru. He is better than me. Your shaykh has superior knowledge. I wish *I* could be his follower." So the follower is a pigeon and he needs proper rearing just like a pigeon does. Once the respect between imam and follower is gone then things are muddied. What happens nowadays? The new imam says, "Don't go back to your old shaykh. I am better than him. I raised him. He was my follower once." So he steals the pigeon and tempts him so that he will stay with him. And this is wrong just as it is wrong in the pigeon world. Codes should be preserved. The code the world over has altered and civilisation dies. The one who would have brought your pigeon back once upon a time now steals it. And so it is with other professions. In a previous age, an apprentice would stay with his boss for fifteen years in order to properly learn his trade. I sent my friend to my other friend, the moulder, and within a week he says he has learned everything he needs to learn from him. I asked him, "*What* did you learn? Can you make this for me?" He said he didn't know how. "So why did I send you there? I wanted you to stay with him for ten years so you could imitate him." There is a famous story here about an ironsmith. A mother sent her son to this ironsmith and after one day of apprenticeship he came back to her, saying, "I have learned the trade." "How could you manage to do so in a single day?" He told her the ironsmith's craft was simple; all he does is make the metal red and then mould it whichever way he wants. The next day the ironsmith knocked at the door of the mother's house. "Where is your son?" The mother replied, "You are a donkey. My son learned your profession in a single day and you have been doing it for the last fifty years." So he asked her, "What did he say?" She replied, "It's very simple. You burn the metal until it's red-hot and then mould it any way you like." Then the ironsmith yelled at her, "So not only did this bastard learn the profession but he taught it to his mother too." And this is our society. They all claim mastery of their profession in a single day. I went back to my friend and found him playing on his computer. He thought he had stolen a pigeon from me. He thought he had learned from me how to make alloys. I am sure he has not managed to take so much as an atom from my profession, as sure as the pigeon man is sure he knows where his bird lands. I am a pigeon man. We are all pigeon men.'

'You are a genius!'

'I am not a genius, but I've been here forty years. I don't know what is happening in London, I'd need ten years there to know for sure, but I am living here.'

§

Sulaymān reawakened in me all that I already knew and which I had allowed to hibernate. Speaking to him it was as if all the connections that were weak were made strong again and I could see through the mental haze. The sparks flew, and, if I may get fanciful for a minute, I might have been flying above Damascus, above the country as a whole, with everything below clearly visible as if spread over a single plane, and also, because time itself was flattened out, as thinly as the layers on a *baklạva* pastry, my memories could hone in wherever I wished them to. Or I might have been the poet, musician, horologist, artificial weather simulator, glass manufacturer, astronomer and engineer, 'Abbas ibn Firnas, who in 247/852, was reputedly the first man to experiment with flying. He leapt from the minaret of the Grand Mosque of Córdoba, using his massive wing-like cloak as a parachute, and suffered only minor injuries. In 875, aged 65, he almost perfected his technique, constructing a hand glider made of silk and vulture feathers, and, jumping from the Mount of the Bride near Córdoba, stayed aloft for ten minutes. This time, for want of a tailwing, he suffered spinal injuries.

'What man-made machine,' he asked, 'will ever achieve the complete perfection of even the goose's wing?'

There is a crater on the moon named after him.

All the people I met in Syria would now find their correlatives in what flies up, makes circles in the air, and returns home. It is a not wholly sensible scheme, granted, but as an *aide-mémoire* it's better than tying strings to one's toes. It is not at all certain my subjects, many of whom would insist on a clear division between species, will be pleased. Still it's worth a gamble. What breed of pigeon would Abū Walīd be? It would have to be a street one for sure, old and ruffled, a few feathers jutting out of place. Apparently he reported me to the British Embassy, saying I had made a million dollars out of him and now he was after his rightful share. And Fatina, what kind of dove? She'd be the whitest of all doves. We already know her voice is a coo. And what of those giggling Yezidi girls with whom, in 1996, I got a ride in a tractor-pulled wagon at whose centre was a pyramid of freshly picked pomegranates? Those ancient young goddesses with their playful antics, a couple of them poking at me, were they not the Aleppo Tumblers which, in 1851, Reverend Edmund Saul Dixon, himself a pigeon fancier, called 'the prettiest of the pretty', and then, actualising their movement with language, wrote: 'Pirouettes, capers, *tours de force*, and *pas d'agilité*, all come alike in turn. Other pigeons certainly can take any course in the air, from a straight line, that would satisfy Euclid as being the shortest distance between two points, to circles and ellipses that remind us of the choreal orbits of the planets round the sun; but the Tumbler, while it is rapidly wheeling past some sharp corner in a tightly-compressed parabola, seems occasionally to tie a knot in the air through mere fun.' Yes, surely they are those girls from the village of Basofan, one of whom took me by the hand to her father's house, where later, unknowingly, I ate sheep's testicles. And who shall be the Rihani, an elegant bird of most gentle nature, if not Farīd whose name means 'unique', who'd be almost thirty now, and who, aged eighteen, in the Roman ruins of Bosra, read me his verses. 'What would you abolish?' he asked me. 'What would you instigate?' So serious, is he still so? Did he become the poet he said he would be? Somehow I think so. And who'd be the Damascene whose eyes the ornithologist Willughby compares to the large, dark eyes of the Syrian people? Might it not be Sulaymān himself, my holy fool, who is wise beyond wise? The biggest and the darkest his eyes ever got was when he sat trance-like before the tomb of Ibn al-'Arabī. The Damascene is the bird Syrian fanciers most prize. And there are those birds, too, that conjure up not just faces but whole landscapes, the Halabī, for instance, with its pale colours that bring to mind the Dead Cities, more specifically the village of Mushabbak where – and this I really did see – in the shell of a fifth-century Byzantine basilica church a skinny mule brayed at a congregation of sheep. The children of that village had sandy hair and blue eyes, Crusader blood maybe, and among them were a few who had six fingers and six toes. There was one boy in particular who stood barefoot on the back of a mule, his arms stretched to either side of him as if he were crucified on air and he kept that position while the mule jounced over rocky landscape. And then there was the kindly Druze couple, from the village of Amra, in the Jebel Hārūn, whose neighbour presented me with an olive branch he had just picked from one of his own trees, saying to me, 'Please, take this to your Mr John Major'. After battle, it is said, it's the olive tree that takes longest to recover its original form, which is why it is considered an emblem of peace. I need hardly say which male bird that neighbour is, but if you really must know then make enquiries of Fatina's female dove. May they together beget peace. As for the Druze couple themselves, I can't decide which breed they are. I shall go back to the *Encyclopaedia of Birds* but perhaps they are not there. My street philosopher, Abed, will be rather more difficult to pigeonise, although maybe, because he swings between extremes, between darkness and light, he'll be the Barbarīsī with its plumage alternating black and white. Yasser will require a solid flier that can wing a message all the way from the centre of old Damascus to his ancestral Turkmen home. And Kosay, what about Kosay? Which bird shall be given security clearance?

Did I really excogitate all this at the time, or is it not a mighty conceit that I now let spill onto the page? Well, yes and no – yes, because there really was a delineation of sorts whose colours would be added at a later date, and no, because there comes a fresh disturbance in the air this prose breathes. Memory is a ruthless cheat, tailoring everything to its own purpose. It asks that whatever one takes from it be given back in dividends. I invent what I see. The recording of Sulaymān's voice brings me back to a rickety table in the Hejaz Café. Suddenly the Barbarīsī, the Halabī, the Rīhanī, the Damascene, the dove, which breed of dove I'm not sure, and the Aleppo tumblers fly up from the page and make their way home to a rooftop in Damascus, which is where I first saw them, just as the call to prayer was being sounded from a nearby mosque.

§

'So what about all the violence and murder?'

Sulaymān paused for a minute or two, pulled the Jabra SP500 Bluetooth Speakerphone from his ear and threw it on the table.

'I don't think the violence is ever over a pigeon. It comes of agitation and teasing and of a need to preserve one's pride. A couple of days ago, I was putting oil in my car, which I bought from someone other than the person I usually go to. My regular man started to curse me, "Why didn't you buy oil from me?" And his insults got worse and worse, such that I was ready to kill him. Actually I had an iron rod with me. I might have acted against my will, but I controlled my nerves in time. I washed and prayed, but *still* I wanted to kill him. I went to a police station and told them my problem and a lieutenant then reconciled me with this man. So I took a wise decision because the argument would not be resolved otherwise. The wars are not over pigeons alone. When I was young, we had a bully in my neighbourhood, Hasūn, who terrorised everyone, a real criminal, always going in and out of prison. Some birds are called *hason* by the way. There was another young man in my neighbourhood called Abū Ṣakhr, which translates as "the father of stone". One day Abū Ṣakhr found himself on Hasūn's terrace. Hasūn had just come out of prison. He said to Abū Ṣakhr, "Get lost!" Abū Ṣakhr stayed put, and because this bully was accustomed to people being afraid of him he slapped him across the face. After receiving that slap he went to his father's house and picked up his father's gun which was fully loaded. Abū Ṣakhr's father was a policeman. Abū Ṣakhr and Hasūn set up a meeting in the wilderness, each with his own friends, this man with his Satans and the other man with *his* Satans. Hasūn was carrying a knife. I saw all this! Although I expected violence, I did not predict this. They attacked each other, one with a gun and the other with a blade. Abū Ṣakhr shot Hasūn as he approached with his knife. Hasūn kept coming for him and the bullets entered him one by one and he died. Abū Ṣakhr was imprisoned for fifteen years. I bumped into him recently. I said to him, "Do you remember when you killed Hasūn? I was a little boy. I watched you kill him." Abū Ṣakhr replied, "And I watched you pray." Now he is a vegetable seller in the market. Abū Ṣakhr is a nice person. Maybe he was offended by the slap or maybe it was destiny. The other man was disrespectful of other people, wicked, a hyena.'

'So would you extend this to the whole Middle East?'

'The one wearing a belt of explosives is the same. The suicide bomber, he, too, is the father of stone.'

'Not Hasūn?'

'No, because Hasūn was merely bad.'

There was something in me, an unwillingness, perhaps, to be fed answers I wouldn't like, which might feel too much like justification, as if to understand would be to be party to acts so utterly vile. At the same time, I knew it had to be Abū Ṣakhr. A bully would never have such diabolical courage.

'You take a jobless man and wherever he goes the path is closed to him, his own society persecutes him, so he too, although in a different context, becomes the father of stone. Any nervous breakdown and this person will reach the stage of being able to blow himself up. If he wants to be free of his problems, this will be a comfort for him. Analyse this psychologically, and you will find it is the same.'

I argued against this, saying most suicide bombers were calm in their resolve, often from comfortable middle-class backgrounds, and either believed in what they were doing or else were brainwashed into thinking they would go to Paradise.

'You will find it is the same. This man, whatever his circumstances, reaches a stage in life where he finds everything's meaningless and so he thinks maybe the hereafter is better for him. Some people in order to reach paradise will sponsor an orphanage. This man uses a bomb as a shortcut there. You will never know how he analyses things inside or where he thinks his comfort lies or what his circumstances are. Allāh has ways as numerous as the breaths of every creature on this earth. By being patient, as I was with the man who used to sell me oil, maybe I'll reach my goal quicker than the suicide bomber. After he explodes himself he won't feel a thing but me, every single day I am dying a thousand times. This man dies just the once, I die many times. It is easy to make a bomb of oneself. I am trying to create solutions. I want to create something from nothing, to help people. The Prophet Muḥammad, peace be upon him, could have turned his followers into suicide bombers. At the battle of al-Hūd he ordered his companions not to descend from the mountains but they did so for the sake of a few spoils and so lost the battle. Strength is not war only – it is dialogue, fruitful dialogue. Once upon a time, the Prophet made a treaty with some unbelievers. On this sheet of paper the Prophet Muḥammad was mentioned. The unbelievers asked that the word "prophet" be erased from the treaty. They said, "If you were a prophet in our eyes, we would never have fought you." Muḥammad, who was illiterate and did not know where to find the word on the page, ordered one of his companions to erase it. The companion didn't want to, but the Prophet insisted, saying, "We'll have dialogue now." The meaning of this is that war is not by sword only. There is psychology too.'

Sulaymān now turned his sights on the great pre-Islamic hero, Antar, whose deeds were to become a model for every Muslim.

'They said to Antar, "Your brother defeats you in battle." So he stretched his hand out to him and said "Bite my hand" and he told the other to stretch his hand and he'd bite it too. The one who screamed first would lose. This is what is going on in the Middle East now. Whoever screams first loses. So both Antar and the other man were biting each other's hand. Finally Antar screamed so loudly his whole tribe heard him. Antar asked his adversary, "Why didn't you scream?" And the other replied, "I would have screamed even louder than you, but I screamed inside." This is what is happening here. America is Antar and those who scream inwardly are the ones whom America persecutes. They may appear speechless, but they scream inside. America is the one screaming out loud and everyone hears her. The plan was to defeat Saddam and go home, but instead they imprisoned him and stayed on.'

'So the pigeon wars have spread throughout the Middle East?'

'My father, may God have mercy on him, thought Saddam would win. I told him it was impossible. "Why?" he asked. I told him that if Allāh were an unjust deity then the whole universe would be annihilated. Abraham, the father of prophets, told Allāh, "If I have problems, this is because of me, while you, Allāh, want every good for me." So we should follow Abraham's line. If we are in torment, this is because of our sins. Allāh intends only good for us. Saddam committed terrible wrongs and so the great centipede of the world moved against him. George W. Bush thinks he is moved by God, that he alone is righteous. They *all* think they are righteous. Ibn al-'Arabī said if you want to know the truth go to the common people. When I want to learn the truth I go into the old city sometimes, and I watch and mingle with the common people. Soon enough, everything is revealed. Ibn al-'Arabī says the common people are righteous. The elite used to disagree with each other, and it's the same with the different Sufi sects, Catholics and Protestants too, but if you go to the grassroots you will understand the truth. When I bought my motorcycle on the very first day I got a flat tyre. I was happy. I smeared my motorcycle with mud so no one would look at it. I would use it only for my daily needs. If I brighten it up, it might be stolen. I leave a hole in it so that nobody will envy or look at it. Every beautiful thing is endangered. Look at the beautiful girl.'

There were no women present in that smoky, very male, preserve, of course, but Sulaymān the alchemist conjured one with words alone.

'You will be converted from husband into guardian.'

Suddenly he pulled from his pocket a thin broken arc of metal, silvery with a golden tinge, with jagged ends that suggested easy breakage and presented it to me.

'Oh, no! Sulaymān!'

The old, crazy gleam was back in his eye.

Another gift, I'm not sure what kind of metal it is.

'Oh, my God,' cried Abed, 'he's back at it!'

'No, not quite,' Sulaymān corrected him, 'but I'm into alloys. Some things I just can't leave alone. For other people, it's pigeons.'

§

My friend with his Jabra SP500 Bluetooth Speakerphone had all the while been carrying another message, which took me several months to decipher. When finally it caught my eye, there was a perfect sun in my skies, and all kinds of connections were being made. The night before, I had a terrible dream: I found myself in my childhood home, which was suspended high above the earth, and I was clinging to something though I couldn't see what exactly. The floor had been left behind, and I could see the earth below as one by one the objects fell from the walls and slid from the shelves and plunged down through the gaping bottom of the house. I had been struck across the side of my head, which left me, for the remainder of the dream, hard of hearing. Where would Ibn Sīrīn have put this in his dictionary of dreams? The Arab dream interpreters say that often things seen in dreams mean their opposite. Wholeness out of chaos? A dream world was torn asunder and the horror of it weighed upon me throughout most of the next day and then, staring at the word 'Jabra' which I'd scribbled somewhere, something clicked. This was an Arabic word!

Our word 'algebra' is derived from the Arabic *al-jabr*, which strictly means 'the reunion of broken parts', and then there is *al-Jabbār*, one of the 99 names of Allāh, 'the Mighty' which also means 'the one who makes things whole again' and then there is a scientific theory, which by now may be discredited, its substance being that sooner or later the universe will go into reverse, and that time itself will go backwards and that maybe it is worth saving one's broken china, and then, just to return to the Arabic for a moment, in modern medical use, when turned into a verb, *al-jabr* can signify the healing of broken bones. Also it can refer to one who can withstand and remain whole in the face of much pain – an epithet which, most worryingly, had been applied to Saddam – but then, when employed with great care, which is one the wonders of the Arabic language, that is, the way the meaning of words can be stretched, it could be made to refer to the mending of a broken spirit, which is what Abed and thousands more like him so badly require.

§

The night before, Abed told me of such progress as he had made over the past year or so. I wasn't sure who he was trying to convince.

'We have this thing in Sufism called *fatḥ* which means "opening" or "revelation", such as you find in Ibn al-'Arabī's *The Mecca Revelations*. A Sufi may have many kinds of *fatḥ*, depending on who he is or what he has done. Usually it means you have been through a great deal of pain, yet despite this you remain patient and you pray. When I fell down the lift shaft and onto my back the first thing I said was "Allāh, please don't make me an atheist." Such a situation can make one curse God. Six months later, I met Rachel and after our separation I experienced great psychological pain. It was at that point, during my breakdown, that I had my first *fatḥ*. This was absolutely *not* a delusion. Although I didn't see the Prophet Muḥammad as such, I saw his hand pointing at my *nafs*, again, another important word meaning one's "self". It is your worst enemy. One must kill it. Some Sufis see their *nafs* as a snake, others as a dog. In my *fatḥ* the Prophet's hand pointed to a wolf with seven children and he told me to put them into a cage and lock them inside. This helped me because I now knew what my enemy was like and could therefore fight it. Why is adultery forbidden? Why is homosexuality forbidden? Nobody really knows because the answer lies somewhere beyond human logic. Those things are forbidden in the Torah, the Bible and the Qur'ān. The list of things that we shouldn't do is called *ghayb* meaning "absences" or "the invisible", things that are beyond the reach of the human mind. Such things you know only in your heart. Each person has his defects – wrongful desires, envy, hostility or whatever. It all has to do with what we call these absences. The Prophet Muḥammad says once you know your *nafs*, you know God. This wolf I saw had to do with things beyond reason, defects which I had to stop and put inside a cage. The Prophet was logical with me. He knew I couldn't kill all the wrong in me. You can't kill it, so, okay, put it in the cage and lock it up. This was five years ago. I went through six different periods of isolation (*khalwa*). I stopped eating food for three days at a time, saying "Peace be upon the Prophet" many thousands of times. All of those isolations were good, and each of them healed some part of me. The second *fatḥ* was during my best ever isolation. This last happened to me during the last day of Ramadan, after four days without food. Every six hours I ate one tomato and some olives. I was hungry and praying all the time. We believe Allāh is the healer, which is one of his names. A doctor is a tool in the hand of God, but the real healer is Him. As you know, I had had these terrible delusions, the poisons of psychotic depression and schizophrenia. This is deeply rooted in me. The doctors don't know why. I had thought deeply about my secret and my identity and decided that they ought to be covered. They were my assets, secretiveness and identity, and they should be covered, otherwise they will be stolen or I will be envied. How best to cover them though? Your identity is not physical. Your secret is not physical either. This is all madness, by the way! I am describing my delusions. One cover was to behave crazily in the street so that people would think I was mad and they wouldn't envy me or think me a man of secrets. So in my madness, I behaved as a madman. I already had this deeply rooted in my psyche. During that last isolation, Allāh convinced me that this was the wrong approach. After a while I went to the doctor, and he told me I had to rid myself of certain mental aspects that were moody and psychological in nature. They were like a cancer. Psychological illness is dangerous. You can be killed by it, out of depression, but Allāh always saves me. Allāh convinced me that this path I had chosen was wrong. He said, "Stop kidding yourself, Abed!" *Al-ḥamdu lillāh!* My mental problem lifted after which the doctor and the medicines were of secondary importance.'

'So it is the same idea they had in the *māristāns* [hospitals] in the Middle Ages, that one can be spiritually cured?'

'Yes. I have endless thanks for God. There are a lot of people like me in this society but they don't have doctors or medicines and wouldn't be able to afford them in any case. They don't realise they are sick, which is a big problem. And they think they are sane. I was saved. Allāh wanted this. During my fit I was about to beat my mother, but Allāh protected me from doing so. I thought she was incestuous and desired me. She phoned the doctor and when he came I told him she was a dèbauchee. He put me back on a full dose. Aggressiveness, withdrawal from society, these are all symptoms of mental illness. It was like when I ran into the baby in that man's arms. The baby cried and I laughed. You remember this from last year. At that point, although I never stopped my prayers, I declared to a couple of people that I had ceased to be a Muslim. You understood my situation. You forgave me.'

Abed spoke to me of his gradual restoration. Would that it were true, that he'd be made whole again.

§

When it came time for me to leave, I told Abed he need never feel alone. I was ready to choke on my own platitude. Sulaymān was easier to say goodbye to, there being no eternal separations in his universe. Clearly Abed had begun to backslide, and nowhere in his face could I see the resolution of the night before. We said our goodbyes, in darkness, at the foot of the stairs of the new footbridge that so many times took us to our rooftop café. Ugly though it is, a child's artefact painted a sickly blue, I am grateful for its construction. It affords a reasonable chance of survival whereas in years past one had to weave one's way through speeding traffic with as much dexterity as possible. When I first knew Abed, he would take me by the hand and drag me, saying one should never hesitate. 'If you change your mind, the driver won't have enough time to change his.' 'What if I get run over?' I protested. 'No problem! Whoever kills you pays a heavy fine.' Abed, so slender once upon a time, cut through the traffic like a blade. I shouldn't wish to try that again, not when an inch can mean the difference between life and death, and not with the added swell to both our waistlines.

We embraced one last time, and as I walked away I heard him call to me, 'I'll be a comma . . .'

'What was that, Abed?'

A lorry had just rumbled past, swallowing up the rest of what he said and I couldn't be sure what I heard was right either. What kind of silly joke was this? Did he really see himself reduced to the wispiest form of punctuation, man's life as a single, brief pause?

'I'll be in a coma after you've gone!'

Epilogue

I found this in my notebook: *Today I saw a most beautiful image, a woman in black, carrying, at a slight angle, four trays of perfectly white eggs.* Would I have remembered her had I not jotted down that note? I would like to think so. She might have come to me one night, unbidden, as I was about to go to sleep. She might just as easily have slipped into the mundane, while I was in a queue, say, waiting to pay for my groceries or waiting to catch the bus home. Equally she might never have come at all. There may not have been sufficient cause to summon her or for her to volunteer herself to an embryo cause. There is no saying when those small electrical impulses in the brain will suddenly flare, but much depends upon the random or upon how one thing inadvertently sparks off another, which points not only to the likelihood of a wealth of uncalled for images but also, with one thing bullying out the other, to the unlikelihood of having any kind of thought at all, so that, at best, one walks about with a head full of broken phrases.

My scribbled entry allows for no such chance. It sits on the page stark, unarguable, and unalterable. I see her clearly through those few words of mine, more so, in fact, than the words themselves describe. She was very lovely, and, to adopt the Arabic cliché, slender like a gazelle. I should mention, too, the black she wore revealed only the oval of her pale face. She would not have made such an impression otherwise. Although covered from head to toe, she made ancient seem modern and the reason for this surely had to have been in the drape, in the way the cloth fell from her body which was arched slightly backwards and a little to one side so as to accommodate the weight in her one arm, the four layers of eggs all so perfectly white. I remember seeing, in Milan, northern Italian renaissance sculptures of the Virgin bearing the

Christ child, her body arched just so, an artistic innovation that came of close observation, of seeing such women in the marketplace. The Italian has a rare genius for the common touch. The Arab, I believe, wants always to stay above the commonplace. What allowance, if any, does he make for the profane? All he does speeds him towards Allāh where the light is so bright he can no longer see. Small wonder his culture blew a fuse. I say this, knowing full well how fatal it is to generalise. What struck me was the confidence with which she, in Damascus, held those eggs aslant, which probably were close to a baby's weight, while looking straight ahead and certainly never, not even once, acknowledging my gaze.

And now, through the window of my newly rediscovered prose, I see more and more of the surrounding scene. All is swept into the present tense. What *was,* suddenly *is.* This small area of Damascus spreads away from her, more precisely, from her slightly jutting hipbone. She is covered from head to toe, save for her oval face. She is waiting to cross the street where Sharia Choukrī al-Quwatlī and Sharia ath-Thawra meet, one of those hideous intersections the town planners will take centuries to disentangle. If they do so at all, it will not be without first making it worse.[1] A blown fuse. What people were ever worse prepared for the future? They have gone into it, forgetting to take with them the graceful Arabic line, which is the keynote to their culture, which informs everything from their script to their music to their architecture. I generalise no more than my Syrian friends do.

As Sulaymān says, *We Damascenes no longer smell the roses.*

A pedestrian, I always get stuck here. I am standing on the other side of the street from her, the lady with the eggs, and I am not so impatient to move this time. I will happily breathe the fumes for a while. There is a flyover, a concrete eyesore built much too close to the old city, and beneath which only the very poor market their wares. Whoever will buy the sad trifles they have for sale? The only hope is for the man who sells a gadget that sculpts vegetables into flowery shapes.

---

1 This area has in fact changed. A footbridge has been installed and the old crossing which I describe removed.

I wonder if he sells enough of them, though, to be able to pay for the seemingly endless supply of carrots, radishes and cucumbers he topiarizes in order to demonstrate his gizmo's magical properties. Should I buy one? A semi-circle of people seems entranced either by it or else by the man's melodious cries. Could it be he advertises in verse? Nearby, an old man sits before a potted plant, which nobody seems to notice. A truly miserable specimen, desperate for water, if it doesn't sell soon it will surely die.

If one draws a line from the woman with her eggs to the man with his sculpted vegetables and extends it further, for which action I seem to recall there is a mathematical formula, what comes next is yet another so-called 'thieves' market' where, so my informant tells me, even the massive refrigerators are of doubtful provenance.[2] All the furniture seems huge. A rococo headboard, pale green with gilt, could have been designed for some hideous palace, and, if it really were stolen, which I am beginning to doubt because who could be human and want to possess such a thing, then the thieves have done its previous owners a service. The best place for it is the fire. A man pushes a trolley bearing a wardrobe. It's time to move on a little. What's this, hanging at the entrance to one of the shops? An imported Chinese spade its metal, most unaccountably, the colour of gold. Actually it's a kind of gold sprinkle. I wonder if this makes it more of a pleasure to use, when the black earth's flung from its Midas blade. There comes a moment when I seriously consider buying it.

2 This area has also been tidied up considerably although the refrigerators and furniture remain.

What's this racket, which throws a hook into my nerves? Unconsciously I walk towards it or rather it tugs at me. At a booth selling cassettes a thin music blasts out of poor speakers, a singer's voice like a woman's but really it is a young boy's, desert music with disco contaminate. There is something haunting about that voice, though, which cuts through the cheap pop overlay like, yes, a golden Chinese spade. The boy singers of Arabia are a musical tradition going back who knows how far in time. This time I make a purchase.

The thieves' market is impossible to romanticise. It is truly hideous, an area to get through as quickly as possible, and yet to ignore it would to be disallow a great part of existence. We cannot feed on the picturesque alone. We go places, and automatically we edit out what we don't like. The world is composed to the shape of our own desires. I find myself where no tourist ever goes unless it is to take the shortest route elsewhere. What are the stories here? If I can't describe what happens here, what right have I to speak of anywhere else? I go deeper into where the market becomes, briefly, a food one, where there are open sacks of round white cheeses, sprinkled with herbs, which I have never tried, baskets of strawberries, beautiful to look at but reportedly unhygienic, and pistachios which, once tasted, really hook one, but what I'll do now, because the reception is beginning to weaken here, is go back to her, the woman with the eggs one of which is punned in the oval of her beautiful pale face.

Absurdly the crossing where she waits, at Sharia Choukrī al-Quwatlī and Sharia ath-Thawra, and where I stand watching her on the opposite side, is manned by four traffic policeman, two on either side, the greatest concentration of traffic policemen I have seen in Damascus, and whose presence here has no discernible effect whatsoever. They are a comedy routine. One of them likes my hat and a few days ago he sought to make an exchange. My Panama failed to go with his khaki. The policemen, seeing the futility of their position, usually do nothing at all, but just now, that is, in the time of this prose, they appear to be recalled to some original sense of purpose. They are frantic. They wave their arms and blow their whistles. What do they suppose they'll be able to achieve? They alone will not be able to stem this human tide. Pedestrians, ignoring them and their shrill whistles, dart back and forth between the moving cars, but not so the lady with the eggs who remains a picture of perfect poise. The world will need to stop for her.

Why are all the eggs white? And what could she possibly want with so many at the same time? What concerns me most, however, is the wonderful image she makes. An architect I met told me that whenever he goes places he makes sketches of what he sees, and that later, when he returns to those sketches, even if they are only the briefest of outlines, they enable him to recollect the scene more clearly than had he taken a photograph of it. A great photographer would have caught the lady in black quickly enough to be able to beat the resultant scowl on her face. She would have been a perfect study in black and white. Most photographs are like so many discarded tissues, made in lieu of actually looking, which is why, in most people's hands, the camera's a complete waste. All this has been said before, I'm sure, but we surround ourselves with gadgetry that renders our senses passive. What the architect told me must surely be true, and what he said further is that in all likelihood it is the physical act of making the sketch, and not the sketch itself, that serves to fix the image in the mind. And so it was, I believe, with the note I made.

I could not have looked at her for more than a few seconds, although here, in the safety of this prose, I continue to stare, without fear of retribution, and the feeling I have for her is one of both melancholy and pleasure. There is nothing in it of what we'd call desire. The eroticism, while it is certainly there, is what Cervantes describes somewhere as being like a fire seen on a distant hill. I have scanned the pages of *Don Quixote* several times, looking for that line. All I can do is apprehend her with a philosophical eye. She wouldn't have time for this nonsense, of course, she who is about to produce a hundred omelettes. May Allāh preserve her hipbone. Could it be her beauty is merely a cipher for something else? At the corner of Sharia Choukrī al-Quwatlī and Sharia ath-Thawra what *is* slides back into what *was*. An abstract argument nudges me. Suppose she had been holding the four trays of eggs square, rather than at an angle, would I be feeling now what was beyond my being able to articulate then, the fragility of our existence? Certainly the melancholy I felt then was connected to matters other than those of accumulating age. I'd picked up a bug somewhere. It was an epidemic that struck at the hearts and minds of the Syrian people, even those as unworldly as Abed and Sulaymān, neither of whom I had ever heard, in days past, make a political utterance. It was upon such scenes as this, not so very far away, and perhaps at this very moment, that Smart missiles were doing their not so very smart business. Great care, so one heard from men whose voices one can squeeze like sponges, was being taken not to hit mosques and places of historic interest. And so what do they hit instead, blind spots such as this one? I hesitate to say what I imagine for fear it might come true. *Today I saw a most beautiful image, a woman in black, carrying, at a slight angle, four trays of perfectly white eggs.* I remember reading somewhere an account of the London Blitz and of how, amid the absolute destruction of several houses, a single, perfectly sound egg was seen to survive.

Select Bibliography

There is no single work in English that goes into any great length on the history of pigeons in the Islamic world. The book most central to my writing of the historical chapters, and which provided me with numerous leads, was Youssef Ragheb's *Les messagers volants en terre d'Islam*. CNRS Editions, Paris, 2002.

Sources other than those specifically mentioned in the text include:

Hansell, Jean. *The Pigeon in History; or, The Dove's Tale.* Millstream Books, 1998.

Irwin, Robert. *The Middle East in the Middle Ages – The Early Mamluk Sultanate 1250-1382*. Croom Helm, 1986.

Jalalu'ddīn a's Suyuti (trans. H.S. Jarrett). *History of the Caliphs*. J.W. Thomas, Calcutta, 1881.

Levanoni, Amalia. *A Turning Point in Mamluk History*. E.J.Brill, 1995.

Nathan, Tobie. "The Djinns: A Sophisticated Conceptualization of Pathologies and Therapies" in *Integrating Traditional Healing Practices Into Counselling and Psychotherapy*. *ed.* Roy Moodley and William West. Thousand Oaks, London, 2005.

Parmelee, Alice. *All the Birds of the Bible – their stories, identification and meaning*. Lutterworth Press, 1960.

Petry, Carl F. *The Civilian Elite of Cairo in the Later Middle Ages.* Princeton University Press, Princeton, 1981.

Rosen-Ayalon, M. "The Sultans in the Mamluk Sultanate" in *Studies in Memory of Gaston Wiet.* Institute of Asian and African Studies, The Hebrew University, Jerusalem, 1977.

Schiltberger, Johann. *The Bondage and Travels of Johann Schiltberger, a native of Bavaria, in Europe, Asia, and Africa, 1396-4127. trans.* J. Buchan Tilfer. Hakluyt Society, London, 1879.

Volney, C.-F. *Travels through Syria and Egypt: in the years 1783, 1784, and 1785: containing the present natural and political state of those countries, their productions, arts, manufactures, and commerce: with observations on the manners, customs, and government of the Turks and Arabs.* G.G.J. and J. Robinson, 1788.

Wiet, Gaston. *Baghdad – Metropolis of the Abbasid Caliphate.* University of Oklahoma Press, Norman, 1971.